SHADES OF WHITE FLIGHT

SHADES OF WHITE FLIGHT

Evangelical Congregations and Urban Departure

MARK T. MULDER

RUTGERS UNIVERSITY PRESS
New Brunswick, New Jersey, and London

Library of Congress Cataloging-in-Publication Data

Mulder, Mark T., 1973–
    Shades of white flight : evangelical congregations and urban departure / Mark T. Mulder.
        pages   cm
    Includes bibliographical references and index.
    ISBN 978–0–8135–6483–8 (hardcover : alk. paper) — ISBN 978–0–8135–6482–1 (pbk. : alk. paper) — ISBN 978–0–8135–6484–5 (e-book)
    1. United States—Race relations—History—20th century.
2. Evangelicalism—United States—History—20th century. 3. Race—Religious aspects—Christianity. 4. Identification (Religion). 5. Racism—United States—History—20th century. 6. African Americans—Illinois—Chicago—History—20th century—Case studies. 7. Whites—Illinois—Chicago—Migrations—History—20th century—Case studies. I. Title.
    E184.A1M78 2015
    305.80097309'04—dc23   2014021722

A British Cataloging-in-Publication record for this book is available from the British Library.

Visit our website: http://rutgerspress.rutgers.edu

Manufactured in the United States of America

For Dad and Mom, in appreciation of your steadfastness, commitment, faith, and love

CONTENTS

MAPS

PREFACE AND ACKNOWLEDGMENTS

The tale of these Christian Reformed Church congregations in the Chicago neighborhoods of Englewood and Roseland has been percolating a long time. The continuing and seemingly intractable nature of racial residential segregation, along with dynamic urban and suburban housing patterns, ensures that the story remains relevant; even as poverty seems to shift to inner-ring suburbs, segregation persists. Established traditions, habits, and religious practices continue to matter in the milieu of the urban United States. I hope here to make a little more sense of the complex manner in which faith practices, in particular, influence the structures and residential patterns of the metropolitan United States.

The narrative here tells an episode from the history of my own religious and ethnic tribe. The larger significance of it, though, resides in what we can learn that enhances our understanding of residential segregation. With that in mind, the reader should not necessarily perceive this book as a judgment. (Indeed, the crafting of this account included a good deal of self-interrogation as to whether I would have the courage to relinquish my own white privilege in similar circumstances.) This book is less about the people involved than it is about the organizational and institutional forces that continue to shape cities. Moreover, it is about illuminating religious practices, structures, and agency within the shifting sands of residential inequality. In the end, I see it as a call to become ever more attuned to the subtle distinctions that exist in religious life and habits and how they might manifest in meaningful ways throughout society.

Aspects of Chapters 6 and 7 of this volume were published as "Mobility and the (In)Significance of Place in an Evangelical Church: A Case Study from the South Side of Chicago," in *Geographies of Religions and Belief Systems* 3, no. 1 (2009). In addition, significant material in Chapters 8 and 9 appeared earlier as "Evangelical Church Polity and the Nuances of White Flight: A Case Study from the Roseland and Englewood Neighborhoods in Chicago," in *Journal of Urban History* 38, no. 1 (2012).

I am honored to have had the opportunity to speak with individuals involved in the events depicted in this book. Pastors Charles Terpstra (now deceased) and Derke Bergsma generously offered time, stories, and perspective regarding what they had both participated in and witnessed. I am grateful to these two gentlemen. In addition, I would like to recognize the unnamed laypeople who agreed to be interviewed about their experiences. On their porches in Roseland, they offered me hospitality and insight.

During the research and writing of this book, I benefitted greatly from participation in two Seminars in Christian Scholarship at my home institution, Calvin

College. The first, under the guidance of Steve Warner, offered the opportunity to examine congregational diversity in North American religion. The second, with Michael Emerson, examined the continuing significance of race in congregational life. Both seminars resonate through the pages here, and both Steve and Michael deserve hearty thanks. I offer my gratitude as well to my colleagues who participated in those seminars for the rapport-filled environments. I am also grateful to my colleague, John Witvliet, director of the Calvin Institute of Christian Worship, who was instrumental in organizing those seminars and has been influential in supporting my line of research in recent years.

Professors Victor Greene and Amanda Seligman challenged and helped improve many of the arguments here. I have appreciated their mentoring. At Calvin College, a very special thanks goes to my colleagues in the Department of Sociology and Social Work. The collegial environment there nurtured this process, and it is good to labor among fellow travelers. In addition, the department's Deur Award supported the latter stages of crafting this volume. Early on, the Calvin College Center for Social Research provided a grant to fund transcription. I offer my thanks to Neil Carlson, director of the center, for the continued and consistent support in numerous avenues of inquiry.

Very little of this history could have been told without the assistance of faithful archivists. My thanks to Hendrina Van Spronsen and Dick Harms at the Heritage Hall Archives of Calvin College; Geoffery Reynolds at the Joint Archives of Holland, Michigan; Marci Frederick at the Dutch Heritage Archives at Trinity Christian College, Palos Heights, Illinois; and Russ Gasero at the Archives of the Reformed Church in America at the New Brunswick Theological Seminary, New Jersey. In addition, it should be noted that Bob Swierenga's prolific writing about the Dutch in the United States, along with his careful wisdom and advice, proved foundational to the volume here.

My good friend Jamie Smith offered encouragement years ago regarding the potential of this project and its significance. Since then, he has been unfaltering in his prodding and wisdom. I owe him deep gratitude. I would also like to thank Peter Mikulas, who demonstrated a keen interest in this manuscript and shepherded it though to publication. Though he no longer teaches at Calvin, my friend Kevin Dougherty and I spent three years together in neighboring offices. He has continued to offer great encouragement. I am also grateful to Gerardo Marti for his thoughtful counsel regarding this project.

Thanks as well to my children Seth, Case, Noelle, and Maya. Their joy and inquisitiveness inspire me. Of course, none of this would be possible without my wife, Dawn. In ways too many to count and depths too profound to measure, she has been an encourager, a friend, and a confidante. Finally, I dedicate this book to my parents, Harold and Gert Mulder. They have supported me unflaggingly and have been models of love and steadfastness.

SHADES OF WHITE FLIGHT

1 · INTRODUCTION

The Irony of Religion and Racial Segregation

Racial inequality and oppression are persistent themes in the study of the urban United States. In-depth analyses have revealed persistently segregated cities and suburbs that offer disparate opportunities on the basis of race and location. Concealed behind the gleaming skyscrapers of the downtown business districts and the SUV-flooded parking lots of P. F. Changs, Pottery Barns, and megachurches in suburbia reside bleak and depressed communities. Inarguably, the vast majority of these neighborhoods tend to be populated by racial minorities.[1] Dilapidated homes and closed-down industrial plants and warehouses dot the landscape of these districts. The detritus and shadows of a long-gone manufacturing economy remind the unemployed and underemployed residents of these neighborhoods of the broken promise of the American dream. With poor housing stock and few walkable amenities, revival of these neighborhoods (both urban and suburban now) seems profoundly unlikely. For better or worse, these places will probably never see an influx of coffee shops, bicycle stores, and hipster pubs.

The causes and dimensions of such pervasive urban poverty, discrimination, and segregation now dominate the attention of many social scientists. Although the 1990s represented a decade of unprecedented economic growth for the United States, statistics from the 2000 census reveal the fact that African Americans residing in ghettos did not experience a corresponding stabilization of their finances. Since then, the 2010 census indicates that the economic downturns of the early twenty-first century have disproportionately affected these same urban African Americans. In short, poor African Americans living in marginalized neighborhoods received the least of boom economies and the worst of bust economies. In the face of this seemingly obstinate discrepancy, scholars have attempted to reveal the antecedents of continued racial injustice and concentrated poverty.

The claim I will make here is that religion and faith traditions matter in these inequalities. This case study of congregations from the South Side of Chicago further complicates the notion of "white flight." More particularly, I will be examining the contours of evangelicalism in the United States and its relationship to the racialized society. In fact, it seems that the relative successes of white evangelicalism had unintended consequences on the segregation and decline of urban neighborhoods. It is a rich irony that the strength of institutional religion led to weakness in cross-racial relationships and in local economies.

RESIDENTIAL SEGREGATION AND ITS SIGNIFICANCE

Though the field of inquiry has been mined by numerous scholars such as Michael Emerson, Mary Patillo, and William Julius Wilson, the most comprehensive and compelling contention has been articulated by Douglas Massey and Nancy Denton, who have asserted that residential segregation is the foundation of persistent inequality.[2] Moreover, they assert, the problem has been compounded by the fact that over the last few decades residential segregation has lost its salience as a public issue since problems concerning economic opportunity, educational achievement, and political representation have risen to the fore in its place.

Massey and Denton contended that despite the major 1968 civil rights law that banned discrimination in housing sales and rentals, remarkably little has been modified to disrupt the pattern of African American residential segregation, which has continued to be at the root of problems that afflict the impoverished segments of the African American population. According to Massey and Denton, the sources of residential segregation are in the northward migration of African Americans from the South. Such an influx threatened the established social structures of northern cities. In response, white homeowners initially implemented intimidation and residential zoning laws to restrict African American mobility. When such maneuvers failed to stem the tide, many of the white homeowners left for the suburbs. That process has been broadly labeled "white flight."

Though it has mutated to fit circumstances, the pattern has endured into the twenty-first century. That model of residential fluidity for some has ultimately functioned to create and maintain the African American ghetto. Conventional wisdom surmised that the combination of limited economic opportunity and choice remained the primary causes of ghetto creation. However, Massey and Denton countered by insisting that ghettoization has a much more institutional basis. The authors provided evidence that banks and real estate agencies operated as the primary vehicles for establishing segregation practices such as "redlining" that severely limited African American housing options. Such a predicament inevitably led to the concentration of African Americans within certain districts of the city. Furthermore, that residential configuration continued so persistently that one-third of all African Americans at the end of the twentieth century resided in isolated residential areas that Massey and Denton described as "hypersegregated."[3]

Although Massey and Denton compellingly asserted that institutionalized segregation was the "structural lynchpin of American race relations," they failed to delineate how comprehensively institutionalized the phenomenon could be. They identify government agencies, lenders, and real estate agents, but I will argue that other institutions—congregations—were also involved. In many cases, churches not only failed to inhibit white flight but actually became co-conspirators and accomplices in the action. The complicity of churches in the residential shifts of the 1960s and 1970s remains relevant today as the urban United States experiences what the political scientist Alan Ehrenhalt has described as the "Great Inversion"—the return of the affluent and the elite to central cities.[4]

As religion continues to play a vital role in the social life of the United States, how will the attendant practices, cultures, and traditions affect the urban residential landscape?

THE CASES OF ENGLEWOOD AND ROSELAND

The episodes considered in these pages occurred in the middle of the twentieth century in the Chicago neighborhoods of Englewood and Roseland. Both places included an enclave of Dutch ethnics. Many of these Dutch American residents belonged to various Reformed church communities that could be best described as Calvinist in theological tradition and evangelical in ecclesiastical practice. These Reformed Dutch found themselves in the throes of a social upheaval that had been building for decades. As the "Black Belt" neighborhoods approached from the north, the Reformed Dutch members of these communities faced what they saw as the only two options: to make a stand in their neighborhood and respond to the demographic change through adaptation or to relocate to the suburbs and reconstitute their faith communities in a new locale. Holding true to precedent, they initially struggled to remain, but ultimately departed for the outlying locations of Evergreen Park, Oak Lawn, Orland Park, and South Holland.

The people under consideration in this book held membership in the Dutch-dominated Christian Reformed Church in North America (CRC). The CRC had been in existence for about a century, still maintained much of the ethnic flavor of the mother country, and yet had evolved within the U.S. religious scene to become evangelical. When the block-by-block advance of African Americans infiltrated their communities, seven congregations removed themselves to the suburbs. In their wake, they left behind remnants in the form of two "Home Missions" centers. The role of church polity and culture is seen even more clearly when comparing these seven CRC congregations to the six Reformed Church in America (RCA) congregations that resided in the same two South Side neighborhoods.

For an observer unfamiliar with the history, theology, and practice of the churches, the CRC and RCA would be largely indistinguishable. In a recent volume discussing the two denominations, the authors indicated that distinctions remain so subtle that only insiders can discern them: "Southern Baptists from Alabama or Lutherans from Minnesota may struggle to comprehend just what constitutes the important differences between the two denominations."[5] The denominations shared Dutch ethnic roots, subscribed to the same Reformed/ Calvinist confessional doctrines, and employed similar worship rituals. Close scrutiny, however, reveals differences in terms of church polity and cultural orientation. First, although both denominations claim Presbyterian-style polity, it would be more accurate to describe the CRC as congregational. In other words, authority rested at the local level: any hierarchical apparatuses wielded little or no real influence on these congregations when their neighborhoods changed. In contrast, the RCA congregations had to receive permission from the denominational structures in order to sell off any church buildings and relocate. In the end, this subtle disparity in church polity predisposed the CRC congregations toward higher levels of mobility and suburbanization as the neighborhoods changed racially.

Second, the CRC and RCA engaged in different social practices. CRC congregations tended to form more closed communities, while the RCA members involved themselves more broadly in the urban milieu of Chicago. Perhaps the most vivid illustration of the discrepancy arose in the area of education: while RCA families tended to utilize local public schools, CRC families generally enrolled their children at Christian schools almost entirely populated by students from the denomination. Such a divergence allowed for the CRC to be more insular, and thus more apt simply to recreate the largely closed community in suburbia. In fact, the CRC congregations epitomized the "closed community." The networks within the churches had such a high level of density that the congregations became fragmented from the larger community.[6] The RCA congregations, less closed, tended to stay years, in some cases decades, longer. Because the two denominations share so much in common, the RCA operates as a fertile point of comparison in how congregations responded to neighborhood change.

At first glance, the episode of Dutch CRC mobilization would seem to offer little material for scrutiny—the flight of white families and individuals from central cities has been well documented and had a national character. However, a closer examination of the mobilization from Englewood and Roseland operates effectively as a case study of the processes of white flight that has much insight to offer on how different religious orientations influenced the larger process. These two neighborhoods served as a locus for the intersection of race, religion, ethnicity, and community-rootedness. All four of these themes played dominant roles in the social structure of twentieth-century United States. In the end, the case study of CRC congregations in Chicago illuminates how a dominant form of evangelical church polity—namely congregationalism—functioned within the larger social phenomenon known as white flight.

COMPLICATING "WHITE FLIGHT"

It should be noted that there does exist a developing literature that finds the term "white flight" problematic due to its unnuanced connotations. Amanda Seligman asserted that the term fails to express the variegated nature of white departure, particularly from the West Side of Chicago.[7] She contended that the term incorrectly implies that whites left the instant that African Americans appeared in their neighborhoods and that the whites played no role in attempting to buttress local infrastructure. In addition, "white flight" fails to convey the fact that not all departing whites left for the suburbs—some, in fact, moved to other neighborhoods in the city proper. More recently, Rachael Woldoff vividly portrayed an urban neighborhood experiencing changes in racial and economic composition in the 1990s. She also complicated the notion of "white flight" in her finding that not all whites actually fled. Woldoff discussed the white "stayers" and why they chose to remain. Beyond that, she richly related the interracial bonds that grew between the white stayers and black "pioneers."[8] In sum, the term "white flight" fails to adequately convey the finely granulated processes of racial residential transition.

Others have argued, however, that typical understandings of the term "white flight" remain too thin. Kevin Kruse broadened the definition of white flight. He argued that it should include not only geographic and spatial notions, but should be understood as a political transformation, as well. That is, white flight included the crafting of a new type of conservatism that left behind racist demagoguery and focused on the language of "rights, freedoms, and individualism." Such seemingly benign vocabulary allowed for more insidious practices. In that way, Kruse argued, white flight is most accurately understood as a physical relocation and a political revolution.[9]

The intent of this volume is to further complicate the term "white flight" in explicating how subtle differences in faith/religious traditions manifested in different responses from whites as African Americans moved into their neighborhoods. Beyond that, I attempt to demonstrate how a uniquely American brand of evangelicalism contributed to the mid-century desertion of many rust-belt cities by white families. As the intermingling of race and evangelicalism continues to be a dominant social force in the United States, this volume is a step in unpacking how religious practices exacerbated the decline of many cities.[10]

The Roseland and Englewood dramas starkly display how religion—often assumed to foster community and social connectedness—can actually help to disintegrate neighborhoods. Nancy Ammerman articulated the ways in which congregations typically respond to neighborhood demographic change.[11]

Some will simply persist—radical transformations are unlikely from largely static organizations such as congregations. Some will attempt to adapt. Risk levels related to loss of resources make this a largely unpalatable strategy. Others will relocate—some figuratively by transforming their niche identity and attracting attenders from wider locales, and others quite literally. The seven CRC congregations studied here chose the latter option of shuffling to the suburbs. Their story reveals the difference between being rooted in neighborhood and being rooted in church. Old neighborhoods remain difficult to simulate, houses of worship less so. The Dutch CRC represented an insular social circle that utilized the local church and Christian school instead of the local park or square or market as the unifying focal point for the community. Such a formation abetted an easier detachment and relocation to the suburbs: constructing two new buildings (church and school), while daunting, is not an insurmountable proposition for recreating a social network twenty to forty miles to the south and west.

This case of white flight also offers insights into how a religious history can find new expression in social movements. In essence, religious identity can have profound implications for later courses of social action or, in some cases, reaction. This particular Dutch denomination had a history rife with schism. The narrative of the CRC resonates with squabbling and subsequent high mobility. That kind of disruptive pattern erupted again in Englewood and Roseland, and ultimately helped to allow an almost seamless departure.

Further, the episode offers new insights regarding ethnic communities and the tension between conformity to the larger society and ethnic integrity. These Dutch American members of the CRC found themselves in a United States full of radical social change. They struggled to maintain the balance between heritage and assimilation in a country that periodically displayed a penchant for nativism (especially during the two World Wars, when the Dutch found it wise to distance themselves from their German cousins). Moreover, the social forces of the civil rights movement, the burgeoning importance of the automobile, the rising materialism, the new availability of suburban life, and the specter of nuclear war gave these Dutch enclaves numerous issues to confront.

Finally, the case of CRC relocation from Chicago and its antecedents help to bolster and offer nuances to the argument presented by Michael Emerson and Christian Smith in their important book, *Divided by Faith: Evangelical Religion and the Problem of Race in America*.[12] These two authors posited that the very nature of evangelical Christianity has prohibited it from being an effective agent in racial reconciliation. Indeed, they asserted that in fact the very opposite was true: evangelical Christianity actually contributed to construction and maintenance of a racialized society. Though not necessarily intentional, the nature of white evangelical religion—with its inability to address fundamental and structural stratifications—has functioned to perpetuate racial barriers and systemic injustice.

In essence, white evangelicals have been opposed to individual racial prejudice while failing to understand the structural/institutional character of racism in the United States. They are, in other words, "antistructural."[13] Emerson and Smith argue that the social reality of many evangelicals prohibited them from understanding and assessing the lack of equal opportunity in the United States based on race. Moreover, by denying the existence of a racialized system, the white evangelicals have fostered and perpetuated it. The inhibitive factor seems to be based in the white evangelical understanding of spirituality: each person is responsible for his or her salvation through Christ and the maintenance of that relationship. Emerson and Smith describe the evangelical "cultural tool kit" as lacking the instruments necessary to understand structural racism and discrimination. Such a cultural blind spot also sees no incongruity between the autonomous individual and historic Christianity.

That individualistic religiosity is directly reflected in the congregational nature of evangelical denominations and churches—that is, with authority resting at the local church level (in fact, many evangelical congregations have no denominational affiliation). Such a polity allows the congregations to own their own worship buildings, which contributes to an increased mobility of church bodies. In the CRC polity, which ostensibly follows a Presbyterian model, the congregations did indeed own their buildings. Thus the very nature of the organizational structure of the denomination precluded any major impediment from a church hierarchy or other deliberative bodies to the mobilization and subsequent suburbanization of individual congregations. The story of the CRC tells us much about wider evangelicalism, individualism, and congregationalism.

Taken as a whole, the case of the CRC congregations in Englewood and Roseland reveals that the manifestation of congregational church polity allowed for an easier departure of whites from central cities. Though they initially considered defending their places in manners somewhat similar to Catholics, the CRC congregations eventually found it much easier and more attractive to leave the core city. The Catholic parish model functioned to inhibit the movement of parishioners. The local congregational model that became more prevalent within conservative Protestantism during the twentieth century offered no such constraints.

In summary, the CRC congregations found relocation to the suburbs a palatable proposition because of precedence, polity, and conception of place. First, the denomination had a history of schism and mobility. The consistent search for and maintenance of theological purity predisposed the congregations to detach and move easily when events and surroundings became unsavory. The maintenance of the closed community remained a leading objective. Moreover, that history of fissure led to a polity that more closely resembled a more evangelical congregationalism than the Presbyterianism of the denomination's roots. Thus while the denominational hierarchy fretted about the erosion of the city and racial segregation, they were ineffectual in prohibiting the abandon-ment of the city by member congregations. In addition, the history of division led to the development of a closed, insular society. The constant inward turn of the CRC congregations created an almost exclusive dependency on the school and church; these two institutions largely represented the whole of CRC social life. Instead of embracing the larger community, the CRC subculture shel-tered themselves and their families within these two places. Having such little attachment to the larger structures of the community, it became relatively unproblematic for the congregations to sell the buildings and replace them in the suburbs.

THE CONTINUING SIGNIFICANCE OF RELIGION

This case study of these Christian Reformed Dutch Americans delivers a new chapter in the story about religion in the United States and its sometimes ambivalent relationship with democracy and the public good. The United States remains a nation of church-goers. Secularization theory has largely run its course.[14] Studies have indicated the existence of more than 300,000 congrega-tions. Moreover, two out of every three American adults claim to be members of a congregation, and a scant 15 percent *never* attend religious services.[15] Since the time of Alexis de Tocqueville's tour in the early 1830s (when he noted a par-ticular prevalence of faith within the American population), religion has been both an instigator and mitigator in the effort to broaden and extend democracy in the United States. The same Bible that defended slavery also, in the hands of the abolitionists, condemned the institution. While some churches played a key role in the civil rights movement, other congregations fled the same movement's beneficiaries.

Religion and race have had a convoluted history in the United States. Matters have often been further complicated when ethnicity has had intimate connections with religion in creating both individual and collective identity. The episodes of the Dutch CRC congregations in Englewood and Roseland and the reaction to African American influx lend a new perspective to the discourse. Their response exemplified how the political structures and social networks of a particular religious tradition could abet the process of white flight. The CRC congregations' strategy of minimal losses and coordinated retreat resulted in almost undetected wholesale removal from the city to the suburbs. In the end, the religious background of these CRC congregations helps to explain how they left their city neighborhoods for the suburbs. Racism was undoubtedly a motivating factor. Fear of depreciating house values undeniably exacerbated the situation. However, those reasons fail to assess adequately how these people left urban centers. To fully understand the larger movement of white suburban migration, there needs to be an accounting of religious backgrounds.

In some ways, the movement of these CRC congregations is well explained by the model of "congregational ecology." That is, churches remain subject to the ecology of a local environment, both demographically and economically. Just as animals in nature need certain habitat and dietary conditions to thrive, congregations need certain resources from their local context. With the shifting population of the urban milieu, congregations remain vulnerable to less nutrient-rich environments. As that ecology changes, it *naturally selects* which congregations will remain. Thus, we should not be surprised when churches either follow their resources (attenders) or reach wider (attracting attenders from a more metropolitan region).[16]

However, the "naturalness" of the congregational ecology model falters when using it as lens for understanding the congregations of Englewood and Roseland. At least one CRC congregation purchased land in the suburbs as preemptive maneuver, encouraging attenders to relocate to a certain locale. In that way, the congregation practiced an agency that belies the notion of simple response to ecology. That tactic functioned to shape the environment. So, yes, urban political economy explains how the "wizards," to use Omar McRoberts's term, of business and government operated to cultivate an artificial Black Belt that could only grow in a constrained block-by-block advance.[17] However, I will argue here that some churches contributed to the monolithic nature of segregation as they either sanctioned it by following attenders to the suburbs or, in some CRC cases, actually directing attenders to a certain outlying area wherein they would reassemble.

It should also be noted that within the sociology of religion, as secularization theory has lost its sway, the "new paradigm" that has emerged has found it useful to focus on the disestablishment of religion in the United States. The new paradigm highlights the voluntary nature of religion and the manner in people choose or "shop" for church. Thus, the paradigm frequently relies on economic or marketplace imagery. In the instance of these congregations in Chicago, the economic frame works up to a point. For those outside churches who would woo or pursue CRC families, it was a closed economy. The Dutch Reformed mostly remained bound to their inherited faith and practices, and there existed little chance that these families would defect to a different religious tradition. It would have been a serious social rupture to leave the denomination, since CRC families exhibited high levels of commitment to the shared circles of church and school. In that way, perhaps, the only real competitors for CRC families would have been other CRC congregations—and there was no one to regulate that internal market.[18]

In some ways the CRC experience is akin to a franchise that has a loyal yet very narrow customer base. If that franchise knows that it has limited appeal to one well-resourced group of people, it will, of course, follow those customers around the metropolitan region. To remain in the old area with new customers who have fewer resources and a lack of familiarity with the brand would be a sizable financial risk. However, that marketplace imagery loses salience when CRC congregations bought land preemptively in the suburbs and directed attenders to consider moving to that area. Customers might be loyal to a particular brand or business, but those allegiances typically fall short of that type of residential influence.

THE PROFOUND LEGACY OF SEGREGATION

We are now roughly a half century removed from the events described in this book. However, we are also a half century removed from the Civil Rights Act and the Fair Housing Act. Some have proclaimed that the election of Barack Obama signaled that advent of the postracial United States. De jure segregation no longer exists. Despite all these ostensible instances of social progress, extreme and debilitating residential segregation based on race continues to plague communities across the United States. Moreover, that segregation is a malignancy— the consequences for those who suffer from these patterns are deleterious. Patrick Sharkey contended that quagmire of African American poverty is directly attributable to residential segregation based on race.[19] That is, "the story of neighborhoods and race in America is one of enduring, *inherited* inequality."[20] The persistence of the urban ghetto based on race has had a ripple effect that manifests in areas of employment, health care, education, and transportation discrepancies. In other words, the seemingly intractable residential immobility experienced by African Americans functions as a foundational source of contemporary racial inequality and injustice. Indeed, in *The Great American City: Chicago and the Enduring Neighborhood Effect*, published in 2012, Harvard social sciences professor Robert Sampson singled out Englewood and Roseland as places of continuing profound marginalization. He described Englewood as "extremely distressed" and as having the third highest foreclosure rate in the city in 2009.[21] Of Roseland, he wrote that the neighborhood showed signs of distress as well, and that it faced a "tenacious crime problem."[22] Thus the residential patterns that developed in the 1950s, 1960s, and 1970s continue to matter. The legacy of white departure continues to haunt the affected neighborhoods. And neighborhoods have consequences. In many urban areas of the United States, African Americans have disproportionately borne the brunt of enduring poverty for generations in the same places.

The residential stasis of large numbers of African Americans, however, should not be misinterpreted to mean that neighborhoods never change. That is not the case. In the early twenty-first century cities and suburbs continue a dynamic relationship of population flow. For example, as the housing tastes and preferences of the middle class and affluent continue to evolve, they may actually displace poor racial minorities in the process of gentrification. While largely speculative to this point, there are studies that indicate that the dominant urban demographic trend of the post–World War II United States (white departure from core cities to outlying suburbs) may have ebbed. In fact, some authors have concluded that the United States is on the precipice of a dramatic "demographic inversion." That is, we might be seeing a return of middle- and upper-class whites to cities—a movement that would push the poor and racial minorities into adjacent inner-ring suburbs.[23] Indeed, studies now indicate that poverty has started a migration to the suburbs. If we are to fully understand and anticipate urban and suburban population movement today and in the future, it remains important to better understand how the metropolitan regions of the United States came to look as they do today.

I argue in this book that the peculiar nature of evangelicalism in this country abetted the exodus of white families from cities. This question regarding the role of religion in the "white flight" of the 1950s, 1960s, and 1970s has resurfaced today: some are asserting that the demographic inversion of the early twenty-first century contains a religious component. James Bielo of Miami University has argued that there has actually been a movement of "re-urbanization" among evangelical Christians.[24] That is, a religious tradition almost synonymous with sprawl, megachurches, and malls may now be returning to urban centers. More than that, Bielo asserted that the cohort of re-urbanization evangelicals tends to voice a cultural critique of the modern suburban lifestyle in the United States. These findings are preliminary, of course, and it remains too early to ascertain whether the movement of evangelicals back into cities indicates a leading edge of a larger movement or an insignificant diaspora. However, it also remains profoundly important to better understand how evangelicals are affected by church practice when making residential decisions.

Whatever the case regarding evangelicals and location, the U.S. population as a whole continues to churn through various geographic locations. Some urban cores seem to be in the midst of a renaissance while their older suburbs absorb more poverty. Outlying suburban areas continue to largely thrive as they remain an emblem of the American dream. All the while, the United States continues to be a place where faith and religion matter. The issue of how residential segregation and racial inequality intersect with religion remains as relevant as ever. The story out of Englewood and Roseland is a step toward a better understanding of how institutions, including churches, created and maintain a system of racial inequality.

MAP OF THE BOOK

Chapter 2 will be an examination of the history of the CRC and its embrace of a form of congregationalism. To fully understand the exodus of these seven CRC congregations from Englewood and Roseland and how the story lends itself to the discussion of race, religion, and residential patterns, one must know the history and context of these people. In *A Portrait of the Artist as a Young Man*, James Joyce noted: "The past is consumed in the present and present is living only because it brings forth the future."[25] Joyce's comment has direct and compelling implications for both scholars of race relations and members of the ethnically Dutch Christian Reformed Church in North America today. Since the late 1950s, members and congregations of CRC persuasion have demonstrated a high degree of mobility. Especially in the greater Chicago metropolitan area, a trend of outward movement from city centers continues to the present. Such a phenomenon of congregational transfer offers lessons as a case study that demonstrates that past, present, and future are all entwined. More explicitly, it reveals how a history of past ecumenical schism can translate into a present of closed communities. Beyond that, it exhibits that church polity may have direct consequences in neighborhood affairs. It displays that the sacred machinations of the church can be utilized to either integrate or disintegrate the local neighborhood. Finally, the case of the CRC congregational departure raises interesting questions concerning the distinction between institutional racism and individual racism.

In Chicago, that history and precedent of fissure and schism mutated into a highly systematized pattern of social insularity for the CRC congregations. Chapter 3 will highlight how almost all social activity was conducted under auspices of the church. Because of that isolation, the Chicago CRC communities of Roseland and Englewood remained stable and homogeneous for over one hundred years and for about eight decades, respectively. However, the social forces of the middle half of the twentieth century would eventually overwhelm these CRC communities. Leaders would have to make a decision regarding the maintenance of isolation and homogeneity, and whether those even existed as laudable goals by the late 1960s.

A controversy that tested the closed community of the CRC in the face of racial change will be the basis for Chapter 4. In the late 1960s a group of African American families attempted to enroll their children in a CRC-affiliated Christian school. The controversy that erupted revealed volumes about CRC culture and church polity.

Chapters 5 and 6 will discuss how the social transitions that affected Chicago proper had particular consequences in local neighborhoods like Englewood and Roseland. The massive influx of African Americans and the struggle for housing had devastating consequences for communities. The perceived erosion of the quality of life in both Englewood and Roseland was attributable to radical residential isolation based on race. In both communities, the local CRC congregations were conspirators in the racial transition that left a legacy of deeply entrenched segregation. As the neighborhoods became increasingly African

American, the CRC families followed the trend to find an ostensible comfort and security in the surrounding suburbs.

Utilizing congregational meeting records, council minutes, denominational materials, and field interviews, the next chapters will reconstruct the actual departure of the churches from their respective neighborhoods. The Roseland and Englewood dramas demonstrate how religious practice has resonance for the fate of neighborhoods. The social totality of the CRC church and school monopoly negated any opportunities over time to develop ties in the community outside those two institutions. In essence, these CRC congregations operated as fully functional communities. In Chapter 7, I will delineate the largely spiritual nature of CRC culture—there did not exist an emphasis on community being connected to "place." Such a dynamic abetted an easier detachment and relocation to the suburbs.

Chapters 8 and 9 will consider congregational polity. Beyond their narrow conception of place, the CRC congregations also exercised a high mobility for the suburbs because of church polity. The congregational structure of the denomination left primary authority with local churches. Even if the larger assemblies of the CRC had expressed extreme consternation on the wholesale departure of seven congregations from Chicago proper, they had no apparatus for preventing the exodus. In Chapter 9, I outline the significance of congregational polity in sanctioning white departure from Chicago. I make the case that congregational polity (a very evangelical structure) allowed for an easier departure from Chicago for these churches and their attenders.

In Chapter 10 I note how congregations in the CRC's sister denomination, the RCA, responded to the same racial changes in Chicago. It is here that we see the nuances that faith practices lent to "white flight." With a marginally different culture and church polity, the RCA responded differently from the CRC.

CONCLUSION

Though there are some unique features of the CRC exoduses from Englewood and Roseland, there also exist strong elements within the narrative that transcend this microhistory and link it to broader elements within U.S. religion. That broader feature is the individualism and congregationalism that existed within the CRC, American evangelicalism as a whole, and even with groups as disparate as Orthodox Jews (whom historian Gerald Gamm referred to as having the "purest form of congregational authority").[26] A dominant theme of American social life has been individualism and independence. Likewise, a central motif within religion in the United States has been congregationalism. Recent studies have indicated the continued pertinence of congregations in American lives: "Since the beginning of the nineteenth century, the proportion of the US population enrolled in local religious bodies has climbed steadily from less than 30 percent to well over 60 percent at latest count."[27] In addition, when one ascertains that there exist over 300,000 congregations in America, it becomes very difficult to study social patterns without taking these institutions and their practices into account.[28] The cultures and practices of congregations continue to resonate throughout U.S. metropolitan patterns.

PART I   # THE EVOLUTION OF AN EVANGELICAL DENOMINATION

2 · MOBILITY AND INSULARITY

To fully understand the exodus of these seven Christian Reformed Church (CRC) congregations from Englewood and Roseland and how the story lends itself to the discussion of race, religion, and residential patterns, one must know the history and context of these people. Since the late 1950s, when confronted with neighborhood change, members and congregations of the CRC persuasion have demonstrated a high degree of mobility. In Chicago, whole congregations tended to move. In contrast, a few hours to the north in Grand Rapids, Michigan, the smaller scale of the city allowed the numerous CRC congregations there to remain in the same locale, while attenders could move out of changing neighborhoods and still easily commute for meetings and worship services at the church.[1] Though they manifested in ways tied to the geography of the urban environment, in both cases the CRC tended to practice a mode of congregational transfer. In Grand Rapids the resources (the attenders and members) remained fairly accessible because most commutes from the suburbs to the core city neighborhoods would remain less than twenty minutes. These congregations would have to nurture niche identities to pull from the metropolitan region. In Chicago, vast expanse of the metro region, combined with the growth of the Black Belt, made a wholesale relocation of the congregation the more palatable option.

Such a phenomenon of congregational movement reveals how a history of past ecumenical schism can translate into a present of in-group preoccupation and larger community rupture and fragmentation. Beyond that, it exhibits that church polity may have direct consequences in neighborhood affairs, to either integrate or disintegrate the local neighborhood. Finally, the case of the CRC congregational departure raises interesting questions concerning the distinction between institutional racism and individual racism.

As the Great Migration during and after World War II brought so many African Americans around and into their communities, the CRC congregations in Chicago struggled to maintain their churches, neighborhoods, and identity.[2] Since the church operated as the strongest influence in their lives, the question now became, how would the clergy and laity respond to that influx of African

Americans? The response of Chicago CRC communities to their new neighbors discloses much about the intersection of race and religion.

Inarguably, race and religion have often functioned as divisive elements throughout U.S. history. Perhaps nothing has haunted the urban United States more than the seemingly intractable chasm between whites and African Americans (although the dynamic changes in urban minority demographics is making this a much more fluid issue and is by no means merely two-sided).[3] Moreover, religious distinctiveness continues to function as a mechanism for self-identification. Historically, however, religion has also functioned to promote reconciliation and cooperation. Examples include white northerners inspired by their faith instigating the abolition movement, settlement houses and women's associations at the beginning of the twentieth century, and the churches that played key roles in the civil rights movement of the 1950s and 1960s.

Unfortunately, this case study of the Christian Reformed Church in Roseland and Englewood adds to that lamentable dynamic where religion has fostered alienation and segregation. Initially, I envisioned this project as a volume to complement and lend nuance to the argument offered by Etan Diamond in *And I Will Dwell in Their Midst: Orthodox Jews in Suburbia*.[4] Diamond contended that because of their religious commitments, Orthodox Jews who moved to the suburbs possessed an innate ability to maintain a sense of community. In direct contrast to the studies that derided the suburbs as "outposts of loners," Diamond insisted that religion could be a variable that mitigated suburban isolation. The strictures of Orthodox Judaism demanded a proximity that led to community bonds.

Though they are not entirely analogous, I initially intended to draw comparisons between the Christian Reformed Church and the Orthodox Jews. I knew that CRC congregations had left Chicago proper for the suburbs—perhaps they, like the Jews, had been able to maintain a distinct ethos of community because of the nature of their Protestant faith. However, closer inspection revealed that a more primary story had to be told. Before any examination of the CRC in the suburbs could be conducted, I would first have to study the factors that facilitated such a wholesale relocation. In essence, the question now centered on whether there was something unique about the Christian Reformed faith that allowed the congregations to be so highly mobile. Moreover, with suburbanization being such a dominant social process of the twentieth century, it seemed necessary to explore whether this CRC episode offered any broader insights on the relation between religion and the central city exodus—whether faith abetted or abated the exodus, or remained an insignificant factor.

Thus, my research now had to fit within the framework of studies that considered the in-migration of African Americans to northern cities during the post–World War II era and the subsequent out-migration whites to the seemingly fairer pastures of the suburbs. The episode I study here concerns the migration of seven CRC congregations from the south Chicago neighborhoods of Englewood and Roseland, beginning in the late 1950s. The impetus for such movement assumed the usual aspects: the northern-bound Great Migration of African Americans that had intensified after World War II left these CRC-ers watching apprehensively from their front porches as the African American ghetto approached on a "block by block" basis. By 1972, all seven churches had exited these two urban neighborhoods. In their wake they left a couple of "Home Missions" gospel centers that had the responsibility to evangelize those who now resided in the houses and neighborhoods that had once been filled with people discussing John Calvin, predestination, sin, and God's grace—sometimes in Dutch, if not, then in a heavy Dutch brogue.

ROOTS IN THE NETHERLANDS

As has been noted, the denomination's past shows a predilection for both fissure and mobility. The precedent of a people only too willing to rupture social ties and remove themselves from the situation stretched back over both a century and an ocean. They demonstrated themselves to be a people intensely committed to the particulars of faith and doctrine. Threats to those specifics were met with schism and mobility.

The foundations for the CRC's existence in the United States extended back to 1795 in Europe, when drastic modifications occurred within the Reformed Church of the Netherlands. The Reformed Church, as its title suggests, originated during the Protestant Reformation and based its doctrines on the thinking of John Calvin, a French Reformation leader. The church found expression of its doctrines in the Belgic Confession, written in 1561 in response to Roman Catholic persecution of the Reformed Dutch; the Heidelberg Catechism, approved in 1563 by Elector Frederick III and considered to be the epitome of orthodox Calvinism; and the Canons of Dort, formulated by the Synod of Dort in 1618 and 1619 and noted for espousing strict predestination dogma.[5]

In an effort to ensure the maintenance of these Reformed standards, the church in the Netherlands required all ministerial candidates to sign a Formula of Subscription. The Formula stated that all who signed concurred with "the articles and points of doctrine contained" in the three aforementioned documents and "fully agreed with the Bible."[6] The Formula also established church government and authority. The organization of the church maintained the Standard Reformed or Presbyterian hierarchy.

Because of strict adherence to the Formula and the doctrinal standards, the Reformed Church remained largely unchanged from 1583 to 1795. Throughout that time, it enjoyed official support as the national church of the Netherlands. Although the government required that officials maintain membership, the church remained largely autonomous as the state acted only as a trustee in property and financial matters. The relationship allowed the Reformed Church to be at once both an established and a free church.[7] The situation would not last, however, as international developments swept into the Netherlands.

The French Revolution established the Batavian Republic and the subsequent incorporation of the Netherlands into the Empire of France. The Reformed Church was demoted into equality with all other denominations in 1795. French rule, however, remained brief—less than twenty years. The victory over Napoleon at Waterloo in 1815 secured William I, the Prince of Orange, as the king of Holland.[8]

King William immediately set himself to the task of restoring the nature of the Dutch kingdom as it had existed before Napoleon's rule. He quickly elevated the Reformed Church to its previous position as the established national church. In doing so, the government liberalized the doctrine and discipline of the church. William altered the polity of the church by filling the hierarchy with royal delegates in place of the usual congregation-elected representatives. He also modified the church's adherence to the three confessional standards. The National Synod that met under William's direction composed a new Formula of Subscription that allowed ministerial candidates to virtually ignore the doctrinal standards.[9]

In response, a number of clergy and congregations seceded from the national church to form what they felt to be a better expression of Reformed or Calvinist theology. In turn, the government created an atmosphere of religious oppression for the "Seceders." Coupled with a severe economic depression, the lack of religious freedom in the Netherlands led many Seceders to begin considering emigration.

After some leaders initially suggested relocation to Java, they ultimately decided on the United States. In April 1846, to better organize the international migration, two ministers named A. C. Van Raalte and Antonio Brummelkamp formed the Society of Christians for Dutch Immigration to the United States of America. Shortly thereafter, they published a pamphlet entitled "Why We Encourage Immigration to North America, and Not to Java."

MERGER WITH THE RCA

Tales of freedom and prosperity in the United States quickly spread within Seceder circles and plans for movement to North America began in earnest. Little did these Seceders know that their inaugural migration would set an oft-repeated pattern for their descendants in the United States. In order to make the transition as efficient as possible, the Seceders called on members of the Reformed Church in America (RCA) to aid them in their move. The RCA had almost 100 percent Dutch constituency and had been formed in North America by immigrants at the time of their initial arrival in America in 1623–1624, during the First Dutch Immigration.

The RCA responded by creating the Protestant Evangelical Holland Emigrant Society. The society functioned to "open the way for members of the Dissension Church who are devoted to the old belief of the Reformation."[10] While leaders in the Netherlands and United States exchanged views and attempted to establish a common strategy, numerous articles appeared in the RCA's *The Christian Intelligencer*, reiterating the plight of the Seceders and the emigration plans.[11] Soon RCA members from Illinois, having read the proposals, wrote to offer their aid. They noted the importance of having a society or committee located near the area where the Seceders would ultimately settle, to complete the arrangement initiated by the Protestant Evangelical Holland Emigrant Society. They volunteered directions to suitable locations for settlement, employment for mechanics, land for farmers to cultivate until they received their own, and anything else to ease the New Immigrants' circumstances. (The Seceders now received the label "New Immigrants" in contrast to the "Old Immigrants" of the early 1600s.)

With knowledge of RCA support in hand, the movement of the New Immigration began—either in congregations or in congregational clusters. Thus, an efficient system of transfer was established. The RCA societies and the New Immigrants in the United States aided those still in the Netherlands preparing to leave. The system worked so well that by 1856 over ten thousand New Immigrants had relocated to the United States. The majority settled within a fifty-mile radius of the southern shores of Lake Michigan.[12]

Though most of the New Immigrants soon enjoyed economic growth and prosperity within the United States, the most important matter to them was the welfare of their families and churches. In both institutions, their faith was continually expressed. Families conducted prayer and Bible reading at all three meals and even at coffee breaks. Outside of the family, the church dominated social life. The people demonstrated commitment to corporate worship, meeting twice every Sunday for an hour and a half. Many would often make a day of it and take along a lunch to eat at church between services. Only the most indispensable labor could be conducted on Sundays. All baking, cooking, and cleaning had to be accomplished on Saturday, and most frowned on leisure activities such as boating, diving, and swimming. The New Immigrants believed Sunday to be exclusively a day for worship of God at church.[13] In effect, the closed Sabbath day epitomized their closed society: almost every activity on Sunday revolved around the worship services, and the rest of the week most social functions orbited through the church community in some manner.

Beyond that, the New Immigrants seemed to believe that it had been God's providence that brought them to their respective settlements. Though they had encountered many hardships and struggles, they considered the initial stages of immigration and settlement to be a success. Most had endured the worst of the journey and the primitiveness of early establishment, and remained largely unscathed. They also realized that the RCA had played a crucial role in the success of their venture. In the minds of the New Immigrants, the RCA had been an instrument of God to benefit them in their immigration. For those obvious reasons, a warm relationship existed between the New Immigrants and the RCA.

The newcomers felt that they could accept a close relationship with the RCA, because the RCA had been born in the Netherlands when the Reformed Church remained entrenched in the older Reformed doctrine to which the New Immigrants so fiercely clung. The RCA had strong roots in the Hudson River Valley and in New Jersey, as those were the areas of earliest settlement during the Old Immigration from 1623 to 1664. In 1848, the RCA made its initial overtures to the New Immigrants about the possibility of union. By April of 1850, a large collection of the immigrant congregations convened to formally approve union with the RCA. They noted that they had been strengthened and encouraged in their dealings with the RCA ever since their arrival in the United States. They went on to say that while they considered all Christians brothers, they would be most comfortable in a denomination that implemented the same Confessional standards and fundamental principles of church government. Finally, the New Immigrants indicated that they had felt nothing but love and acceptance from the RCA, and so now desired to "make manifest the fellowship" and merge with them.[14]

Many of the New Immigrant congregations soon affiliated themselves with the RCA. There seemed to be a genuine sense of gratitude to the RCA for allowing the union. The RCA had cared for and advised them upon their arrival in the United States and the relationship now continued under more formal auspices. The New Immigrants often expressed how they cherished the "feeling of love and brotherly fellowship" and that they desired that the union with the RCA would "grow closer and more cordial."[15] The story of the New Immigrants had come almost full circle: they now again enjoyed the fruits of affiliation with a large, organized denomination.

A SCHISM WITHIN THE RCA

From all appearances, the formalization of the relationship between the New Immigrants and the RCA seemed well received by all those involved. The upper echelon of the New Immigrant hierarchy especially seemed to enjoy the newfound support and fellowship. However, many of the laity distrusted the union and eventually would actively pursue their misgivings. Indeed, by 1852 a number of New Immigrant congregations began to clamor for secession from the RCA, lodging numerous complaints. Charges arose that the RCA had departed from the Reformed theological tenet of "election"—also referred to as predestination—when its ministers promoted a book entitled *A Call to the Unconverted*. They contended that the book denied election in favor of universal grace and that the author argued for salvation on the "merit of outward works" instead of grace alone.[16]

By September of 1855, a New Immigrant congregant leveled more accusations at the RCA concerning open communion—that is, that anyone might partake, as opposed to closed communion, which allowed only members of a church to partake. The New Immigrants had long been fervent believers in closed communion. Moreover, other New Immigrants also charged the RCA with failing to observe the Canons of Dort, the significant expression of the Reformed doctrine that espoused a strict interpretation of predestination. Beyond that, still other New Immigrants expressed dissatisfaction with the RCA's implementation of the Heidelberg Catechism—another tenet of the Reformed doctrine that had been typically utilized as a basis for many sermons.[17] It seemed inevitable that the history of fragmentation within the New Immigrant community would rise to the fore once again.

By April of 1857, the crises within the New Immigrant congregations of the RCA climaxed as a number of different churches announced their withdrawal from the denomination. Some of the churches took the opportunity to list their grievances, including the RCA's collection and use of over eight hundred hymns, which were being implemented contrary to Reformed church order; the RCA's policy of open communion—inviting "men of all religious views to the Lord's supper, excepting Roman Catholic"; and finally, the RCA's failure to mandate that the Heidelberg Catechism regularly be the basis of both sermons and instruction for classes.[18]

Soon the separated churches affiliated themselves and became the denomination known as the True Dutch Reformed Church—later to be changed to the Christian Reformed Church. Initially, the CRC struggled because of both a lack of revenue and ministerial candidates. In addition, the mother Seceded church in the Netherlands maintained formal relations with the RCA. The Seceded church tended to be dismissive of the CRC and concurred with the RCA that the Secession in the United States tended to be based on "arbitrariness, quarrelsomeness, assumed and never proven error."[19] The Secession of 1857 thus did nothing to settle the controversy within the Dutch immigrant community in the Great Lakes area. Rather, it merely marked the commencement of a twenty-five-year period that saw increasing tension.

The close proximity of the CRC and RCA denominations in the Great Lakes area and the fact that they interacted and conducted business together made it only natural that their theological differences would be frequent subjects of discussion, both informally and formally. That constant contact ensured the liveliness of the debate. Apologists from both camps composed numerous pamphlets and brochures defending their position and reproving the other. Much of the discourse considered the legitimacy of the CRC. However, as the years passed, the RCA also became the subject of scrutiny as it repeatedly failed to take a position on Freemasonry when petitioned by Classes from the Great Lakes region to condemn lodge membership as antagonistic to church membership. That omission cultivated a tension that came to a head in 1882 and ultimately solidified the existence of the CRC. The CRC had used that quarter century to identify and distance itself as uniquely different from the RCA.

Because of Freemasonry's secret rituals and declaration of oaths, the CRC and, indeed, almost all of the New Immigrants found it to be a suspicious organization. Most condemned the lodge as "a work of darkness and thus unlawful for a church member."[20] Jacobus Brandt, a justice of the peace and communicant of the church in Forest Grove, Michigan, summed up the assertion of most New Immigrants when he claimed, "Nothing compared so completely and accurately to the spirit of the anti-Christ as Freemasonry." He explained, "In the Masonic Lodge the name of Jesus may not be used, not even in their prayers. They have a few references from scripture in their books, but these are mutilated by carefully leaving out the name of Jesus. Freemasonry is also a religion. They have priests, altars, prayers, songs, death and resurrection to a new- or rebirth."[21] Thus, many New Immigrants decried the lodge because of what they construed as anti-Christian implications.

However, the RCA consistently refused to condemn Freemasonry, a fact that frustrated the New Immigrants within the denomination and embittered the CRC, which had so coveted an alliance with the Seceded Church in the Netherlands. Soon that omission by the RCA catalyzed a second secession. Beginning in 1881, New Immigrant congregations of the RCA in the Great Lakes began to formally announce their disaffiliation with the denomination and their subsequent union with the CRC.

Better still for the CRC, it now gained the recognition of the mother church in the Netherlands. Since 1857, the Seceded Church in the Netherlands had been voicing its disapproval of the CRC. However, in 1882 they dispatched a missive to the General Synod of the RCA relating its "deep felt sorrow that many members of your church belong to those secret orders, hiding in the darkness, and that even your ministers and professors openly confess that they belong to the lodge."[22] From that point on, almost all Reformed immigrants from the Netherlands shunned the RCA and joined the CRC upon arrival in the United States.

THE CRC FINDS ITS FOOTING

The Masonic controversy proved to have great benefits for the CRC. The influx of former RCA congregations and new Dutch immigrants tripled the size of the denomination during the 1880s.[23] Though debate still raged between the RCA and CRC, the two denominations then fought on a more equal ground. Indeed, the scholar Paul Conkin has noted that CRC would remain "intensely confessional," "rigorously orthodox," and would grow throughout the twentieth century to a size comparable to the older RCA.[24]

As the CRC grew more firmly entrenched in the United States, it sustained the conservative flank of Reformed Christianity in the United States. The church leadership worked to ensure that the confessional standards, the rigid Calvinism, and the antirevivalist spirit resonated throughout the denomination. In fact, some have noted that the CRC had historically shown a palpable hostility toward the more American-style new evangelicalism.[25] For example, when revivalist Billy Sunday toured through Michigan in 1915, one CRC author wrote that his lack of dignity "made Christianity a laughingstock," his sermon had a "superficial" quality, and his methods resounded with "individualistic" tendencies."[26] James Bratt (a historian who has written extensively on the denomination and the ethnic subculture) also noted that other CRCers clucked disapprovingly as the evangelicals placed emphases on Sunday school rather than catechism, prayer meetings instead of Bible study, topical discourses instead of catechetic sermons.[27] For the CRC, all such movements signaled a departure from the intellectual for a more impulsive, emotion-based religious experience and had no place within the church.

Moreover, the members of the CRC clung so fiercely to both their Calvinistic faith and Dutch ancestry that the denomination functioned as an enduring ethnic subculture: "The Dutch-Americans who worshipped in CRC congregations . . . created a host of separate ethnically homogeneous institutions—financial, political, educational, welfare, medical—to preserve cultural identity and resist absorption into the American melting pot. Such segregation was necessary if Dutch Calvinists were to retain their religious beliefs and patterns."[28] While the RCA presented a much more welcoming and genial face within the American community, the CRC prided themselves on "strictness of creed and code" and continued to speak the Dutch language at home and in worship.[29]

That "strictness of creed and code," however, did not necessarily engender an ideological monolith, and schism would again shake the denomination. By the 1920s the CRC would be debating the notion of "common grace." One of the most basic tenets of Calvinism remained the dogma of predestination: that God had imparted a saving grace restricted to the elect. In the late nineteenth century a Dutch theologian named Abraham Kuyper began espousing a neo-Calvinism that asserted that God went beyond the "special grace" of personal salvation and demonstrated a "common grace" to all of humankind in general. Kuyper at different junctures of his life would find employment and vocation as a newspaper editor, founder of the Free University, and, eventually, the prime minister of the Netherlands. The essence of common grace probably found its greatest summation when Kuyper declared at the founding ceremony for the Free University that "there is not a square inch in the whole domain of our human existence over which Christ, who is sovereign over all, does not cry: 'Mine!'"[30] The significance of the doctrine of common grace resided in the fact that it called for an engagement with the "world." Kuyper maintained that positive good still remained in the world—that common grace operates to restrain the evil of sin.

Such a notion functioned as a departure from the separatist/pietist tendencies of the CRC. In fact, some members viewed the conception of common grace to be indicative of a church attempting to reconcile with the "broader" views of the secular world. A notable pastor in Grand Rapids, Herman Hoeksema, vehemently insisted that Kuyper's espousal of common grace directly contradicted the Calvinist precept of total depravity—that is, through the sin of Adam and Eve all of humankind have been totally corrupted. Hoeksema found common grace to be irreconcilable with his notion of salvation for the elect and the "inevitable destruction" of all others.[31]

In 1924, the CRC Synod issued an official declaration that supported common grace.[32] The Synod stated that God indeed bestowed a non-salvific grace on all humankind in three manners: "1) The bestowal of natural gifts, such as rain and sunshine upon creatures in general; 2) the restraining of sin in human affairs, so that the unredeemed do not produce all of the evil that their depraved natures might otherwise bring about; and 3) the ability of unbelievers to perform acts of civic good."[33] Such a statement left little room for question as to where the majority of CRC congregations stood on the issue.

In response, Hoeksema departed from the CRC and several congregations and pastors followed. In 1925 they established the Protestant Reformed Churches. In the end, the fissure further demonstrated the CRC pattern of mobility and schism.

THE TENSION OF ASSIMILATION

Beyond the common grace dispute, the 1920s would prove to be a pivotal decade for members of the CRC as they cautiously maintained the balance between being Dutch and being American. The issue of assimilation became a controversy that provoked much apprehension. The CRC Dutch consistently refused to be swallowed by the dominant mainstream U.S. culture. Through the first two decades of the twentieth century, almost all CRC worship services continued to be conducted in the Dutch language. These families' earlier generations had come to the United States for two reasons: economic opportunity and conservation of religious values. In particular, they sought the freedom to exercise their faith, implement a private Christian education for their children, and to establish economic security. They did not necessarily have any predilection to embrace their adopted country and its culture.[34]

Instead, the original intent of the New Immigration had been to plant Christian communities. There would indeed remain a deliberate attempt to maintain homogeneity. As late as 1907 an article appeared in the CRC periodical, the *Banner*, which harkened back to the 1857 secession as a necessary preparation before fully engaging the American scene. It carried the title, "Not Ashamed of the Basis of 1857":

> Our great and peculiar duty and calling here was and is . . . to become more and more what God in his providence in the past had designed us to be as a Calvinistic people. . . . To reach this purpose . . . we had no right to be benevolently assimilated. . . . Christian isolation, therefore, was a duty, isolation to develop ourselves quietly and without due haste, to become firmly settled as to our principles . . . until we are prepared enough, strong enough, to cast us with body and soul and all our previous Calvinism as a world-and-life view as well as a religious system, into the arena of American religious and political and social life.[35]

Thus such a noteworthy endeavor demanded at least a modicum of isolation and segregation. However, some scholars have contended that these Dutch constructed for themselves "self-imposed ghettos" only because of their clannishness.[36]

The detached relationship of the Dutch ethnic communities found expression in 1915 with the German sinking of the *Lusitania*. James Bratt described how, at the time, the mainstream press in the United States roundly denounced the belligerent actions of the Germans. However, the Dutch-language periodical of the CRC, *De Wachter*, contended that the United States remained at least partially responsible because of President Woodrow Wilson's false neutrality. Moreover, the editors of *De Wachter* went on to indict the people of the United States for irresponsibility in their simple support of Wilson's policies and their prejudicial treatment of the Germans. Such a tendency continued throughout the early years of the war as *De Wachter* columnists gave much space to pro-German accounts of the war.[37]

After the United States entered the war, however, it became more difficult for members of the CRC to express such convictions without being labeled as aliens or traitors. Thus, a new tension arose. Eventually the tide turned, and the Dutch CRC began to become more patriotic as they understood the United States to be fighting in self-defense. Informal adoption of a position of support for the United States came in 1918 when the Synod of the CRC sent President Wilson a telegram denoting the "righteousness of the cause."[38] The Synod went on to join the Federal Council of Churches (FCC) in order to join that organization's army camp ministries.

The next decade saw the denomination attempting to be more accommodating to the larger social scene in the United States while also starkly delineating how they thought Christian faith should be practiced. Indeed, the social and cultural upheaval of the World War left the CRC members even more deeply committed to their faith, taking on an antimodernist outlook. Moreover, the denomination set a new precedent when it published a condemnation of what it saw as three particularly virulent forms of "worldliness": card playing, dancing, and theater attendance.[39] The importance of this unparalleled declaration lay in the fact that it represented one of the first times that the CRC offered a connection with fellow Protestants who could not claim to be either Dutch or Reformed. In fact, these three sins had been arousing pietists of many denominations for decades. Moreover, according to James Bratt, when the CRC wrote their rationale for prohibiting these worldly amusements, they included obvious hints of Fundamentalist dogma. In addition, earlier in the decade the denomination had made a decisive departure away from Dutch-language sermons toward English. Thus, by the late 1920s it would seem that the Dutch CRC would be slowly extricated from their insulated communities and into the larger arena of religion in the United States.[40] Indeed, they began a slow evolution toward the U.S. evangelicalism that they had heretofore found embarrassingly unmoored in doctrine.

The uniquely Dutch nature of the denomination seemed to be on the wane. The tide of Dutch immigration to the United States slowed during the 1930s. The previously consistent influx of immigrants and the continued utilization of the Dutch language for church services and publications had assured the maintenance of ethnicity. When both began to ebb in the 1930s, however, it would seem that the process of Americanization would only gain momentum.

MAINTAINING THE CLOSED COMMUNITY

The preservation of Dutch ethnicity, though, would again ascend to a prominent position within the CRC communities when the Great Depression and World War II beset the United States. The plight of the "world" left these Dutch Americans somewhat paranoid and intent on reclaiming their distinctiveness. A CRC spokesperson stated:

> We will have to fight and work much harder than we have in the past twenty years if we are going to preserve [our heritage]. The forces that tend to obliterate . . . our distinctiveness are becoming stronger and more numerous. Unless we retrace our steps and dedicate ourselves anew . . . to everything included in our Calvinistic heritage, we shall soon go the way of so many denominations . . . whose glory has now departed.[41]

The CRC became adamant about the conservation of doctrine during this era of strife. Numerous CRC authors doggedly sought to further explicate the rationale of Calvinism. However, that dogma continued to focus inward. The majority of written work demonstrated a preoccupation with what systematic Calvinism meant for the Dutch Reformed family. It seemed to offer little for the world outside of the Reformed faith. Theater attendance, movies, and card playing continued to be decried as vices, while economic depression, cata-strophic war, and genocide remained virtually ignored by Dutch Reformed thinkers.[42]

At the same time, the CRC grew increasingly uncomfortable with its affilia-tion in the Federal Council of Churches. A 1945 report to the Synod declared the FCC to be "wholly controlled by Liberals and Moderns."[43] Feeling disillusioned, the CRC distanced itself from that alliance and instead became more active in the National Association of Evangelicals (NAE)—a body that the denomina-tion had formally joined in 1943. The CRC found the NAE attractive because of its loyalty to the Bible and its stated goal of encouraging the nation to "recover its religious moorings."[44] The NAE sought to ally evangelical Protestants in a man-ner that allowed these more conservative churches to have voice in the conversa-tion that already included mainline Protestants and Roman Catholics.

Despite the alliance with the NAE, the isolationist tendencies of the CRC manifested in 1947. A CRC minister in New Jersey criticized the NAE for preaching and evangelism, the proper duties of institutional church bodies. Moreover, the pastor noted that the association tended to endorse a decidedly non-Calvinistic theology. In 1948 one report to synod asserted that the NAE might be so un-Calvinistic as to actually do harm to the CRC. That same year another report referred to the NAE as "Fundamentalist"—an epithet in CRC parlance.[45] One prominent CRC minister asserted:

> As to a united front with others who hold the so-called fundamentals of the faith with us, it should be pointed out that such a formal united front before the world becomes exceedingly questionable for Calvinists when those with whom we are joined deny the real fundamentals of the Faith, such as: Total Depravity, Uncon-ditional Election, Limited Atonement, Irresistible Grace, and the Perseverance of the Saints.[46] . . . It is ironical, to say the least, that those who deny these Fun-damentals should be called Fundamentalists! What happens to our Reformed witness in the world when, by formal and official representation, we are silent on these salient points of which our Faith is constructed? Are we not denying them publicly by such an organizational union which silences them?[47]

A 1949 report argued that continued membership in the NAE would eventually dilute the distinctiveness of the CRC and that continued cooperation with the association would have deleterious effects on the denomination's "distinctive creeds, distinctive practices, distinctive forms of devotion."[48] In 1951 the CRC left the NAE when Synod voted to withdraw. (The denomination would rejoin the NAE 1987.)

Even as the CRC continued its insular pattern of affiliation and schism, the members of the denomination could not escape some of the larger social forces of the United States. For some of the CRC members living at the halfway point of the twentieth century, the previous two decades of calamity seemed fitting for a nation full of vice and needing to be reproved by a righteous God. James Bratt has argued that the prosperity and comfort of the 1950s, however, left these Dutch Americans somewhat confused. Americanization again became an issue of great import. It seemed that even the most conservative members of the CRC had been swept up in America's growing middle class and demonstrated an eagerness to enjoy the fruits of membership: materialism and suburbanization. Dutch Reformed thinkers revised earlier commentary on the United States and began to spout rhetoric that smacked of civil religion. With the Cold War ever escalating, even previously critical authors began to insist that since God could not possibly support the Godless communists, He must, therefore, have a special plan for the United States.[49]

As they became more Americanized, these Dutch Americans seemed to gravitate to a particular brand of Americanness: conservatism. They hated materialism as they saw it espoused by labor unions. They despised the bureaucracy of government, but registered no distaste for that of corporate life. James Daane, a CRC member who wrote for *Christianity Today*, represented the rank and file of denomination well when he praised "America for having a churchgoer in space (John Glenn), presidents at prayer breakfasts, and evangelists in public print (Billy Graham in the *Saturday Evening Post*)."[50] Another prominent member of the CRC, Lester De Koster, lauded both President John F. Kennedy for proving that Christian politics could occur in the United States and FBI director J. Edgar Hoover for demonstrating the potentialities of the modern police force in the war against communism.[51]

Thus, in the latter half of the twentieth century, the Dutch CRC maintained a tension of preserving heritage while accepting assimilation. James Bratt aptly described the denomination as paradoxically seeming to both embrace and reject Americanization. For example, the evangelical resurgence of the 1970s and corresponding proliferation of "charismatic" Christianity rekindled religious embers for the CRC as well. However, rather than affiliating with the uniquely American brand of religion, the CRC worked ever harder to define its doctrines in contrast. CRC authors indicted the movement for placing emotion over intellect and engaging in Arminanism—perhaps the most heinous doctrinal inaccuracy for these Dutch Americans. In essence, then, the members of the CRC continued to live in a context of strain where they attempted to maintain religious and ethnic identity while accepting at least some aspects of the dominant U.S. culture.

Bratt noted that the reluctance of these Reformed Dutch Americans to accommodate the larger culture has been a notable phenomenon: "Having all the marks of the WASP profile, the Dutch did not melt into American society on schedule; in fact, they vociferously resisted the same. Socioeconomic dysfunction cannot explain the anomaly, for in these areas the Dutch have adjusted well enough. The reason must lie in considerable part in the realm of 'outlook,' 'religion,' and 'mind.'"[52] In essence, the Dutch Americans had created for themselves a largely invisible subculture in which they alternately affirmed and denounced the dominant culture.

They often insulated themselves in their church circles that included two services and catechism classes on Sunday and society meetings throughout the week. Within these tight social circles, however, differing strains of Calvinist ideology began to compete with one another. These subspecies had significant influence on how the church should and would regard some of the social upheaval of the mid-twentieth century. As already alluded to in the Protestant Reformed Churches rupture, these Dutch Calvinists often espoused competing perceptions of how true Calvinism should be expressed. Within the CRC itself, different modes of Calvinism emerged. Roughly speaking, according to Bratt, these would be labeled the pietists, the confessionalists, and the positives. This spectrum ranged from a "flee the world" isolationist mentality to a more Kuyperian engagement of the world that ultimately sought a transformation.[53] Thus even within the closed society of CRC denominationalism, the potentialities of rupture and departure seemed to simmer perpetually.

In the end, as the turbulent middle half of the twentieth century approached, Dutch Calvinists of south Chicago found themselves attempting to preserve the closed community while enjoying the successes of white middle-class life in the United States. However, their history and culture predisposed them to isolation and mobility. With such well-established precedents, it should have been easy to predict the reaction of Chicago CRC congregations, as social forces rapidly transformed their neighborhoods. The CRC represented an ethno-religious tradition which, when threatened external pressures, became ever more vigilant about protecting that which they understood to be in jeopardy. When the Black Belt of the South Side began pushing first into Englewood and then farther south into Roseland, the affected congregations had no templates for adaptation or innovation. Instead, they had a well-rehearsed ritual for protective mobility.

3 · SHUTTERED IN CHICAGO

In Chicago, the CRC's history and precedent of fissure and schism mutated into a highly systematized pattern of social insularity. Almost all social activity was conducted under auspices of the church or the school. Because of that isolation, the Chicago CRC community of Roseland remained stable and homogeneous for over one hundred years and the Englewood community for about eighty. The social forces of the middle half of the twentieth century would eventually overwhelm the CRC in these neighborhoods, however. Leaders of the faith community would have to make a decision regarding the maintenance of isolation and homogeneity and whether those even existed as laudable goals by the late 1960s.

THE EARLY YEARS

Following the 1834 Secession from the National Reformed Church of the Netherlands, in 1849 a group of immigrants from the North Holland province founded an Illinois settlement called High Prairie—later to be called Roseland—some six miles north of another Dutch settlement known as Low Prairie, later to be renamed South Holland, a suburb of Chicago. The Dutch settlers of High Prairie immediately began establishing their farms, erecting barns and then homes. They produced eggs and dairy products to sell and barter with at the local store. For the first summer, they traveled to Low Prairie for Sunday worship. However, the six miles to services were especially difficult since the families had to extend their trip to avoid paying a toll on the Sabbath at Riverdale. Thus, when the first winter came, the settlers of High Prairie made the decision to establish their own church. Eighteen charter members founded the Holland Reformed Church of High Prairie. The next spring (1850) the church built a structure for the Sunday worship services.[1] An influx of immigrants from the Netherlands continued as the settlement of High Prairie grew, and by 1855 the congregation became too large for its original building. They quickly constructed a new larger house for worship in order to accommodate the flourishing young settlement.

By 1860, the government opened a post office and named the area Hope. By 1875 the name would be permanently changed to Roseland. Within one generation the poor Dutch immigrant community had become largely self-sustaining in the country of adoption. Historian Henry Lucas related how one Dutch resident of Roseland wrote back enthusiastically to the Netherlands in 1853: "The country . . . was not a wilderness, but a prairie. Wages were excellent, products sold at good prices, all people were equal; there were few police and few saloons, and there was little drinking. Taxes were low. There was no hunger or want; the Hollanders ate beef or pork thrice a day, and in place of rye bread enjoyed the finest wheaten."[2] The Roseland area gradually drew away from general farming and developed a more lucrative gardening economy in order to take advantage of its close location to the markets of Chicago.

Beyond Roseland and South Holland, other Dutch communities sprang up in the greater Chicago area. On the South Side, a Dutch neighborhood called Groninger Corner developed in 1848, with its inhabitants finding work in the rapidly developing Chicago economy. Later, during the 1880s, a new cohort of Reformed Dutch immigrants established themselves in the community of Englewood, a South Side neighborhood just north of Roseland. Shortly thereafter, two churches—one CRC, one RCA—were founded in the community and developed growing membership rolls.[3]

Englewood and Roseland both maintained intensely Dutch atmospheres. The 1884 *History of Cook County* offered a detailed description of Roseland:

> The boundaries of the hamlet are Halsted Street, Indiana Avenue, and Ninety-ninth and One Hundred and Fifteenth streets. Its inhabitants are sturdy, phlegmatic, industrious natives of Holland; and standing by some of the little squat small windowed houses, hearing the high-Dutch gutturals, seeing the pollards and rectangular enclosures, the square-faced, wooden-shoed, tow-headed little Dutchmen; in fact, observing the 'tout ensemble' would cause one to fancy themselves rather near Amsterdam than fifteen miles from Chicago.[4]

The Reformed Dutch of Chicago had established for themselves a thriving enclave.

SWEPT UP IN INDUSTRIALIZATION

Soon, however, the Dutch Roselanders experienced a dramatic transformation of their environs. By 1880 the Pullman Company had built a series of factories just to the west of Roseland. Eventually, the massive industry employed roughly ten thousand men. Moreover, the entire district quickly became an industrial hub as International Harvester, Sherwin Williams, and Illinois Central constructed factories in the vicinity. Until the arrival of Pullman, Roseland had steadfastly remained an ethnic Dutch community—almost a reproduction of a village that could be found in the Netherlands. The original inhabitants of Roseland now, however, found themselves in close quarters with new settlers, immigrants of Slavic origin.

One result was that the value of the Dutch vegetable farms and their product expanded immensely with a growing customer market. Many CRC and RCA congregants became extremely wealthy from real estate as they sold parcels of land that they had bought for $5 per acre for up to $2,000. With such incomes, the Dutch actually expanded their activities and founded new Reformed and Christian Reformed churches. However, not all of the Dutch felt so comfortable in their neighborhoods within rapidly expanding Chicago: "Hollanders from Englewood and Roseland, who preferred rural life, moved into" northwest Indiana.[5] Thus, a pattern was established before the turn of the century that would be repeated decades later: a sizable portion of the Reformed Dutch quickly relocating to outlying regions when the current situation grew uncomfortable due to a surge of newcomers. As previous generations in the mother country had demonstrated, this traditional Dutch community had no aversion to high mobility.

Despite that exodus, many did stay in Chicago proper. Though they constituted an insignificant minority within the city, they still prospered enough to have established twenty-four different RCA and CRC congregations, along with a number of Christian schools. In 1920, the Chicago Association of Commerce computed that in the 9th Ward (which included Roseland and Englewood), persons of Dutch birth or ancestry constituted 8.37 percent of the total population. However, some scholars have questioned such a low figure and have asserted that census takers failed to include Americans whose ancestors had been of Dutch birth.[6]

MAINTAINING THE CLOSED COMMUNITY

The 1900 census stated that the greater Chicago area held 20,000 Dutch and followed only Grand Rapids, Michigan, in number of persons of that ancestry within a city. As in the rest of the CRC settlements in the Great Lakes, the typical pattern of settlement involved focally located churches and Christian schools. That development template proved critical to the survival of these ethnic communities. In fact, the historian Amry Vanden Bosch made the assertion that the enduring nature of the CRC communities in particular found direct correlation to their "attachment to the church, as well as to their strong race consciousness."[7] For these Dutch, race meant the same as nationality. Just as fervently, they clung to their religion and its attendant traditions and expectations. Dutch American historian Robert Swierenga has insisted that

they were "tribal" in their fierce in-group loyalties, behavior of exclusiveness, and the transplanting of Old Country institutions and the Dutch language and culture. In concert with the other Dutch Reformed communities of the American Midwest, the Chicago Dutch conducted worship services entirely in the tongue of the motherland until the 1920s. But above all they were Calvinists of the old school, dating back to the Synod of Dordrecht (1618–19).[8]

In other words, they distanced themselves from the "religious churn" that Robert Putnam and David Campbell described regarding religion in the United States in their volume *American Grace: How Religion Divides and Unites Us.*[9] Contrary to the dominant pattern, they had sorted into bunkers, not clusters.[10] They feared worldliness and attempted to create for themselves closed communities in which, although they could not avoid limited interaction with Jews and Catholics, they would be able to lives of obedience largely unimpeded by outsiders.[11]

In addition, these Dutch made great efforts to control their economic activity. They had a tendency to patronize only Dutch businesses, craftsmen, and banks. Soon many found their niche in the larger economy collecting cinders—residue from boilers and waste incinerators. The collection of cinders mutated into garbage hauling, a desperately needed service in a city quickly outgrowing itself as well as one immune to economic depression. The Dutch domination of garbage hauling became a virtual monopoly: since Dutch arrival in the Chicago area there have been 350 Dutch-owned garbage collection businesses. Swierenga related: "The owners were often related to one another, they attended the same churches, and they relied on informal understandings and agreements to control contracts and keep out interlopers. Critics aptly called them the 'Dutch Mafia.'"[12] Beyond that, Swierenga noted that the South Side Dutch especially gravitated to carpentry and masonry.[13] The Dutch had clearly carved out a substantial economic foothold within the economy of Chicago.

With so many CRC members involved in blue-collar trades, the rising power of the unions during the 1940s and 1950s inevitably became an issue. The CRC had a history of condemning labor unions as "worldly" and materialistic because of the socialistic underpinnings, ungodly or atheistic principles, and reputation for violent tactics. In Chicago, they would only join unions when pressured and would typically refuse active participation. They often rationalized membership as a necessity for feeding their families. However, the church did not always sympathize, and membership in the Teamsters or AFL-CIO could translate to a forced resignation from congregational leadership in the Consistory (the governing body of a local congregation). Eventually some of the CRC workers in the Chicago area found a solution when they established locals of the Grand Rapids–based Christian Labor Association (CLA). Grocers and building tradesmen constituted the majority of the membership. The Dutch American tradesmen and teamsters from the RCA, however, had fewer issues with unions in general and never offered support for the CLA. Thus, the CLA became a very minor entity with only CRC support. In the end, the CRC workers had again separated and isolated themselves—from even their ethno-religious counterparts in the RCA.[14]

Beyond church and business, the CRC members also established mutual aid societies and social clubs. With few government safety nets, the CRC leadership felt obligated to help those within the "household of faith" who struggled financially. Thus the early societies found their duties to encompass mostly the disbursement of economic aid. Some of these demonstrated a modicum of mutuality with the RCA. The "Zelf Hulp" Burial Fund Society allowed members of the two denominations to cooperate in buying plots in "Dutch Sections" of local cemeteries. In 1913 it had grown to 14,000 members, and records demonstrated payouts of about $150,000 in death benefits. A multitude of other societies surfaced in the Chicago area, as well. The Excelsior Society, for example, campaigned for the establishment of the Holland Home for the Aged, which opened in Roseland in 1914. CRC and RCA congregations also jointly supported a Christian college in Palos Heights and participated together in softball, basketball, and bowling leagues.[15]

The bulk of collaboration, though, occurred within the denomination. The CRC congregations in Roseland cooperated in support and administration of an evangelical mission to Lithuanians in Chicago. Moreover, Amry Vanden Bosch related that by 1927 the CRC churches of Chicago had established not just a mission for proselytization, but one for the indigent as well: the Helping Hands Mission, which included a headquarters and two separate branch locations. In all, the Helping Hands Mission had forty-four beds for transients and during the winter months often fed one hundred men a day. The CRC congregations also routinely conducted clothing drives, with the donations distributed at the Helping Hands Mission. In addition, the administrators expected the men to attend the gospel meetings and Sunday school classes that they offered. In one year the Mission reported holding 407 gospel meetings, distributing 8,300 tracts and 955 gospels, and making 67 hospital visits. Vanden Bosch characterized the Mission:

> The Reformed churches have never tolerated the usual revival methods in their churches and they have never introduced them in their mission work. They rely rather on the more practical and enduring methods of education and continued and helpful assistance to the family. Families are induced to leave tenement districts and take up their residence in a better district of the city, and to unite with some evangelical church.[16]

It would be safe to infer that by "usual revival methods," Vanden Bosch meant high-pressure, emotional pitches for potential converts to make a decision in the moment. For better or worse, the Calvinist notion of predestination or election took some of the emphasis off evangelism efforts.

In addition, the Chicago CRC congregations also established the Chicago Jewish Mission in an effort to evangelize their Jewish neighbors. It would seem that the CRC had no interest in socializing with Jews, but were very willing to proselytize. This particular endeavor, however, elicited a measure of antipathy from its very targets and found little success.[17]

Politically, the CRC remained largely inactive. Vanden Bosch described them as being politically "unorganized."[18] However, when they did venture to a polling place, they almost invariably pulled the lever of the Republican candidate. The CRC members would almost never run for office themselves. Even when RCA members—who did run for office more frequently—campaigned, they could not necessarily count on the support of their fellow ethnics in the CRC, unless they ran as party-backed Republicans. In 1906, the Dutch-language newspaper *Onze Toekomst* attempted to create a voting bloc for Dutch candidates without success. The editors remarked that they found a spirit of cooperation to be "non-existent among our people."[19] At the root of such fragmentation lay the isolated and insular CRC. Though most outsiders would find the differences between the CRC and RCA largely imperceptible, the CRC members felt the religious chasms to be too vast to cross for them to vote for fellow Dutch candidates from a different denomination.

Meanwhile, the first few decades of the twentieth century saw the RCA becoming increasingly socially active. In 1910, RCA members founded the Christian Anti-Saloon League, which eventually changed into the Dutch-American Civic League of Chicago to promote progressive causes. In 1920 an RCA minister founded the Christian Political Society. Again, in 1930 RCA professionals formed the United Dutch-American Voters' League. All the while, the CRC members ignored the activism of their closest contemporaries in Chicago. They even refused to acknowledge the Christian Political Society when the organization endorsed government funds for Christian schools.[20]

The separatist strain among the CRC had such intensity that some parents "considered their children's infrequent marriages to RCA families as 'mixed' or interfaith marriages."[21] Although there was little discernible variation between the faith and theological doctrine of RCA and CRC congregations, CRC parents "wanted their children, especially at the high school level, to socialize with 'their own kind.'" According to Swierenga, remaining in Christian schools augmented the likelihood of marrying within the community.[22] In fact, the CRC members could be so insular that within their own communities they formed subgroups based on provincial heritage in the Netherlands. For some, this remained a practical matter, in that Dutch dialects had wide ranges and mutual comprehension could be difficult. However, even in church voting evidence of provincially based voting blocs could sometimes be detected.[23] In essence, these CRC Dutch could utilize an almost infinite number of methods to carve out an ever more unique identity for themselves in the United States.

THE COMPREHENSIVE CONGREGATION

With such a predilection for isolation, CRC members had to depend on the congregation as the primary vehicle for social interaction. In his magnum opus, *Dutch Chicago: A History of Hollanders in the Windy City*, Robert Swierenga vividly detailed how the church dominated the social life of these families. He noted that they took the biblical imperative to "live in the world, but not of it" very seriously. Pastors often warned of the perils of city life. Laboring and doing business with "outsiders" had to be begrudgingly accepted, but "social life was lived among family and fellow church members."[24]

A study of intermarriage—a common indication of levels of assimilation—demonstrated the limited nature of CRC social circles. Any non-Christians clearly fell outside the pale of potential marriage partners. Marriage to Catholics was infrequent as well because of cultural taboos—Reformation Day sermons that lauded the work of Martin Luther in Germany frequently enumerated the failings of Catholicism. In addition, the CRC doctrinal standard, the Heidelberg Catechism, referred to the "popish mass" as "idolatry."[25] Such language hardly promoted accord with the Catholic parishes down the street.

As stated earlier, the more conservative elements of the CRC even held reservations about marriages to members of the sister denomination, the RCA. RCA members derived their "outsider" status from the fact that they opposed Christian education and had a more open policy for involvement in "worldly" amusements. Swierenga referred to a quotation from a CRC woman: "I married Henry Kickert from the Reformed Church, but he is a good man."[26] Swierenga asserted that the "but" spoke volumes as to the reservations of CRC members marrying into the RCA. As already alluded to, before marriage young CRC people in Chicago received strict admonition not to get involved in "worldly" activities. In fact, the CRC leadership attempted to channel the entire social life of it children "into an exclusively ethnoreligious track."[27] The consistent effort to remain "spiritually separate from the world" meant that movie houses, theaters, cabarets, and dance halls were off limits. The CRC Synod of 1928 condemned theater attendance, dancing, and card playing:

> Synod instructs consistories to inquire of those who ask to be examined previous to making public profession of their faith and partaking in the Lord's Supper as to their stand and conduct in the matter of worldly amusements, and, if it appears that they are not minded to lead the life of Christian separation and consecration, not to permit their public confession. . . . Synod urges consistories to deal in the spirit of love, yet also, in the view of the strong tide of worldliness which threatens our churches, very firmly with all cases of misdemeanor and offensive conduct in the matter of amusements; and, where repeated admonitions by the consistory are left unheeded, to apply discipline as the last resort.[28]

Since the denomination had such strict sanctions against worldly amusements, they created social activities for the young people that kept them both secluded and occupied. Beginning in the 1890s, the denomination created Young People's Societies. Swierenga quoted one minister's rationale: "We believe our young people ought to stay in their own circle and are very glad to see our young people join our Society. In unity there is strength."[29] These societies varied from church to church, but usually included social and religious teaching and organized weekly activities. The minister of the congregation usually provided leadership and intentionally used the Society as a method for integrating the younger generation into the life of the church. For instance, meetings of many Young People's Societies were ordered by Robert's Rules of parliamentary procedure as a precursor to involvement with the Consistory.

The youth of the CRC also had the opportunity to become involved in the Young Calvinist League (YCL). In the early 1950s, YCL morphed into the Boys Calvinist Cadet Club and the Girls Calvinette Club. In many ways, these two clubs operated as religious counterparts of the Boy Scouts and Girl Scouts. Decades earlier, the CRC and RCA had coordinated youth activities with one another. However, the CRC's creation of these two clubs manifested a chasm that had been developing between the two denominations because of differences concerning education: the RCA children tended to enroll at public schools while the CRC children went to Christian schools.[30] This distinction would prove to become an essential aspect of CRC identity. Indeed, when Classical representatives visited a church, they commonly assessed the congregation's commitment to Christian education. (A Classis is a collection of churches within a defined geographic area; each congregation has multiple representatives at the meetings, and the body's decisions are binding for affiliated congregations.) A high proportion of enrollment of the children in Christian school would be lauded as a "commendable covenant consciousness" and indicative of "a strong and robust" church.[31]

Social programming went beyond the youngsters of the CRC. Adults also had societies, missionary fests, and conferences. Beginning in 1937, Chicago area CRC families could even vacation together exclusively at the Cedar Lake Bible Conference and Campground. Activities ranged from Bible studies to evening worship to inspirational speakers to lake recreation. In every dimension, the church dominated social life. Swierenga quoted one female CRC member: "Church societies were a way of life. Our three young ladies' groups were very large. Annual socials were great occasions—mother and daughter festivities, socials for older ladies' aid groups, and also home-talent programs."[32] A typical week for a CRC family in Roseland was summed up: "Before the widespread ownership of cars by our people, families would troop in a body, in rain or shine, to church for services that lasted an hour and a half. Monday nights were for Catechism; Tuesday nights were for Young Men's Society, Young Women's

Society (none of this mixed sexes Christian Endeavor stuff such as the Reformed churches indulged in), and Consistory; Thursday nights were for Choral Society."[33] There was little room in that schedule for any other forms of social life.

The closed nature of the society left the CRC congregations ill-prepared for neighborhood change. There existed few of the "bridging ties" that Robert Putnam discussed in *Bowling Alone*. When Charles Terpstra arrived in 1965 to pastor Second Roseland CRC, he described the scene during his first days in the neighborhood:

> Very few [CRC families] had moved away in 1965 when I arrived, but the very first black family moved into the neighborhood of the church the same week I moved into the parsonage. And they were bombed, with Molotov cocktails, they were right across from the church, kiddy corner across the alley, and they were bombed right after I got there. And the police were parked on that curb by that house for weeks, at the very time my family moved there. And I went to see them one of my first or second days in the neighborhood. And I was severely crit-icized by a [church] member family right across the street who said, 'He went to see the black family before he came to see us.' That was a no-no.[34]

As Terpstra later assessed the situation, he noted the limits of the closed CRC community in responding to the advance of the Black Belt: "The people were not oriented to the challenge at all. It just seemed to me that the teachers and preachers that had preceded me in Roseland had not in any concerted way pre-pared the people to accept the challenge to minister to a different population that was moving into the neighborhood." Terpstra's references to the "teachers and preachers" again demonstrated the primacy of the schools and congregations.

Terpstra also explained that he thought the CRC community in Roseland still envisioned itself as an immigrant community: "The [CRC people in Roseland] congregated on safety and their isolation and living together in close-knit neigh-borhoods and this population change was a big shock and they weren't prepared for it. . . . Their leaders . . . talked about being the church and being there and taking care of themselves and remaining orthodox and faithful and all of that." Certainly a component of the insularity of the CRC communities in Chicago was linked to maintenance of Reformed Calvinist traditions. Terpstra, however, asserted that social patterns also had more banal sources: "They stayed living close to each other and depended on each other and became interrelated and they stayed as homogeneous and as close-knit and as isolated as they could. One reason was preservation and protection of orthodoxy, but I'm sure another rea-son was just plain comfort and pleasure. I mean, it's nice to live together with people that are like you." Thus Terpstra's perspective revealed that the highly internal orientation of CRC social circles had both the manifest function of shielding orthodoxy and the latent function of allowing a high degree of social well-being and comfort.

Although voluntarism is a dominant feature of the U.S. religious scene, it fails to fully account for the CRC closed community. Families and individuals within that denomination experienced a more limited freedom. To leave the denomination would have been to rupture almost all social ties. While they could freely move about within the denomination from congregation to congregation, they risked severe sanction if they departed from the denomination entirely.

In many ways, the CRC families in Chicago epitomized the closed community. They had fewer strong connections to the broader community—even when compared to a very similar denomination, the RCA. The CRC institutional base of the church bred a social isolation in the middle of a vast metropolis. When the urban demographic changes of the urban United States of the 1950s and 1960s arrived in Chicago, these CRC communities had little desire and few resources to respond or adapt.

4 · A CASE STUDY OF THE CLOSED COMMUNITY

The Disrupted Integration of Timothy Christian School

As already noted, the church alone did not claim the entirety of CRC members' social lives. Instead, the church and the Christian school worked in concert. Leaders of the CRC understood the Christian schools they established to be "feeders" or "nurseries" of the church and vital links in the CRC social chain. A test of the closed CRC community would occur in the 1960s when African American parents attempted to enroll their children at Timothy Christian School—an institution on the West Side of Chicago founded and supported by CRC families. The African American families quickly and resolutely found themselves rebuffed by the board of the school: their children would not be enrolled. Although the hierarchy of the denomination scolded and chided those affiliated with Timothy, they had no protocols for enforcing integration of the school or, failing that, any discipline for those who refused enroll the African American children. The Timothy Christian School incident demonstrated the autonomy of the supporting churches and the effectiveness of the closed community in maintaining homogeneity.

Though the church did not operate the schools, the two institutions, according to Robert Swierenga, were equal partners and very closely associated.[1] In fact, one school publication clearly articulated an apology for the Christian schools: "We have reasons to believe that the rearing of our children in the fear of the Lord, including instruction in the Bible, leavening the whole of primary education, largely accounts for the loyalty to our church [CRC] and its doctrines."[2] Thus the Christian school actively partnered to ensure the future vitality of the church.

In addition, these CRC members felt compelled to establish private schools because they fervently contended that education remained the responsibility of parents, not the government. In 1883, the CRC congregations established Ebenezar Christian School, which on its opening day of classes already boasted an enrollment of three hundred students. By 1910 the CRC families had established five Christian schools in the Chicago area. In 1918 they completed their educational system with the establishment of Chicago Christian High School in the center of the Englewood neighborhood. Significantly, the local CRC congregations did not administer or control the schools, as would be the model for both Catholic schools and some other Protestant church-affiliated schools. Rather, the more informal CRC "societies" (the name for the organization of school-affiliated families) retained all responsibility for them. In this way, the associated families ran the school. In essence, the CRC communities sought a private education wherein the teachers articulated Christianity within every subject and insisted that religion stood as the "chief motive in life."[3] Initially, all the schools taught in Dutch in an effort to ensure the vitality of the language in the United States. Only in 1924 did Ebenezar Christian School, the strongest proponent of Dutch instruction, finally reduce teaching in the mother tongue to one afternoon a week. It would seem that in both education and worship CRC members sought to shield themselves from the influences of city life in Chicago.

THE PRIMACY OF CHRISTIAN SCHOOLS

The parent-run Christian schools within the CRC communities of Chicago were understood as a necessity in the vast and hostile environment of the urban United States. The influences of Dutch Calvinist thinkers such as Guillaume Groen van Prinsterer and Abraham Kuyper gave impetus to these schools. Kuyper, in particular, developed a notion of "sphere sovereignty." That is, different aspects of life should be governed by different entities. With that in mind, Kuyper contended that the education of children remained the responsibility of parents, and was "not a prerogative of the state or the church."[4]

In contrast with the insular CRC, which made Christian schools an essential part of religious training, their cousins in the RCA went on the record twice in Synodical decisions supporting public education. The RCA leadership understood public schools as foundational to democracy and argued that Christian students in those schools should be representatives of Christianity. Swierenga remarked that such attitudes were indicative of that denomination's assimilation compared to the CRC.[5] The RCA did, though, express an appreciation for Christian education—within the church, the college, and the seminary. A history of the RCA's Synod of Chicago noted the following: "As part of its program of church extension, the Particular Synod of Chicago was concerned about Christian education in its various forms—founding academies, colleges, and seminaries, promoting Sunday schools, and emphasizing the need for catechetical instruction among the youth."[6] It should be noted that Christian elementary and secondary schools remain conspicuously absent from this statement. Based on historical documents, the Synod of Chicago seemed particularly interested in ensuring that the youth of the church study the Heidelberg Catechism within the congregation to ensure that they remain solid representatives of Christianity in larger society: "The times call for well-trained, well-indoctrinated membership in our churches, in order that they may not be swept aside by every wind of doctrine so prevalent everywhere."[7] For the RCA, formal Christian education tended to be the domain of the church and postsecondary institutions. The church and family retained the responsibility for ensuring that young people had the training necessary to be "salt and light" in the wider world.

On the other hand, although CRC leaders allowed the need for Christians to be involved in secular society, they saw a greater threat from imposition of secularization. CRC parents grew especially suspicious of the inclusion of Charles Darwin's evolutionary theories and the liberal social values of modernism in the public school curriculum. Many believed such thinking to be heresies. Moreover, the inherent religious neutrality of public schools forced an accommodation of "all shades of belief."[8] In response, CRC Christian school advocates met in Chicago to develop their own textbooks.[9]

The consistory of First CRC of Englewood summed up the importance of Christian schools: "We love to speak of the chain consisting of three links—home, church, and school."[10] Though the school did not have a formal relationship with the church, the CRC Synod of 1936 clearly delineated a de facto relationship:

> It is the duty of the consistory to use every proper means to the end that a Christian School may be established where it does not exist, and to give wholehearted and unreserved moral backing to existing Christian Schools and a measure of financial help in case of need. . . . If, in the judgment of Classis, a Consistory does not support the cause of Christian Schools, Classis should continue earnestly to admonish such a consistory publicly in its classical meetings and privately through church visits until in truly repents.[11]

The Chicago CRC congregations took the instructions from Synod very seriously. By 1940, the seventeen area churches had 89 percent of their children enrolled in Christian schools. Swierenga noted that in many congregations the refusal to send children to Christian schools meant social exclusion at church. Another man who had grown up in a CRC congregation and in the Christian schools of Roseland asserted that membership in good standing in the church "all but presupposed sending one's children to Christian school."[12] Moreover, some have argued that the schools as institutions

> were the most critical link in the chain that maintained cultural and ecclesiastical oneness in the church; they kept alive the Dutch language until the 1920s and

transmitted Calvinist theology and cultural values for many generations. The schools stood in the shadow of the churches, and this naturally concentrated the families nearby, which strengthened community and church life immeasurably. The Christian high schools also provided a place to find a marriage partner within the greater Chicago Reformed communities. Christian schooling thus kept the children within the cocoon of the church.[13]

Such an insulated and isolated demeanor did not bode well for the CRC Dutch who resided in Chicago proper on the eve of the some of the most radical social restructuring to sweep across the industrial core of the United States after World War II. It would be these changes that would began to cause fissures in the edifice of the CRC community in Chicago.

THE ATTEMPTED INTEGRATION OF TIMOTHY CHRISTIAN SCHOOL

As African Americans arrived in CRC community neighborhoods in Chicago on the wings of the Great Migration, one particular Christian school became a battleground that would vividly illustrate the limitations of the insular social circles. While the CRC communities of Englewood and Roseland would eventually see a mass exodus of congregants, the CRC community in Cicero also faced a concurrent racially charged issue. Previously, those same congregations in Cicero had begun a "home missions" church in the neighboring community of Lawndale. At the time, Lawndale had a reputation as an African American ghetto riddled with crime. In 1963 the mission formally organized as the Lawndale Christian Reformed Church and counted twenty-four members and thirty-five baptized children.[14] By 1965, some parents from Lawndale CRC decided to attempt to send their children to the local CRC society-supported school: Timothy Christian School. The school board, though, refused to enroll the African American children from Lawndale CRC. At Calvin College in Grand Rapids, Michigan, a college owned and operated by the CRC, the school newspaper (*Chimes*) distilled the events:

> On April 14, 1965, members of the Lawndale Christian Reformed Church of Chicago requested admission for twenty-one of their children to Timothy Christian Schools of Cicero. They were refused. The school board justified its refusal of the Lawndale parents' request on the grounds that the community in which the schools are located could be hostile to the presence of these children in their city. The cause of the refusal and the predicted hostility: the children are black.
>
> This seemingly simple request for entrance into the Christian school has spawned a controversy that has since grown to crisis proportions. The black parents have continued to request admission; the school board has continued to

refuse it. As a consequence of the obstinacy of both sides, the entire Christian Reformed community in the Chicago area has become polarized. Vicious hostility arising from deep-seated attitudes has tortured the community on the rack of bitterness and recrimination. Tolerance, magnanimity, and practically all hope for solution have evaporated; the threat of violent explosion pervades the situation.[15]

The Timothy school board defended its actions with the argument that they simply sought the well-being of the African American children in question. They cited the City of Cicero as a place of intense hostility toward African Americans. William Buiten, vice president of the school board, remarked, "The board's decision is not based on animosity; just on the community problem."[16] In other words, the board's official statement of defense centered on a concern for the safety of the African American children in the openly racist community of Cicero. They argued that they perceived concrete threats from the citizenry of Cicero. One school board member allowed, "A few of the school parents are racist, yet most fear for their children's safety."[17] Implicitly in that defense the board hoped to distance themselves from the smell of racism.

Residents of Cicero at the time did have a reputation for consistently opposing integration. The working-class Italian and Polish descendants had moved to Cicero in the wake of blockbusting by unscrupulous realtors—the practice of preying on white fear of home depreciation because of proximity to neighborhoods of racial minorities. One local CRC pastor even argued that the Cicero residents "hated blacks" because they associated them with losing their homes (and thus the assumed appreciated value of the house as well) in previous neighborhoods. The same pastor noted that these residents worried about "the enormous crime rates which 'the colored' bring to a neighborhood."[18]

Proponents of allowing the African American children to attend Timothy noted that Cicero had allowed African Americans to work and shop in the city. However, a board member quickly countered that allowing children to attend school in area remained a much different matter than simply working or shopping. He stated that residents feared that African American families would eventually desire to move closer to the school that their children attended. A letter to the editor of *Cicero Life* seemed to substantiate the claim of the board member: "I see in the paper that Timothy Christian School is going to bring twenty Negro students to attend classes and they are seeking the approval of neighbors for this. . . . Where are those twenty students going to eat lunch? Where will they play while the other students go home for lunch? People of the area take heed. If you don't put a stop to this mad scheme now you had better have For Sale signs printed up because you will be needing them soon afterwards."[19]

In 1968 the Timothy board sent out six hundred letters to families living in the immediate neighborhood of the school. The board wrote the letters to solicit feedback concerning the possibility of having African American children attend the school. They received 244 written responses and divided them into categories. Only 13 respondents expressed encouragement. Ten reacted with hostility and threats of violence, and 85 expressed opposition without reason. Opposition was expressed by 132, who gave various reasons. Two letters chided the board for attempting to pass responsibility for the decision on to area residents. In sum, there seemed to be three dominant explanations for opposition: 1) eventually African American parents would follow their children to Cicero, buy homes, and "the neighborhood would be ruined"; 2) children should always attend school close to their present home; and 3) it would present a danger to the children, the Christian school society, and the general populace of Cicero.[20]

THE SCHOOL BOARD DENIES ENROLLMENT

On September 24, 1965, the school board announced that they had decided to refuse to admit the African American children from Lawndale CRC. They justified the action on the basis of the safety of the children. The board minutes articulated a rationale: "The board realizes that the children from our Christian Reformed Church in the Lawndale area should be accepted for admission. . . . However, enrolling them in our schools in the Cicero area . . . [involves] dangers that all those in touch with the prevailing racial attitudes are well aware of."[21] After the announcement, the board received a standing ovation from the parents in attendance.

On the other hand, many Lawndale CRC parents reacted in shock and found the board's defense somewhat dubious. Many expressed deep suspicion regarding the claim that Cicero did not, in fact, have enough law enforcement personnel to ensure the protection of African American students. Indeed, after the Timothy board issued a public statement as to why they had refused admission to the Lawndale children, the Cicero town council responded by promising complete protection of the African American students: "We will definitely protect the students. We've got to protect everybody whether they're residents of Cicero or not; that's the law."[22]

Dissatisfied with the Timothy board ruling, the Lawndale parents continued their fight. One Lawndale mother, Dorothy Roberts, wrote to the CRC denominational periodical, the *Banner*: "We are black Christians, members of the Christian Reformed Church. . . . But—and here is our problem and our pain— our covenant children below the high school level have been denied admission to the Christian school located only three miles from the church."[23] Even the use of the term "covenant children" demonstrated a strong familiarity with the CRC, as that is a term that is part the denominational lexicon. The editor of the *Banner*, Lester DeKoster, responded with sympathy to Ms. Roberts, but also noted that if the racial situation in Cicero was as volatile as reported, the Timothy board deserved the benefit of the doubt and prayer rather than "criticism and condemnation."[24]

At the CRC Synodical meetings of 1968, the events in Cicero weighed heavily on the proceedings. Ultimately, Synod 1968 wrote a Synodical Declaration on Race Relations:

> Fear of persecution or of disadvantage to self or our institutions arising out of obedience to Christ does not warrant denial to anyone, for reasons of race or color, of full Christian fellowship and privilege within the church or related organizations such as Christian colleges or schools . . . and that members of the Christian Reformed Church advocating such denial, by whatever means, must be reckoned as disobedient to Christ and be dealt with according to the provisions of the Church Order regarding admonition and discipline.[25]

Undeterred by the firm statement of Synod, the Timothy board maintained the status quo.

Soon, however, the cacophony of dissent grew louder. First, four teachers from the school sent letters to the school board, the church Consistories of Classis Chicago North, and parents of their respective students indicating their inability to accept the refusal of the school to enroll African American students.[26] Teacher Karen Cox wrote:

> In direct opposition to the teaching of our Lord and in open conflict with the position of the Synod of the Christian Reformed Church, the Board has refused to admit black covenant children to Timothy Christian Elementary School. As an employee of the Board, I am put in a position of compromise. I cannot accept this policy. I have been deeply troubled. I do not believe the Lord will bless my teaching under these circumstances.[27]

In response to the fact that the 1969–1970 academic year began without the admittance of African American students, another teacher, Elizabeth Westerhof, wrote:

> There is no more time to be hopeful; the thing we prayed and hoped would not happen is now happening, and our Christian conscience cannot be silent. The Board's refusal to change its policy puts it in direct conflict with the position of the highest deliberative assembly in the denomination, and in direct conflict with the demands of discipleship to Christ clearly laid upon us by God's word.[28]

Both teachers requested that the school board take immediate steps to enroll African American children by October 20, 1969. Eventually, four teachers and the principal would resign in protest over the board's decision.[29]

In addition, the Lawndale parents turned to Classis Chicago North to pressure Timothy into accepting their children. The Classis did meet multiple times about the issue but refused to accept the Lawndale overture to declare the Timothy board's actions as "sinful" because of its implicit racial discrimination. The Classis did, however, appoint a Classical Advisory Committee on the Lawndale Educational Needs. At the committee's first meeting, the attendees began working on a plan to sue, on behalf of the Lawndale parents, Cicero public officials who could not or would not provide protection. The committee noted that a successful suit would almost guarantee the presence of federal marshals in Cicero. Upon report of these activities, the Timothy board responded with vehemence that not only would they not support such a lawsuit, they might also be compelled to hire their own attorney to argue against it.[30]

Reeling in frustration from the lack of cooperation by the Timothy board, the committee reported to Classis Chicago North:

> We can come to no other conclusion than that the Timothy Board . . . [is] simply not interested in identifying themselves with our fellow believers in Lawndale in their effort to obtain and enjoy "all the privileges of full communion with the people of God." . . .
>
>   We find it to be intolerable when we, as Christians, allow black-hating racists to determine, in effect, the admission policies of our Christian schools. Our collective apathy and indifference to this evil situation has caused untold damage to the feelings of our black brethren and has seriously undermined our ministry of the Word in the black community.[31]

At the same Classical meeting a motion "to declare to be sinful the present policy of the Timothy Christian Board by which black covenant children are excluded from Timothy schools in Cicero, and to declare that this policy cannot be continued with willful disobedience to Christ" was defeated.[32] (A similar motion had been defeated at Classis a couple of months earlier as well.) Ultimately, the Classis disbanded the Advisory Committee on the Lawndale Educational Needs. For the moment, it appeared that Classis Chicago North would take the issue no further.

Meanwhile, the pages of CRC-affiliated journals continued to debate the topic. The editors of *The Reformed Journal* dedicated the entire March 1970 issue to the matter. The series of articles ran under the title, "An Event That Shames Us All." The first piece by Henry Stob declared the necessity of repentance for the entire CRC denomination over the issue of race. Nicholas Wolterstorff, a Calvin College philosophy professor, wrote an article entitled, "Is the Christian Reformed Church Serious?" The professor wondered whether the denomination actually meant to be more inclusive of other races or whether the official pronouncements had a hollow ring. Wolterstorff contended that the pronouncements of Synod concerning race coupled with the actual activities at Timothy constituted "the grossest hypocrisy."[33]

As the intellectuals of the denomination debated, the situation for the Lawndale parents grew intractable. Classis Chicago North stood pat even as Synod called upon it to "bring its policy and practices into harmony with the deliverances of Synod without further delay. Failure to comply will cause Classis Chicago North to be in contempt of Synod and in open disregard of the church of Jesus Christ."[34] In 1970, the Classis met twice and had the opportunity to respond to the directive of the Synod. The Classis refused to take any action of censure beyond a pastoral letter of concern to the Timothy school board. In fact, the Classis at one point actually asked Synod to change its race policies and amend past statements concerning the Timothy-Lawndale situation.[35] The position of the Classis caused agitation across the denomination. Martin LaMaire, a contributor to *The Reformed Journal*, asserted that that "local assembly of churches [Classis Chicago North] continued to refuse to recognize that racial exclusion (among Christians) is disobedience to Christ. Classis demonstrated no empathy with black fellow believers who suffered discrimination because of racial prejudice."[36] Thus the withering glare of the denomination expanded from the Timothy board to include Classis Chicago North.

In October of 1971 the situation became even more polarized when three African American families from the Lawndale community filed a lawsuit against the school. Complicating the matter, the CRC's Synodical Race Committee provided the suing families financial aid and counsel in pursuit of the litigation. The suit asked the court to issue an injunction forcing the Timothy board to enroll African American children and to take legal action against any citizens of Cicero who proved to be obstacles to such a move. By late November, U.S. Federal Judge Hubert L. Will criticized the Timothy board:

> It is just as unconstitutional to be discriminatory under alleged discrimination or coercion as it is to be discriminatory enthusiastically or voluntarily. Discrimination isn't discrimination depending on the motivations. It is discrimination depending on what your conduct is, and nothing that I read in the complaint . . . as to why the Cicero situation is different, the tensions in the community and so forth . . . are not justification for unconstitutional discrimination.[37]

Despite the court opinion, most of the African American parents of Lawndale refrained from enrolling their children at Timothy Christian School. Duane VanderBrug, the pastor of Lawndale CRC at the time, noted that "It is true that (admitting black students) into the school would have been risky and tense; no one doubted that." However, the minister also indicated that the Lawndale congregation's council and education committee anticipated that as they petitioned on the basis of Christian discipleship, the board would eventually relent and enroll the African American students in a "courageous, biblical stand."[38] The school board, however, would not acquiesce.

RESOLUTION WITHOUT RECONCILIATION

Within a couple of years, Lawndale parents opened their own Christian school. At the same time, Timothy began the process of selling its Cicero facilities in an effort to move the entire system farther out to Elmhurst. While these developments alleviated some tension and the practical problems of Christian education for Lawndale children, the episode in general left an ugly legacy in the area for the CRC. It became an emblematic episode of the failures of a closed community. Beyond that, it clearly demonstrated the local authority that dominated the CRC.

In the end, Martin LaMaire succinctly laid part of the blame in the type of shuttered societies that the CRC had been fostering in the United States since the denomination's inception. In his discussion about Classis Chicago North's steadfast refusal to acquiesce to the demands of Synod, he noted,

> Another factor which accounts for the continued recalcitrance of this body [Classis] is its Insular Mind. Regarding its handling of the Timothy-Lawndale issue, Classis is resentful of interference by "outsiders." It is up-tight because Synod, and the rest of the denomination, is looking over its shoulder and disapproving of its actions. It wishes to live on its own island of detachment from whatever the rest of the Church might say or do. Its general attitude can be summed up tartly: "What right does Synod—or the rest of the Church—have to meddle in Cicero?"[39]

Though LaMaire only singled out Classis Chicago North for indictment, the ethos of the "insular mind" could be rightly said to pervade every CRC community in the Chicago area. From the establishment of Christian schools to the hesitance to intermarry with the RCA to the heavily programmed societies for all ages, the CRC in Chicago actively sought "sufficient isolation." Klaus Schooland, a CRC professor, had earlier articulated that with such a mentality. "Calvinists should construct a holy community within and against the larger society. . . . Through them [separate organizations] we shall become more conscious of our position over against the world."[40] Thus, Schooland trumpeted the merits of the "closed system." He posited that for the CRC, isolation gave strength. The fervency of the closed community should be noted in Schooland's use of the word "against." In this way, the CRC families in Chicago practiced an urban form of Emile Durkheim's "mechanical solidarity."[41] That is, some societies maintain cohesion because of homogeneity in background, belief, and experience. For certain CRC communities, the mechanical solidarity demanded a sense of not just being outside of the larger society, but also a rebuke to the failures of that society. Such a practice of "othering" allowed the communities to remain unadulterated.

The maintenance of internal homogeneity remained a primary effort of CRC communities in Chicago. Though social upheaval surrounded them, the majority attempted to stay the course within the tradition. They displayed a limited desire or ability to adapt to the demographic transformations sweeping the city. Even those within the same ethnoreligious denomination who dared challenge the actions of these communities found themselves quickly dismissed as interlopers. Such an attitude allowed for easier maintenance of internal uniformity in these Chicago CRC communities.

PART II CITY AND NEIGHBORHOOD CHANGE

5 · CHICAGO

A Brief History of African American In-Migration and White Reaction

The closed and insular CRC congregations in Chicago would eventually become actors in a drama that had begun decades earlier. The changing demographics in Englewood and Roseland were part of a larger social phenomenon that drastically altered the residential patterns of Chicago and other core cities across the United States. The creation of the African American ghetto in Chicago that would eventually subsume both Englewood and Roseland began during World War I. At that time, African Americans from the South, attracted to the work available in northern steel mills and packinghouses, became participants in the Great Migration. Thousands of African Americans came to Chicago in hopes of "bettering their condition."[1] However, upon arrival and settlement, many of these African Americans would experience bitter disappointment.

In Chicago, African Americans often found limited housing and work choices. Even during the early influx of World War I, newly arrived African Americans were forced into highly segregated ghettos that were actively enforced by whites. In the end, many of the migrants' hopes foundered on the inconsistencies of both business cycles and outright racism.

THE ARTIFICIAL GHETTO

Much has been made of the urban crises that seemingly erupted in the mid to late 1960s as major race riots exploded in numerous U.S. cities. However, those flash points are better understood as symptoms of a crisis that had been brewing for decades as African Americans were systematically excluded from housing and economic markets. In other words, residential segregation and deindustrialization of the urban core conspired to create the urban crisis, not the riots.[2] As African Americans migrated to the urban North "they would suffer disproportionately the effects of deindustrialization and urban decline."[3] In the end, the promise of steady and secure employment in the North proved to be an illusion for many African Americans.

As debilitating as restricted employment was, however, residential segregation became the most "visible and intractable manifestation of racial inequality." In many northern metropolises, African Americans "found themselves entrapped in rapidly expanding yet persistently isolated ghettos."[4] Federal housing policies had a complicit role in starkly demarcating the residential areas of U.S. cities into bifurcated racial zones. Beyond that, local businesses and residential institutions also colluded in artificially creating what historian Arnold Hirsch has referred to as the "second ghetto" in the years following World War II.

Between 1940 and 1960, the African American population of Chicago nearly tripled. Such an influx strained the resources of the existing African American community and gave impetus to seek housing in neighborhoods that had previously been all white. As the Black Belt of Chicago began to expand, white homeowners responded in sometimes violent manners. At the same time, downtown business interests began to fear that the decay surrounding them would eventually suffocate the Loop commercial district. In response, they sought government support for an urban renewal project that would reclaim the Near South Side of Chicago as a white middle-class neighborhood.[5] The solution included racially segregated housing projects that extended for miles. Redevelopment, renewal, and the construction of public housing all fed into the growth of residential segregation in Chicago. In that way, public policy "played a key role in fostering, sustaining and, not infrequently, intensifying the separation of the races even in the absence of Jim Crow legislation."[6]

The government sanctioned and supported the creation of the post–World War II ghetto in Chicago. The government's role in urban redevelopment and massive public housing programs had a tremendous impact on the evolution of the ghetto. In Chicago, such programs tore down decaying neighborhoods, and former residents often became "fugitives" whose only alternative was the high-rise public housing projects. Others sought refuge in nearby residential areas. That "spillover" process hastened racial succession in the neighborhoods like Englewood and Roseland.

In the end, institutions played a complicit and conscious role in creating distinct racial residential segregation. Those institutions included banks, real estate agencies, and varying levels of government. The end product was a racially stratified residential pattern in many U.S. cities that had operated as terminuses for the Great Migration.

THE PARTICULARS OF CHICAGO

As the African Americans migrated to Chicago, they found little to satisfy their search for economic equality and social justice. In fact, Chicago businesses often exploited African American workers, employing them only for the worst jobs and as strikebreakers. These practices led to antagonism between African Americans and white workers. The situation left one scholar to conclude, "Black migrants moving North were too many to assimilate, too poor and vulnerable to return South, and too American to support ethnic enterprise. In the aggregate, they reaped none of the possible benefits of labor migration."[7] Indeed, the economic and social promise of the urban North would prove unfulfilled for the majority African Americans making the journey from the southern United States.

Initially, Chicago became a focal point of the Great Migration because of its stockyards, steel mills, foundries, and easy accessibility via the railroad. Scholars of the movement have pointed to three basic catalysts for the African American migration. First, the agricultural market of the South had been devastated by the invasion of the boll weevil. The lack of crop made African American workers expendable and, thus, unemployed. Second, many African Americans became frustrated by the legitimized discrimination that existed in the South in the form of Jim Crow. Third, World War I broke out, leaving departing servicemen's jobs open, cutting off the immigration supply for labor, and creating the wartime boom economy: a perfect storm of industry radically ramping up as the workforce became depleted.[8]

Thus, the impetus for leaving the South was largely economic in character. In the early years of the twentieth century, the economy of the South became dependent on the manufacturing base of the North. That is, the raw materials of the South needed the factories of the North to be transformed into finished products. In that way, the South's "local products were undercut by cheaper, northern ones; its labor transformed from artisan to wage labor; and, in general, its terms of trade with the North were made unfavorable."[9] These alterations in the economy left certain sectors of the southern population as expendable and superfluous.

At the same time, the boom economy that accompanied World War I offered African Americans the opportunity to enter northern industrial employment for the first time. The combination of increased orders, loss of European immigrant employees, and loss of labor personnel to the military left northern industrialists with a greatly diminished labor pool. In response, they did the previously unthinkable and offered factory positions to African American southerners.[10] Hoping for better lives, hundreds of thousands of African Americans left the South every year, destined for northern cities that included Chicago.

LIMITED OPPORTUNITIES

Once in Chicago, the newly arrived African Americans experienced extreme ghettoization. In other words, they found themselves forced to live in homogeneous communities and had infrequent contact with those outside. White hostility created and ensured the maintenance of the segregation. African Americans were consistently barred from white neighborhoods by tactics that ranged from the subtlety of restrictive covenants (agreements among property owners that prohibited signers from selling or renting to African Americans) to the conspicuousness of physical bullying and intimidation. The ghetto became more entrenched as there seemed to be no hope for mobility in Chicago. The neighborhood color lines received rigid enforcement and escape remained unrealistic for African Americans.[11]

Beyond the ad hoc activities of white neighbors and neighborhood associations, the Chicago Real Estate Board enforced the residential color line, as well. The board adopted a practice of selling houses to African Americans only on blocks contiguous to other African American blocks. This intentional practice appears to have begun in 1917, when the board noted with alarm that southern-origin African Americans poured "into Chicago at the rate of ten thousand a month" and that they would "do more than $250,000,000 in damage" to property in the city.[12] Moreover, the board reflected the sentiments of many white Chicagoans when it petitioned the City Council to pass an ordinance prohibiting further migration of "colored families" to Chicago until such time that the city could develop "reasonable restrictions" sufficient to "prevent lawlessness, destruction of values and property, and loss of life."[13] Though that particular petition failed because of a clear lack of constitutionality, the agitation by the board continued.

Compounding the debilitating effects of the compulsory residential segregation was the fact that the African Americans in Chicago did not have the ability to develop a true enclave. Traditionally, in a functional enclave society the migrants would have had the ability to sustain and support themselves through the development of ethnic enterprises. The African Americans in Chicago, though, had no opportunity to develop an economic independence— they relied on white employers and thus never acquired self-sufficiency. Not surprisingly, those limited economic prospects led to inferior community institutions and facilities.[14]

The plight of African Americans in the Black Belt of Chicago offered a striking contrast to European immigrant communities. Whereas the Irish, Dutch, Poles, Jews, or Italians banded together to enjoy a common linguistic, cultural, and religious tradition, "the blacks were forced together by a systematic pattern of discrimination that left them no alternative."[15] In fact, it has been argued that African Americans in Chicago felt less connected to each other by common cultural heritage than by a mutual set of grievances. The racial solidarity of the Black Belt thus actually functioned as a response to a negative environment rather than a positive choice: "it was an attempt to preserve self-respect and foster self-reliance in the face of continual humiliations and rebuffs from white society."[16]

The presence of the African Americans in Chicago also fostered the development of a united white front. Regardless of ethnicity, religion, class, or political affiliation, the whites in Chicago partnered in the effort to keep African Americans segregated both socially and spatially.[17] The violence and intimidation of whites toward African Americans prohibited the latter from the following the path of other immigrants out of the tenements and into the wider city. In essence, the African Americans in Chicago felt a constriction more intense than that of any other immigrant group.[18]

Forced into the ghetto with no chance for moving out into white neighborhoods, the best that African Americans could do was push out the borders of the Black Belt. The boundaries simply extended out into the contiguous territory. Eventually, the Black Belt would have to be measured in square miles, as opposed to blocks. Even while the territory expanded, the housing densities remained extremely high. Beyond that, African Americans tended to inherit some of the oldest and most primitive housing in Chicago. Eventually, even the limited better housing deteriorated with overcrowding.

Though African Americans in Chicago acquired what would hardly be considered prime real estate, they continually met resistance in their outward expansion as they found themselves surrounded by hostile white communities. Some whites in these communities even asserted that there existed "nothing in the makeup of a Negro, physically or mentally, which should induce anyone to welcome him as a neighbor."[19] Furthermore, the whites living in the neighborhoods on the fringe of the Black Belt feared that the presence of African Americans would taint their local communities. The whites began to organize more frequently against the spreading ghetto: "violence often met the black who strayed beyond the stipulated lines," and "it became commonplace for mobs of fifty to two hundred chanting people armed with bricks, bats, and lengths of pipe to surround the home of a black 'invader,' deface the exteriors, and smash all the windows."[20] Such threats and violence resulted in consistent overcrowding in the older areas and constant tension on the edges. The situation became more agitated as African Americans continued to arrive in Chicago. By 1919, a dramatic housing shortage existed. Returning servicemen seeking housing exacerbated the predicament.

RACIAL ECONOMIC TENSION

In addition to tension over housing, there was also labor strife in Chicago. Often, newly arrived African Americans from the South found work as strikebreakers during World War I. In fact, the terms "negro" and "scab" became "synonymous in the minds of numerous white stockyard workers."[21] Much as with housing, the Armistice and impending return of military personnel only made the competition for jobs between whites and blacks that much sharper.

The racial tension in Chicago culminated in a weeklong race riot that began July 27 and ended August 2, 1919. During the violence, the city experienced intermittent "killing and maiming and burning."[22] The aftermath left 38 persons dead, 537 injured, another 1,000 left homeless.

Despite that hostility, African Americans continued to arrive in Chicago during the Great Migration and had no intentions of returning to the South. It seemed that both the white Chicago and African American Chicago had resigned themselves to living in a state of perpetual tension of contested housing. In the years of interlude between the two World Wars, the African American population in Chicago continued to strain for adequate housing, but had little difficulty in securing employment. After some initial struggles in the fallout of the riots of 1919, African Americans in Chicago enjoyed an economic boom with the rest of the city.[23] News of the opportunities in Chicago spread down the network to the South. As a consequence, the African American population of the city increased by 114 percent during the 1920s.[24]

During the 1920s, the Black Belt included about eight square miles of Chicago proper. Between 1925 and 1929, the Black Belt enjoyed what has been referred to by some authors as the "fat years." During that era, the Black Belt became a vibrant city in its own right. African American–owned businesses and newspapers thrived, and residents had the opportunity to be represented politically by fellow African Americans.[25]

However, late 1929 would usher in the "lean years." The Depression that took its toll on the United States in general ravaged the Black Belt of Chicago as well. Within the African American community there existed a sentiment that they were always the "last hired and first fired." The paucity of jobs was exacerbated as more African Americans continued to migrate from the South. In fact, between 1930 and 1940 the African American population of Chicago grew by more than 43,000.[26]

Although consistently disappointed by the housing situation in Chicago, African Americans there still held hope for economic opportunity. By 1939, residents of the Black Belt began to anticipate a war boom economy. Initially, however, most of the African Americans expecting to get called to work were disappointed: the Depression had caused thousands of white Chicagoans to lose their jobs as well, and they were the first to secure jobs as the economy began to gain momentum. Angered by the apparent hypocrisy of the war effort, African Americans in Chicago picketed with signs that read "Hitler must own this plant; Negroes can't work here."[27]

However, such discontent quickly subsided. First, President Franklin Roosevelt issued an executive order in 1941 that demanded an end to racial discrimination in hiring by government agencies and manufacturers holding defense contracts. Second, the Japanese bombing of Pearl Harbor and the subsequent acceleration of production in the United States required unprecedented amounts of industrial labor. Necessity allowed African Americans to be reintegrated into Chicago's industrial base. In fact, the wartime economy demanded so much production that Chicago would eventually face a labor shortage. In response, a new wave of African American migration from the South began trekking for the Midwest. As 60,000 African American migrants arrived in Chicago between 1940 and 1944, they found no shortage of jobs, but little of anything else.[28] In fact, many were "literally unable to find shelter in the ghetto."[29] Housing continued to be inadequate, and the Black Belt offered overpopulation, poor recreational facilities, and overcrowded schools.[30]

AD HOC RESTRICTIONS ON
AFRICAN AMERICAN HOUSING

Though the city maintained an ostensible peace in the immediate post–World War II era, with no days-long riots as in 1919, racial antagonism continued to be manifest in short outbursts of violence. Most of the riots were spontaneous and unplanned in nature: "White residents—often including women, older men, and teenagers—reacted to the attempted integration of their neighborhoods with name calling, rock throwing, arson, and assault."[31] Arnold Hirsch referred to this epoch as one of "chronic urban guerilla warfare."[32]

In addition to violence, some neighborhoods organized property owners' associations in an effort to "prevent further Negro invasion in their territory" and "to stimulate all those already there with the desire to get out." For example, in the neighborhoods of Hyde Park and Kenwood, the association had an organized list of methods. These included: "A. The prevention of loans to colored people to buy property. B. Prevention of the renewal of mortgages on the property of Negroes. . . . C. Prevention of lease renewals; and the loaning of funds to white agents for the improving of their property, making it accessible and desirable for white tenants. D. Getting the Hyde Park hotels to agree to not employ Negroes unless they lived in the Negro district."[33]

Even as white residents attempted to enhance their segregation and concentration, African Americans sought relief from the congestion of the Black Belt and began to investigate housing in previously restricted areas of Chicago:

> As migrants from the South crowded into the Black Belt, landlords converted more and more apartment buildings into kitchenettes to accommodate them. The neighborhoods became poorer and denser, and the black middle class became discontented and tried to get away from the slums by expanding the Black Belt southward into previously white neighborhoods—a difficult process, because nearly all of the white neighborhoods were segregated by fiercely maintained custom and, in many cases, also by force of law, through "restrictive covenants" that barred blacks from buying houses and were then perfectly legal.[34]

The restrictions on African Americans in the Black Belt had debilitating consequences. Because of the industrial demands of World War II, the African American population in Chicago doubled from 250,000 to 500,000 in the decade beginning 1940.[35] With such crowding and constriction, the Black Belt often became a "dumping ground for vice, poor-quality merchandise, and inferior white city officials."[36] The "quarantining" of African Americans intensified their "differentness" from white Chicago and "curtailed their chances for improvement." Thus they became "the victims of circular reinforcement."[37] The only hope for relief was a block-by-block advancement of the Black Belt. Once a home had been purchased in a previously all-white area by an African American, others would quickly move to the area and create a "beachhead."[38] In that pattern the Black Belt grew and subsumed white blocks, frequently touching off hostilities.

Eventually, however, white homeowners would have little recourse beyond that violence. In the 1948 case of *Shelley v. Kraemer*, the Supreme Court handed down a ruling that made restrictive covenants unenforceable. In response, many white families began leaving for the suburbs. Armed with Federal Housing Administration and Veterans Administration loans, white families contracted builders to construct 300,000 new housing units in the suburbs during the decade. The evidence revealed a mass departure of whites for the suburbs: between 1950 and 1956, 270,000 whites left Chicago proper.[39]

As the housing market expanded outward in suburbia for whites, the economic growth of the World War II era allowed some African Americans to purchase the recently vacated homes. (African American families found the suburbs closed to them: from 1946 to 1963 only nine African American families moved into previously all-white suburbs in the Chicago area).[40] The African American middle class increasingly sought relief from the disinvestment and deterioration of the Black Belt. Many began to accept the financial and physical risks, and bought homes located in the previously all-white neighborhoods that surrounded the traditional African American neighborhoods. The block-by-block advance of the Black Belt continued.[41]

However, the expansion of the Black Belt still remained severely constrained and segregation thrived unabated. African American families became victims of a dual housing market.[42] Affordable housing for African Americans was consistently located in areas contiguous with the ghetto. Once a white neighborhood had been "tainted" with the presence of an African American family, realtors and speculators (frequently referred to as "blockbusters") arrived to profit from the transition. These agents exploited the situation by offering below-market values to white sellers who hoped to salvage as much of their investment as possible. In turn, the agents would sell the home to sometimes desperate African American families at an above-market price, for a sizeable profit. A document published by the Church Federation of Greater Chicago noted the "predatory" nature of the real estate industry: "Further offenses of the real estate dealers include the encouraging of Negro invasion of white territory to reduce the selling price of surrounding property, making enormous gains in buying up and reselling to Negroes."[43] The often-repeated process ensured continued segregation. In fact, the initial presence of "'fly by night' realty offices" preparing for "the big financial kill opening up to them" commonly represented the first symptom as African Americans moved in and whites moved out.[44]

THE ROLE OF POLICY AND PUBLIC HOUSING

In an effort to alleviate the congestion and attendant tension within the Black Belt, the City of Chicago began a massive program of urban redevelopment and renewal. A major component of these new programs was the construction of high-rise public housing complexes similar to the projects built by the Works Progress Administration (WPA) and controlled by the Chicago Housing Authority (CHA) in the late 1930s and early 1940s. These new buildings, which Hirsch referred to as "vertical ghettos," supplemented the old ghetto.[45] In the end, they proved not to be a viable solution: "These mammoth steel and concrete developments, many of which were as jarring as the sprawling symmetry of the suburban tract, were surrounded by fields of extreme poverty and so conjured up images of isolation and hopelessness."[46] In constructing the projects, the CHA attempted to blend progressive ideals of European modernism and state governance. Such an architectural disposition led to "dreary high rise blocks and their rows of uniformed windows punched out of cliff-like walls."[47]

Despite the problems associated with the public housing projects, the CHA continued into the 1960s to build the structures at a rapid pace. Between 1955 and 1963, the CHA built 21,000 low-income family apartments; all but 2,000 were of the high-rise variety.[48] Even as the CHA managed the pace of construction, they could not control the location of the housing projects. The city council of Chicago wielded that power and made every effort to keep public housing out of white neighborhoods. In 1949, the CHA presented a plan to build future structures on vacant outlying lands, but saw that proposal roundly defeated. It seemed the council's primary concern had little to do with ensuring adequate housing for the poor in Chicago: "The council insisted that blighted housing in the ghetto be torn down and new housing rebuilt on the same location. The problem of residential displacement and the fact that the severe housing shortage would be little alleviated by such strategy were of minor significance to the council members. The really important task was achieved: Chicago's poor black residents remained segregated."[49]

The placement of the housing projects was not only afflicted by powerful white ethnic leaders who refused to tolerate an African American presence in their neighborhoods, however. African American politicians colluded as well in their attempt to maintain a homogeneous constituency in the ghetto. A mono-chromatic electorate ensured the holding of an office or a position.

The placement of Robert Taylor Homes (opened in 1962) demonstrated perhaps the clearest case of intentional segregation and discrimination. The designated tract that would eventually host the Homes had at one point been described as the "largest contiguous slum in the US."[50] Since the 1930s, most of the units that the Homes would replace had been designated "dilapidated" and lacked both adequate water and sanitation facilities.[51] In the end, however, while the Robert Taylor Homes might have provided better living conditions, they did nothing to alleviate segregation. The process simply shifted the resident African Americans out of older stock housing and into sterile concrete towers.

Though the CHA seemed to believe in the transformative power of the high rise building, they had little opportunity to ensure the viability of projects like the Robert Taylor Homes. The Homes, for instance, were further isolated by the presence of Interstate 94 (also known as the Dan Ryan Expressway): "Mayor [Richard J.] Daley brazenly constructed a large expressway at taxpayer expense, effectively shielding the housing development from the predominantly white community of Bridgeport, where he lived."[52] In effect, the highway functioned as an artificial barrier that ensured the limited access of African American residents to the rest of the city.

As the city council, the mayor, and even African American politicians ensured that the African Americans languished in separate areas of the city, large amounts of federal subsidies guaranteed white families the ability to live comfortably in the suburbs with unprecedented ease. The money that the federal government spent on the interstate highway system, combined with the mortgage assistance made available to veterans, inspired the development of new housing in Chicago's suburbs. Between 1940 and 1950 Chicago proper grew by 6.6 percent while the suburbs grew by 32.7 percent. During the 1950s, the shift to the suburbs increased in intensity: Chicago's population declined by 1.9 percent while the suburbs increased by 71.5 percent. Of the 688,000 new houses built in greater Chicago in the fifteen years immediately following World War II, 77 percent were located in the suburbs.[53]

Their housing choices already limited by white hostility, African Americans in Chicago were further ghettoized by the CHA, Chicago politics, and federal subsidies. The combination left black Chicagoans severely constricted in the ghetto. In fact, since the 1950s Chicago has routinely been cited as one of the most segregated metropolitan areas in the United States. But urban political economy does not fully explain the prevalence of residential segregation. A component of that severe ghettoization involved the decisions, processes, and cultures of religious institutions like the CRC congregations of Englewood and Roseland. As the Black Belt advanced southward to their neighborhoods, those congregations would have to assess what it meant for their respective communities.

6 · THE BLACK BELT REACHES ENGLEWOOD AND ROSELAND

Though government policy and the animus of white homeowners limited their mobility, African Americans who did have some economic success tended to move from the heart of the Black Belt to its fringes—slowly advancing into adjacent white neighborhoods. By the 1950s the neighborhood residents of Englewood began noting the demographic changes advancing southward. Shortly thereafter, the same contiguous expansion of the Black Belt would have a dramatic effect on Roseland as well. The CRC congregations in those two neighborhoods would soon find themselves in rapidly changing communities.

While the CRC congregations on the west side of the city endured extreme scrutiny and criticism from the denomination in the wake of the Timothy Christian School debacle, their fellow denominational members in the South Side neighborhoods of Englewood and Roseland made similar decisions about the African American influx. At Timothy Christian School the board attempted to keep African Americans out of the institution. On the other hand, the CRCers in Englewood and Roseland decided to leave the area and take their institutions with them, despite a fairly long history in both communities.

ENGLEWOOD

In the years directly following the Civil War, Dutch CRCers began settling the open prairies of Englewood for market gardens. The Englewood community lies about six miles south of Chicago's Loop. The spectacular growth of Chicago, however, forced many of the farmers to begin making the transition to urban work in the 1880s. At that time, the township had 2,850 inhabitants, and most business crowded around the intersection of Sixty-third and Halsted Streets. By the mid-1880s, Englewood would be connected to Chicago by multiple railroads and interurban lines. In 1889 the relationship was formalized as the city annexed the much smaller community.[1] The community's defined boundaries became Fifty-fifth Street, Seventy-fifth Street, State Street, and Ashland Avenue. It covered a four-and-half-mile-square area.[2]

As was the pattern with many of the aforementioned communities on the South Side of Chicago and adjacent to the Black Belt, the United States' entry into World War II had deep reverberations for Englewood. As African Americans migrated into Chicago, Englewood became an enticing destination because of its proximity to the Black Belt and the industrial factories there. A general population growth in Englewood during the 1930s had led to an increase in housing conversions. At the same time, however, the housing stock in the neighborhood began to decline in quality. During that decade, white middle-class families began departing for points farther out in the city and to the suburbs as well.[3] From 1930 to 1960, the total population remained fairly stable, only increasing from 89,000 to 97,000. However, these figures fail to convey the tumult and radical demographic shift of those decades. During that period, Englewood shifted from a predominantly white population to predominantly African American. During the 1940s, the African American population of Englewood increased fivefold.[4] In the years 1930, 1940, 1950, and 1960, the percentage of the population represented by African Americans rose from 1.3 to 2.2 to 10.5 to 68.9, respectively. It should also be noted that during the decade of the most drastic racial change, 1950 to 1960, the general population of Englewood only increased from 94,134 to 97,595.[5]

In response to these changes, in 1939 a group of citizens from Englewood created the Southtown Planning Association (SPA) in an effort to create, as they wrote, "ingenious ways of preventing Negros from moving into the area."[6] The SPA was founded and run by realtors, bankers, and the local chambers of commerce. Although most energies of the SPA were spent in crafting and enforcing restrictive covenants, at other times the organization did demonstrate somewhat creative means for maintaining buffers between African American settlements and the white areas of the South Side. These "ingenious" methods included lobbying to create the Illinois Redevelopment Act of 1941. The SPA reaped the reward of the act when they received permission to create a subsidiary organization, the Southtown Realty and Development Corporation (SRDC) under its auspices. The new corporation had an aggressive policy to purchase property from African Americans who had bought into the community. Moreover, the corporation obtained "structures for demolition and rehabilitation if those alternatives were deemed necessary to keep property out of black hands."[7] The new association also had the authority to eradicate blight in its neighborhood. In 1946, the SPA attempted to utilize the SRDC as it launched a "build the Negroes out of Englewood campaign" in an effort to rehabilitate an increasingly African American corner of the community. The SPA plan called for the relocation of African Americans to the suburb of Robbins in order to redevelop their currently inhabited settlement in favor of middle-class housing. Another scheme of the SPA was 1947's "Choose Your Neighbor Campaign"—an obvious promotion of restrictive covenants. In fact, that same year the SPA allotted half of its $30,000 budget for the enforcement of covenants.[8]

A flashpoint in the acrimony occurred in 1945 when white students at the local high school went on a "hate strike" to protest the new racial demographics, and local businesses "resisted black patronage in an attempt to placate their white clientele."[9] Though the Supreme Court's ruling of *Shelley v. Kraemer* in 1948 made restrictive covenants illegal, the SPA continued to expand its activities and presence in Englewood as well. Indeed, many local businessmen and property owners understood Englewood to be of significant strategic importance as white Chicago sought to defend its borders from the growing Black Belt. One SPA activist asserted in 1950 that "if Englewood's residential areas remain healthy and stable, all areas of the south and west will also maintain their integrity."[10] Because of its assumed importance as a last stronghold, whites fiercely defended Englewood from the advance of the Black Belt.

Though the population levels remained fairly static in the areas around Englewood, the activities of the corporation conspired with larger government projects to actually reduce residential possibilities and further strain the local housing market. The construction of the Dan Ryan Expressway and demolition of a number of dilapidated structures in the Black Belt collaborated to cause a net loss of 902 housing units between 1950 and 1960. As a result, the growing African American population began seeking housing more actively in previously white neighborhoods in Englewood.[11]

Local whites, however, did not always attempt to reduce African American influx peacefully through associations and corporations. Instead, they sometimes displayed a violent defensive posture in response to the in-migration of African Americans. In one case, a rumor spread that a home within the community was simply being "shown" to an African American couple—in fact, the African Americans were attending a union meeting. Gaining a life of its own, the rumor "called forth large crowds, which registered a destructive protest against the presence of blacks . . . and 'outsiders' in general."[12] Estimates at the time had the Englewood crowds peaking at around 10,000 participants. In actuality, the house of the union meeting sustained little damage as police moved in to protect the property. Instead, the targets of the violence became unrecognized outsiders: "'strangers' who entered the area to observe the white protestors and innocent passers-by were victimized by roving gangs."[13] The riot lasted for three days and any unrecognized whites or African Americans who entered the district could expect to be assaulted. The ferocity of Englewood residents' reaction to a rumor was indicative of the tension that existed in many of the white communities bordering the Black Belt.

Despite the activities of whites, by the late 1950s Englewood was reported as having pockets of both "changing" and "changed" areas. In other words, the residential transition to African Americans had been completed on some blocks, but others remained in process. Even with the change, the community managed to maintain the largest "out-lying shopping area in the City of Chicago." The neighborhood was also described as still having good transportation to the Loop. Some light industry remained, and in the southeast corner of the community Wilson Junior College and Chicago Teachers College still enrolled students. Overall, though, Englewood suffered from "crowded schools and residences, high rates of unemployment and school dropouts, and a disproportionate number of families on Public Aid."[14] By the early 1960s, the residents of Englewood found themselves in a community on the precipice of slum-like deterioration. One local minister assessed the situation: "The problem it faces is whether it is to become another deteriorated and dilapidated slum, populated exclusively by Negroes and headed for mass clearance, or whether it is headed for rebirth in which its substantial human and physical resources will be capitalized, redeveloping and maintaining it as a productive live community."[15] The same minister went on to note that Englewood possessed some positive capital for fomenting a rebirth: the large business district and at least thirty Protestant churches and two Roman Catholic churches. By that time, however, both First Christian Reformed of Englewood and Second Christian Reformed of Englewood had departed for the suburbs, and Auburn Park CRC of Englewood would follow in less than a year.

ROSELAND

Roughly ten years later, four CRC congregations would leave Roseland under similar circumstances. Five miles almost directly south of Englewood, the community would not experience the block-by-block advance of African Americans in Chicago until the early 1960s. By 1972, however, all four congregations had relocated to suburbs such as Orland Park.

The predecessors to the CRC congregations in Roseland arrived in 1848. At that time, the area was best described as a swamp with occasional patches of dry prairie. However, the locale did offer easy access to the markets of Chicago because of a high ridge (at that time called Thornton Road and today known as Michigan Avenue) that allowed for consistently dry traversing. The Dutch settlers situated themselves near the ridge and set about establishing small produce farms. The economic viability of the area soon increased when the Illinois Central and Rock Island railroads laid tracks through the area in 1852.[16]

The 1880s saw Roseland transformed from pastoral village to a burgeoning industrial community. A real estate agent at the time commented: "111th Street might well ... be called 'Dinner Pail Avenue,' for morning and night it is traversed by thousands of shop men going to and returning from work, for most of the shop men live and own homes in Roseland."[17] Crews laid seven more sets of railroad tracks, and the Pullman factory village was established just to the east. Irish, Swedish, German, and English workers and their families began moving into Roseland. After World War I, the influx of workers also included immigrants from Italy and Poland. Moreover, a "handful" of African Americans moved into the northern fringes of the area, as well.[18]

Some even began describing Roseland as a "city in itself." Evidence for such a statement included the fact that its size rivaled "such cities as Bloomington, Danville, or Decatur, with its miles of paved and lighted streets, its three large school buildings, its twenty churches, its three newspapers, several wholesale groceries, a number of factories, and its two enclosed ballparks."[19] A building boom during the 1920s brought brick bungalows, two-story single-family residences, and small apartment buildings.[20] Such structures were necessary as the population of the community increased 53 percent during the decade. One resident described construction: "The abandoned farmland south of 104th Street was split into sizeable lots commensurate with the upper-class residences that would soon be a-building; new asphalt streets and smooth sidewalks . . . provided literally miles of uninterrupted area for roller-skating, scootering, and bike riding."[21]

Growth of Roseland slowed a bit with the economic depression and World War II raging in Europe during the 1930s. However, during the 1940s the population would increase by 29 percent. In the northern sections of Roseland, these increases were largely attributable to African American influx. During the 1940s, white residents in Roseland began to mobilize to protest the Chicago Housing Authority's plan to construct a public housing project that would undoubtedly bring more African American residents to the community. As byproducts of central business district redevelopment, the residents of Roseland viewed the housing projects as threats to the stability of their neighborhood. Much like Englewood, these protests in Roseland sometimes became violent. The historian Arnold Hirsch reported that at an assembly to protest the Fernwood Park Homes project, the police arrested numerous persons with Dutch last names for racial rioting.[22] Despite these efforts by white residents of Roseland, African Americans continued to settle in the community. By 1950 the overall population of Roseland was a little over 50,000, and African Americans accounted for 18 percent of that figure.[23]

Hirsch also asserted that Cornelius Teninga (a conspicuously Dutch last name), a realtor from Roseland, offered the "most articulate" argument to the Housing Committee of the Chicago City Council. Teninga noted the people of Roseland detected a "'disastrous financial burden' in the forced rehousing of thousands of displaced persons but also the 'kindling of alarming racial tensions which will result from the wholly unnecessary dispersal of the colored inhabitants at the center of our City . . . into the outlying areas.'"[24]

Teninga's efforts notwithstanding, in 1954 the Chicago Housing Authority completed the construction of the Governor Frank O. Lowden Homes in the Roseland area. African Americans inhabited the 128-unit housing project almost exclusively. In 1960 African Americans accounted for 23 percent of the total population of Roseland.[25] One resident noted in 1964 that the "Hollanders who made up the greater portion of Roseland . . . are now moving to the suburbs to avoid the next population change in the community." He also related that "the local community improvement association has the avowed purpose of 'keeping the negro out'" and that in his "judgment they will be unsuccessful."[26]

Despite the demographic changes, Roseland continued to be the dominant retail complex for the Far South Side of Chicago into the 1960s.[27] The stores there included Robert Hall, Sears, Roebuck, and Gately's Peoples.[28] A real estate assessment conducted in 1963 found the shopping center to have a vacancy rate of 15 percent and the buildings to be in "fair" to "good" condition. The business district had lost some sales volume to outlying areas. However, at the same time business leaders expressed hopefulness about the customers that would be brought to the area with the southwest extension of the Dan Ryan Expressway and that same road's junction with the Calumet expressway—plans for both bringing them near the Roseland area.[29] Little did they know that instead of delivering customers into communities, expressways succeed at better conveying those customers through and past a business district to more outlying areas.

The 1960s, then, represented the seminal moment in the decline of Roseland's business district. The South Side of Chicago began to experience erosion within its industrial base. More and more traffic would be diverted off city streets of businesses and onto the expressway. The combined effect debilitated the retail stores. Eventually, Robert Hall, Sears, Roebuck, and Gately's Peoples—the four major anchors—would all close their doors.[30]

The demographic transformation and accompanying economic decline during the 1960s devastated Roseland. During the mid-1960s, the in-migration of African Americans gathered such momentum that in 1970 they constituted 55 percent of Roseland's population. The growth in percentage is an indication that many white families had departed. Between 1970 and 1980, the white population of Roseland dropped by almost 96 percent while the African American population grew by 82 percent. By 1980, African Americans accounted for 97 percent of a total population of over 64,000.[31]

Such a rapid racial turnover had deleterious consequences for the community. Business and industry followed the whites to the suburbs. Residents of Roseland found themselves dealing with myriad concerns: "unemployment, inflation, mortgage defaults, business failures, and gang-related problems."[32] In the 1970s alone, the community experienced over 900 mortgage foreclosures. Quality of life declined as the infant mortality rate rose to 26 per 1,000—one of the worst in the city. In 1960, fifty-eight physicians had served the community;

that number dropped to thirty-one in 1970 and eleven in 1980 (all while the total population grew by over 5,000).[33]

A NATIONAL SCANDAL OF BLOCKBUSTING AND THE DUAL HOUSING MARKET

Chicago was not unique in the racial turnover that affected specific neighborhoods from 1950 to 1970. Edward Orser blamed the rapid racial succession process that occurred in Baltimore in part to the real estate practice of "blockbusting."[34] The developer James Keelty had originally envisioned Edmondson Village, though it actually sat in Baltimore proper, as an ideal suburban-like community the emerging white middle class would find affordable. Orser described the community as "flourishing" from its inception in the 1920s until 1955. During those decades, Edmondson Village had a reputation as a stable and secure community.

However, from 1955 to 1965, some 20,000 white residents moved out of the west Baltimore neighborhood of Edmondson while approximately the same number of African Americans moved in to take their place. Edmondson stands as a vivid illustration of how the transition occurred: blockbusting—"the intentional action of a real estate operative to settle an African American household in an all-white neighborhood for the purpose of provoking white flight in order to make excessive profits by buying low from those who fled and selling high to those who sought access to new housing opportunities."[35] Of course, it should be noted that blockbusters were only one cause in the white dispersal from the city. The residential segregation patterns that found establishment in post–World War II America and that persist to the present were the outcomes of a larger "silent conspiracy" that included both individuals and institutions. (I will make the claim that, in some cases, those institutions included churches.)

The collusion ultimately fostered a dual housing market in rust belt cities like Chicago and Baltimore: one for whites, one for African Americans. At the institutional level, it included real estate, finance, and the federal government's refusal to fund housing choices that challenged the dominant patterns of residential segregation. At the individual level, white residents often refused to consider the possibility of residential integration and, consequently, they actively maintained the dual housing market.[36] Such a market ultimately victimized both African Americans and whites. Whites lost their community and forfeited financially when they sold their homes for prices lower than expected market value. At the same time, African Americans faced the injustice of racial discrimination and had to confront excessively high housing costs because of their artificially limited choices.

Blockbusting real estate agents had the opportunity to engage in this type of exploitation in places like Edmondson Village because the community had no cohesive institutional network operating as a bonding agent. Though the population was nearly equally divided between Protestants and Catholics, ethnic and religious discord seemed nonexistent. However, under that façade, Orser discovered flaws that undermined an ostensibly stable community. Though the community was racially homogeneous and seemed to embrace a suburban ethos, it lacked a tangible solidarity. Within the neighborhood, there seemed to exist no larger sense of place. The village legally sat within the borders of Baltimore but, in reality, suffered geographic isolation. Moreover, the residents had no identifiable historical or institutional infrastructure to which they could turn for assistance or, at the very least, for a sense of identity. In the end, Orser concluded that social upheaval that befell Edmondson Village resulted because the community lacked the resources to avoid or confront the exploitation and manipulation of the blockbusting real estate agents.

CRC CONGREGATIONS NOTE THE CHANGES

A lack of resources, on the other hand, fails to fully explain the Englewood and Roseland exoduses. Both functioned as viable urban neighborhoods, integrated into the larger economy of Chicago. There was no geographic isolation. However, in both communities there resided a large number of CRC families with intense in-group networks. In that sense, there existed a social isolation that inhibited reliance on outside institutional infrastructure.

Minutes from Classical meetings reveal that by the mid-1960s the CRC congregations of Roseland had concerns about the changing demographics of the neighborhood. However, at the Classical meeting of January 1966, representatives who had visited the Roseland congregations noted that internally the congregations seemed to be thriving. The minutes describe Fourth Roseland as having a high level of spiritual life and First Roseland as healthy. The reporters who had visited Third Roseland described the congregation as being in "high gear" and "forging vigorously ahead" after having recently completed the construction of a new church building and parsonage.

However, a note of concern related to the neighborhood concluded the reports on Third Roseland and Fourth Roseland. Regarding Fourth Roseland, the Classical representatives wrote: "The movement of colored people to the proximity of the church presents a challenge or problem."[37] The letter describing Third Roseland's circumstances offered the richest detail: "For reasons that are obvious the Roseland area has in recent years lost some families who moved to the Oak Lawn and South Holland areas. Yet in spite of that fact Roseland III has recently gained some families." After that positive note about Third Roseland, the writers addressed the issue of racial transition in Roseland more generally: "It can be said that all the Roseland congregations are holding their own and there is no immediate need for any alarm due to the race situation. . . . Let none suppose that there is any paniky [sic] fear, despair or discouragement on the part of these congregations. The race problem is one we shall all have to face, altho [sic] obviously, it is more acute and pressing in some areas."[38] Thus, the congregations revealed that although they understood the racial transition as problematic, they had a measure of confidence that they would weather the storm, somehow.

The next year the congregational visits revealed a measure of success at Third Roseland. The congregation had a consistent turnout of "neighborhood children" (probably code for African Americans) for both vacation Bible school and after-school programs. Moreover, the congregation demonstrated some initial steps toward integration: "two persons from the community were accepted into the fellowship. . . . Noteworthy in this is that these persons were of the colored race."[39] The cautious optimism of these notes would prove myopic: all four congregations would remove themselves from Roseland in less than five years.

The social transitions that affected cities like Baltimore and Chicago proper had particular consequences in local neighborhoods such as Englewood and Roseland. The massive influx of African Americans and subsequent departure of whites had devastating repercussions for communities. The erosion of the quality of life in both Englewood and Roseland was attributable to radical residential isolation based on race and the manner in which resources followed whites to the suburbs. In both Chicago communities, the local CRC congregations were conspirators in the racial transition that left a legacy of deeply entrenched segregation. As the neighborhoods became increasingly African American, the CRC families followed the trend to find ostensible comfort and security in the surrounding suburbs. By 1972 a total of seven CRC congregations had left Englewood and Roseland and, consequently, Chicago proper as well.

PART III CONGREGATIONS RESPOND TO NEIGHBORHOOD CHANGE

7 · THE INSIGNIFICANCE OF PLACE

In this chapter I argue that the rapid departure of these seven CRC congregations was dependent, at least in part, on a poor conception of place that manifested in weak ties and affiliations to the neighborhoods surrounding the churches. In other words, although the typical white flight issues of racial change and concerns over property values certainly played a role in the rapid departure of these CRC congregations, a more careful examination of this case offers evidence about the historical importance that the concept of place played in the process of white flight. That is, within these highly socially isolated religious communities there are such weak ties to the broader neighborhood that members are easily predisposed to mobility: when they felt their neighborhood threatened by the arrival of African Americans they did not take very long to pack up and reconstitute themselves in the suburbs.

Much has been written about conservative Protestant congregations and the closed communities that they have tended to foster. The theological orientation and emphasis on in-group social ties frequently results in closed networks that inhibit the ability to seek integration with the wider community.[1] In this view, the social capital of a closed community leads to "public bads" rather than "public goods."[2] Here I will extend that argument and demonstrate how the closed community translated into one that also had weak connections to place.

INSULARITY AND PLACE

The members of these CRC congregations in Englewood and Roseland represented an insular social circle that utilized the local church instead of the local park or square as the unifying focal point for the community. The story here reveals the difference between being rooted in neighborhood and being rooted in less geographically determined communities, such as congregations. In a lot of ways, these CRC congregations operated as fully functional isolated

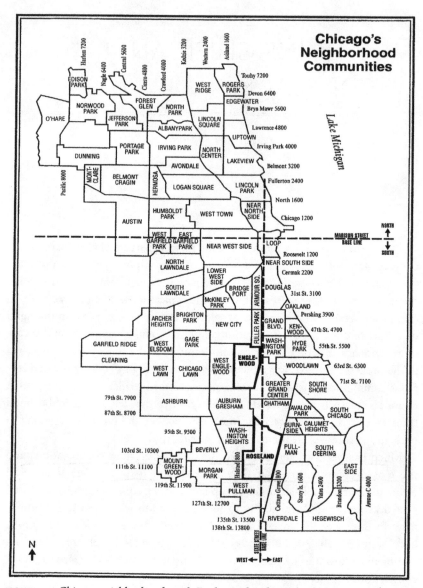

FIGURE 7.1. Chicago neighborhoods with Englewood and Roseland highlighted. (Map by Janice Dane.)

communities. Those communities tended to be largely spiritual—there was no emphasis on community being connected to "place."

Within the interdisciplinary field of urban studies, there has been a burgeoning literature concerned with the notion of place and its relationship to community. Yi-Fu Tuan wrote perhaps the classic tome on place, *Topophilia: A Study of Environmental Perception, Attitudes, and Values.*[3] Tuan created the term "topophilia" to describe the "affective bond between people and a place or set-ting." He argued that culture and environment remain closely linked. He also asserted that human-made environments could provide evidence about the worldviews of the people who inhabited the area in question. One reviewer wrote: "Tuan points out that the impact of architectural space transcends that of much larger natural configuration outdoors; one is led to muse about the aim of the builders, about the responses of clients and other observers."[4] In essence, places reveal much about a people and their values—place has meaning. One geographer has noted: "It is generally accepted that the art museums, along with universities, are established primarily to pursue and display intellectual achieve-ments and meanings, whereas prisons, law courts, factories, and offices mostly create and sustain social relations. Place helps constitute and balance this basic structure of nature, social relations and meaning."[5] In addition, place both con-strains and enables. Place has effect: "The easiest way to understand how places work is to recognize that they all, large or small, thick or thin function to include or exclude different elements of forces of the world."[6]

Being pervasive, place has a crucial role in developing social connectedness—yet it can also be configured to have a coercive effect. In either case, place does not remain neutral. Rather, it takes on conscious characteristics and meanings that have importance within the urban arena. For our purposes, it would seem the CRC congregations of Englewood and Roseland first manipulated their places in an effort to remain exclusive. When such strategies became unviable, however, the seven congregations displayed a visceral indifference to their larger communities and mobilized. Not only does this case study of the CRC congrega-tions of Englewood and Roseland further our understanding about how commu-nities understand place but it also lends further insight into how religious bodies participated in white flight. The historians John McGreevy, Gerald Gamm, and Eileen McMahon have all discussed how Catholic parish identity led some white Catholic families to fiercely defend their neighborhoods as African Americans moved in. McGreevy especially noted that the manner in which Catholic com-munities in northern U.S. cities defined their surroundings in religious terms had profound consequences on the emerging residential patterns of the 1960s and 1970s. In contrast, the CRC communities within Englewood and Roseland on the South Side of Chicago accorded their surroundings less religious or spiritual significance. Thus when their place/neighborhoods started changing, they mobilized for the suburbs.

ENGLEWOOD CONGREGATIONS RESPOND TO NEIGHBORHOOD CHANGE

The social transitions and resultant turmoil of the 1950s, 1960s, and 1970s in Chicago had drastic effects on some of the most significant institutions, including the churches and schools. Many of the local congregations reacted with alarm to the changes occurring near and within their once-stable white environments. One church newsletter reported that the expansion of the African American ghetto had caused "panic bordering on hysteria." The same periodical reported that as bordering communities saw widespread white flight, residents of the Englewood area felt a "shadow of fear" hovering and lurking in their midst.[7]

Numerous sociologists have noted that one strategy for congregations in changing neighborhoods is to adapt to a worship style more welcoming to the newcomers in the area.[8] In this case, these CRC congregations never seemed to consider seriously an alteration in congregational style in response to the changing community. Derke Bergsma (a local CRC pastor) noted that while they did not prohibit African Americans from attending, there exists little evidence that the CRC congregations sought out new membership among their African American neighbors. The CRC congregations in Englewood established policies of inviting African American visitors to meet with the pastor and members of the council after the service. Bergsma noted that no such policy existed for white visitors and that the leadership conducted the procedure to screen African Americans with the excuse: "to consider with them their motivation."[9] The policy indicated that the leaders of the congregations doubted that their churches could simply be attractive to African Americans.

Bergsma suggested that the councils defended the separate protocols by noting that in 1960 a civil rights group had announced intentions of organizing sit-ins to draw attention to white churches in Englewood that had demonstrated an unwillingness to welcome African American worshipers. In that sense, the post–worship service meetings with African Americans served as reconnaissance missions where church leaders ascertained whether they might be targets of the sit-ins. At the same time, some parishioners also noted that African Americans "invariably came in late, after the services were well underway, and this was disturbing."[10] First CRC of Englewood locked their doors shortly after services began in response to the problem with interruptions—a rather severe response that probably violated fire codes.[11]

As early as 1957, Second Englewood formed a committee to study the effects of the changing community on the future of the congregation. Bergsma noted that although the committee devoted some time to community and congregational preservation, they also considered the alternative of relocation. In 1960 the committee commissioned the creation of a map that revealed the residence locations of member families. The map clearly demonstrated a pattern of membership drift to the southwest suburbs of Chicago.[12]

That same year, First Englewood established a Long Range Study Committee to examine the "present situation and the future of our congregation in regard to our changing neighborhood."[13] According to Bergsma, the committee seemed to immediately set about the task of assessing the feasibility of relocation. Less than a month after its formation, the committee recommended that the council send a questionnaire to ascertain the membership's opinion on buying property elsewhere as a future site for the church.[14] The majority of member families indicated via the questionnaire a disposition to remain with church—particularly if a new structure were to be built in the southwest suburban area. Subsequently, less than four months after the formation of the Long Range Study Committee, the council approved the purchase of property in the suburb of Oak Lawn for the future site of the church.[15] In this case, congregational leaders preemptively strategized to retain church membership in a new location, even though a majority of the families had indicated a willingness to remain committed to the church in Englewood. Thus, to use the religious marketplace imagery, the congregation changed the location of the business long before all the customers had moved. Thus economic frame fails to fully explain the relocation of First Englewood.

On the other hand, the economic imagery works better for Second Englewood. Although Second Englewood had begun the process three years earlier, not until October 1960 did their Long Range Planning Committee actually send out a congregational questionnaire. The poll asked whether the respondents thought the church should move and, if so, where. Sixty-eight families responded to the questionnaire. Fifty-nine of them expressed a desire for the church to move and overwhelmingly recommended relocation to the southwest suburbs.[16] According to Bergsma, the council registered these responses as a mandate from the congregation and began actively to pursue both the sale of the current structure and the purchase of property elsewhere.[17]

In the end, the leadership of both churches began to realize that only relocation would allow for a continuation of the current congregational identity. In 1959, First Christian Reformed had a membership of 1,001 and Second Christian Reformed a membership of 708.[18] Membership rolls remained in steady decline, and Bergsma noted that many of those who had not transferred drove to Englewood from their suburban homes on Sunday mornings and evenings past other CRC congregations. In fact, many of the members of the councils had become suburbanites themselves, so there remained very little inclination to continue existence in Englewood. By 1963 both churches had dedicated new edifices in the suburb of Oak Lawn.

Meanwhile, the question of the viability of the CRC schools arose. By 1959, these two CRC congregations displayed a new level of consternation when they organized the Church-School Committee for Community Action (CSCCA). The congregations joined with the Chicago Christian Grade School and Chicago Christian High School—two institutions supported by members of the CRC churches—in an effort to deal with community problems in a concerted, organized manner. "Problems," in this case, had to do with the in-migration of African Americans and the subsequent expansion of Chicago's Black Belt into Englewood. The churches and schools charged the new committee with devising strategies that would nurture the local area as a favorable environment. Bergsma would later assert, however, that "preservation" would become the most accurate description of the committee's duties. Though officially titled with the term "Action," the new organization was frequently referred to as the "Committee for Community Preservation" in council minutes and subsequent interviews.[19]

It should be noted that the CSCCA did take the step of recommending that both CRC congregations join the Organization for the Southwest Community (OSC). As a community organization, the OSC sought both to inhibit block-busting through building code enforcement and to lobby for a more robust police presence in the area. The organizers of the OSC conceived of it as a "new experiment in urban community life."[20] Through it, they sought to align groups with similar interests, including churches and community organizations. Bergsma observed that the two CRC congregations joined the organization under the pragmatic assumption that the OSC would nurture an environment in which members of the churches would want to continue live. Soon, though, the two CRC congregations found themselves at odds with the OSC for scheduling meetings on the Sabbath and for sponsoring fund-raising dances, both forbidden within CRC culture at the time. Moreover, they harbored suspicions that OSC did not share their level of alarm regarding the changing demographics of Englewood. Within eighteen months the CSCCA recommended that the two CRC congregations withdraw from the OSC. Both congregations quickly discontinued their membership in the organization.[21]

The withdrawal from the OSC signaled the end of the CRC congregations' broader community alliances. It seemed that because of their lightweight nature, their bridging ties frayed quickly when stretched by outside cultures and patterns of behavior. However, the congregations maintained the CSCCA as an internal organization for addressing neighborhood-wide concerns. The CSCCA responded in 1959 when rumors circulated that the board of trustees of Chicago Christian High School in Englewood had been considering the sale of its facilities to the Board of Education of the City of Chicago. Such a possibility meant the inevitable removal of the high school to an area farther south and beyond the African American influx. The committee quickly sent a missive to the Christian High School board that urged the members to not sell the high school facilities.[22] The committee feared that the departure of the high school to a suburban location would be a catalyst in the removal of families with teenage children away from Englewood. The relocation of the Christian schools would create a vacuum for the CRC families in Englewood that would eventually draw them to the suburbs. Such a movement would have dire consequences for the two churches. From a congregational ecology perspective, the churches would lose the close proximity of their most cherished resource: families. To remain viable, they would have to adapt to new resources in the neighborhood or follow their traditional resource to the suburbs.

In the end, the Christian High School agreed to sell their property to the Board of Education.[23] The Christian High School board had concerns about the future sustainability of the school in Englewood. Enrollment had been on the decline as the neighborhood changed. With that in mind, the board began the process of relocating to Palos Heights.

ROSELAND CONGREGATIONS RESPOND TO NEIGHBORHOOD CHANGE

Somewhat later, Roseland's rapid residential transformation precipitated a serious socioeconomic crisis. The CRC churches left Roseland en masse, playing a role in this drama. In the end, a manipulation of and disregard for place operated to facilitate the massive exodus.

Though the four CRC congregations (for locations, see Figure 7.2) did not approach the changing demographics of their neighborhood monolithically, the patterns contained enough commonality that a reporting of the activities of Second Roseland and Fourth Roseland, the two that would eventually merge as Orland Park CRC, serves well as a case study. Fourth Roseland would be the first church to leave, and Second was the last, the two bookends of the departure of the CRC from Roseland.

In February 1964, the Evangelism Committee at Fourth Roseland reported at the council meeting that they had discussed "bringing the gospel" to and taking a survey of the "church membership of the colored folk in the near neighborhood."[24] In a somewhat tentative step, the committee thus demonstrated a willingness to, at the very least, engage the newly arriving African Americans. Of course, it should also be noted that members of an evangelism committee within a CRC congregation would not necessarily be representative of the rest of the church. That early tone that seemed to signal an embrace of the newly arriving African American population had changed somewhat when, over a year later, the council took up the topic again. The council discussion reportedly revolved around a number of questions that portended very different potential future courses for the church. The first two questions dealt with remaining in Roseland as a racially diverse congregation: "1) How does our congregation feel about possible future integration? 2) In view of the fact that we may lose a number of families due to the changing neighborhood should we seek to increase our neighborhood evangelism?" The first two questions demonstrated a sense that the church would have to adapt to survive in the current context. Fidelity to traditional congregational rituals and habits in the same place would mean the demise of the institution. The second two questions dealt with relocation: "3) Should we as

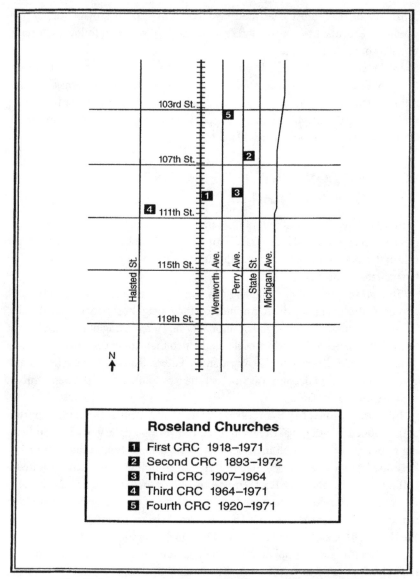

FIGURE 7.2. The CRC congregations of Roseland, 1893–1972. (Map by Janice Dane.)

a congregation seek to move to a new location and encourage our membership to move to a particular location? 4) Should we seek to buy land for the future and appoint a committee for this purpose?"[25] We see here the control that the congregational leaders felt that they had over the residential decisions of member families.

After the discussion, the members of the council decided to go on record as concluding that they would encourage membership to stay within the community. However, the recorded minutes of the meeting offer no evidence that the council discussed how they would encourage families to remain.

Meanwhile, throughout 1966 the Evangelism Committee continued to discuss the matter of "working with the colored in the area."[26] In October, the committee broached the subject of obtaining a store for a meeting place explicitly for African Americans. Such a discussion raises questions regarding whether the congregation thought it plausible that they could become integrated. The use of a separate facility connoted a sense of discontinuity between the church and its outreach to African Americans. In December of 1967, the committee discussed obtaining "a man to work the area due to changing racial conditions."[27] However, by July of 1968 the committee tabled both attempts at racial outreach for at least a year.[28] Though not explicitly stated in meeting minutes, this "tabling" of racial outreach raises questions about the tenuous presence of the congregation and its future commitments to the neighborhood.

While the council and Evangelism Committee wrestled with challenges associated with the evolving local community, the Building Study Committee of Fourth Roseland discussed the congregation's space needs. The inaugural meeting of this committee occurred in January of 1965. The minutes of the meetings reveal that debate about constructing more meeting space had been hotly contested within the church for a number of years. For the first few months of the year, the committee considered sketches of the potential addition. However, by May the committee made the decision that it would be difficult to justify any construction due to the "prevailing and possible later developments with respect to the stability of our membership as a result of significant population changes which may take place in our area." In light of that attitude, the committee ultimately recommended that the congregation not be presented with any proposals having to do with physical expansion for the next year and that trends be evaluated "with respect to the stability of our membership in view of the developing population changes."[29] Thus, by 1965 the entrance of African Americans into the Roseland area took a prominent place in the leadership dialogue of Fourth Roseland. In a deliberate manner, the church began to assess the changes taking place in the community. The questions to be addressed had to do with integration and its effect on membership and the production of physical space.

Roughly a year later, the issue turned again to the evangelism of the newly arriving African American population. At the April council meeting, the Evangelism Committee sent a delegate to petition the council to reconsider an earlier decision not to canvass the area north of 103 Street and west of the railroad tracks—an area that had become largely African American. The delegate asserted that such inactivity would bring the church in direct violation of a number of mandates set down by various authorities: scripture (Matthew 22:37–40 and 28:19–20), the Heidelberg Catechism (Lord's Day 2, Question 5), the Church Order (Articles 73 and 74) and "the position of the Christian Reformed Church regarding the race issue."[30] In that manner, the Evangelism Committee used the meeting to suggest that the current course of the congregation related to race amounted to disobedience to God. The committee had grounded its argument on the biblical directive to "love one's neighbor." Based on these assertions, the council agreed to rescind its earlier decision and gave permission to the Evangelism Committee to begin the canvass.

Meanwhile, the congregation's leadership began to make initial plans for relocation. In September of 1967 the council passed the motion approving the recommendation of the Planning Committee that a questionnaire be sent to the membership of the church regarding the relocation of church property.[31] The initial draft of the questionnaire included the following questions:

1) Would you remain where you now reside if Negroes move on your block? [This question was deleted for the final edition to be sent to the congregants] 2) Have you any intentions of moving at the present time? If so, where? 3) Would you join another CRC church or remain a member of Fourth Roseland? 4) If conditions, which in your opinion, require moving elsewhere, into what area would you most likely move? 5) Would you consider it wise for the church to purchase land in some area for future development provided it becomes necessary to vacate the present edifice? 6) If your answer to the above question is yes, in what area would you like to see the property purchased? 7) If you move into another area and transfer your church membership to a church in that area, would you, if the Fourth Roseland Church were moved into the same general [location] in which you then reside, rejoin the church? 8) Would you consider a merger with an existing church outside of the Roseland area?[32]

The council's questionnaire portrayed an organization bent on survival. The multiplicity of options attested to the desperation of the council. Two months later, the Planning Committee returned to the council with questionnaire results in hand. The findings of the survey included the following information: 1) seventeen families had intentions of moving, sixty did not; 2) thirty-one families responded that it would be wise for the church consider land for purchase, thirty did not; and 3) the Lansing and South Holland area received the most votes (fourteen) for the future community to be considered. Upon the recommendation of the Planning Committee, the council passed a motion to establish a Long Range Planning Committee to investigate available land in South Holland for a future church building.[33] The survey results demonstrate the role that the church had in encouraging the departure of its families. Almost four-fifths of the families indicated that they did not intend to leave Roseland. In spite of that, the council established a subcommittee whose only apparent purpose would be to plan an eventual relocation.

While the council went about the business of planning for a future outside of Roseland, they also remained active with the other three Roseland churches in supporting and coordinating the activities of the nearby Pullman Gospel Center. The center operated under the auspices of the four churches, and a report in April of 1968 noted that "Negro adults have been in attendance and they seem to be well received."[34] Less than a month later, the council of Fourth Roseland met and decided that it would now be agreeable to identify the Gospel Center with the Christian Reformed Church.[35] So it seems plausible to assume that the church wanted to maintain an outpost in the area even while they made plans for departure. It should also be noted that the Gospel Center was often referred to as a "mission"—a loaded term—within the minutes.[36] The typical connotation of "mission" usually had to do with individuals ordained by the church to bring the Gospel message to underdeveloped regions of the world. There would seem to be broad and significant implications in the notion that a mission had to be established within a community in which the CRC had had a presence for over a century. In other words, the leadership gave very little thought to making the already established churches in the area more hospitable or attractive to African Americans. The Gospel Center functioned as a proxy for the CRC congregations: it allowed them tangible evidence of outreach to African Americans while not compelling any changes within their respective congregations. In congregational ecology terms, there would be no niche switching to attract the new resources in the area.[37]

By late 1968, the activities of both the Gospel Center and the Long Range Planning Committee pervaded the official business of Fourth Roseland. In October the congregation received letters detailing the work of the Long Range Planning Committee and a proposal to purchase land in the general vicinity of 151st Street west of Harlem Avenue in Orland Park. However, First Roseland complicated matters that month when they sent Fourth a missive inquiring about the possibility of a merger. Fourth responded that they would receive the letter as information and table the issue until the next meeting. It would seem, though, that the die had been cast. Fourth Roseland had little inclination to merge with First Roseland in Chicago proper. The recent momentum had been decidedly toward relocation to the suburbs. By late October, the council had received permission from the congregation to purchase the parcel of land in Orland Park by a vote of forty-eight to seventeen. In November, Fourth responded to First's inquiry by noting that because of the recent decision to purchase property for relocation that it would be "inappropriate to discuss the feasibility and possibility of merging."[38]

Moreover, in late 1968 the coordination between the four CRC congregations of Roseland seemed to ebb. At the same meeting that Fourth refused to entertain

First's request for merger, they also noted that an earlier proposition for the four churches to cooperate to obtain an ordained minister to work in the "inner city" had to be dropped because of a "lack of support by the consistories."[39] Outside of support for the Gospel Center, the congregations began to demonstrate little other than apathy for the Roseland area. Moreover, the problems of the "inner city" seemed to be becoming more prevalent as Fourth had to replace a vandalized sign and cope with cars being "tampered with" during services. The Building and Grounds Committee reported that new locks had been installed and the council began discussing the desirability of posting guards for the parking lot and church basement.[40]

Ironically, while Fourth buttressed their edifice against the local neighborhood and made plans for relocation, they also entertained a noteworthy CRC minister who came to speak to members of the four Roseland CRC churches about the neighborhood conditions. The pastor discussed what could be done to encourage people to stay in the neighborhood. The Fourth minutes reflect that the pastor received a tepid response and that "very few members attended."[41] In fact, it would seem that the pastor in question did little to slow down that momentum of departure, as in February of 1969, the very next month, the council of Fourth appointed a Relocation Committee.

The following month, the Relocation Committee weighed in at council with the following two recommendations: "1) That the Council be authorized to sell the present church properties and 2) They be authorized to plan the construction of new church properties at 152nd Street and 7500 West."[42] The committee went further and offered a rationale for such activity: "rapid decline" of the neighborhood, decreasing membership in the church, and the recent sale of the local Christian school building. The motion passed, and the council decided that the issue would be brought before the congregation for a vote on May 7.

At the congregational meeting, the council offered the following proposition to the assembly and moved for its adoption:

1. The Fourth Christian Reformed Church of Roseland relocate.
2. The Fourth Christian Reformed Church of Roseland relocate to the Orland Park area, specifically to the 2.5-acre site authorized for purchase at the October 30, 1968 congregational meeting.
3. The Council be authorized to obtain bids for and/or otherwise seek buyers for the present church properties.
4. The Council be authorized to start preliminary planning with a view to constructing new church properties.[43]

Each aspect of the proposition passed that evening. Recommendations one and two passed fifty-five to twelve and forty-seven to eighteen, respectively. Recommendations three and four passed unanimously.

That same year, the congregation of Fourth Roseland celebrated the church's fiftieth anniversary. As part of the celebration, the congregation published a history of the church. The booklet benignly presented recent events:

> The church reached the peak of its membership in the year 1954 when it numbered 132 families and a total membership of over 550 souls. In 1958 the Roseland area began to change and many people moved to the suburbs. This was also felt in our church as some of our members joined the movement. In the early 60s this loss of membership was somewhat overcome by the influx of many families who moved into Roseland from the Englewood area and affiliated with our congregation. However, at the close of 1967 our membership had decreased to 99 families. The council appointed a long range study committee, its mandate to find an area to which our people could be directed should they decide to leave Roseland in order to give them an opportunity to remain with our church. The committee was also able to find a suitable site for the church to relocate. . . . In November 1968, the congregation approved the proposal of the council to purchase two and one-half acres at 75th Avenue and 151st Street. . . . This is an undeveloped area adjacent to land purchased by the Chicago Southwest Christian Schools Association. It is expected that many new homes will be built there providing an opportunity for members of our church to migrate to this area.[44]

The history notably described the church as offering direction as to where congregants should relocate. Thus the church did not simply follow its resources to the richer ecology of the suburbs. Instead, the church practiced agency in guiding attenders out of the city. There existed an assumption of housing location choice and a high level of mobility for attenders of Fourth Roseland. The privilege of building houses in suburbia while having close access to a Christian school would prove irresistible.

Though the congregation made definitive plans for imminent departure, they still had local problems to address in Roseland. In June of 1969 the council broached the topic of "The Black Manifesto." The previous month James Forman, a black militant leader, interrupted a Sunday morning worship service at New York's Riverside Church and presented "The Black Manifesto": a demand for that congregation's share of the reparations owed to African Americans by the white religious community in America. The Manifesto had been written in April of 1969 by the National Black Economic Development Conference and the Manifesto phenomenon spread outside of New York and into other cities.[45] The leadership at Fourth discussed various ways to address the potential disruption of Sunday worship by the Manifesto.

By July the Council had made a decision about both the Manifesto and the nagging security concerns. The Building Committee reported that security guards would be utilized in the parking lot (later that year they would formally request police protection), and a motion passed that if ever "confronted with the 'Black Manifesto' our pastor or the minister in charge of the service should dismiss the service."[46] Later that year the council also made a formal request for police protection on Sunday, Monday, and Wednesday evenings "in view of recent happenings in the area of the church."[47] It would seem plausible to assume that some criminal activity had occurred near Fourth Roseland.

At about the same time, the council from Second Roseland reported that they were approached by three "boys" who appeared as representatives of the Barren Town Diplomats. Though the minutes fail to describe the Diplomats, it seems safe to assume that they functioned as a formal organization of African American young men. The Diplomats asked permission to use the church building for meetings. The council refused to commit, and tabled the issue.[48] A rumor of the Diplomats' request apparently circulated through the congregation. At the next council meeting, five men from the congregation appeared, wanting to know whether the elders had given "permission to a black teenage club to use our church buildings for meetings."[49] The council responded to the query by noting that they had not had the opportunity to vote on it. Moreover, they attempted to assuage the inquiring men by asserting that if they granted permission, the teenagers would also require supervision. The council then dismissed the men so they could discuss the matter.

Ultimately, the council of Second passed a motion to deny the request of the Barren Town Diplomats. The council justified the decision on "the grounds that they were not a religious organization."[50] In transparent contradiction, however, the council passed at the same meeting a motion to grant a request to use the church for block club meetings.[51] Two white women had appeared earlier to make the request. Stating that they represented forty families in the immediate area of the church, they went on to note that the newly formed block club sought to "maintain and improve the community."[52] The minutes, however, failed to note any religious underpinnings for the club.

Indeed, a half year after the block club received permission to use the church, the council displayed a stark disinterest in investing in any other larger community programs. In March 1971 the Greater Roseland Organization sent a letter requesting the cooperation of the church on some community projects. With no rationale expressed in the minutes, the council concluded that Second would not participate.[53]

THE MISSION IN THE NEIGHBORHOOD

While Second and Fourth Roseland fortified and insulated themselves against their neighborhoods, the other two CRC congregations revealed their ultimate intentions to relocate as well. The four churches had long shared responsibility for the Pullman Gospel Center (often referred to in the minutes as the Mission, in 1972 it reorganized as a CRC congregation). Part of the responsibility included sending members of the supporting congregations as emissaries to the Gospel Center worship services. They now, however, questioned why they would support it after they left the area. In October 1971 the council minutes of Fourth Roseland revealed that First Roseland and Third Roseland had been deficient in their responsibilities to the Mission: recently they had failed to send delegates on Sunday mornings.[54]

In a written history of the Pullman Gospel Center, the author noted that "the first black faces began appearing" at the mission in 1968. The year 1969 is then described as a "banner year," with ministries aided by a seminarian and a program that brought in CRC teenagers to work in the neighborhood. Then, somewhat cryptically, the history noted that that same fall "everyone left, including the director." The passage in the booklet explained further: "By 1970 the Roseland area was witnessing a mass exodus of white families and an influx of new black residents."[55] With a palpably dwindling enthusiasm for the Gospel center, in April of 1971 Fourth adopted the following recommendation:

That the supporting Churches of the Pullman Christian Reformed Church recommend the work to be continued contingent upon broadening the financial base and the restructuring of the control and direction of the Mission.

Grounds: The work of the Mission can no longer be considered the work of the Four Roseland Churches in as much as they no longer related geographically to the Roseland community.[56]

At that juncture, only Fourth had confirmed plans to leave the area, but the tone of the proposal clearly intimated the sense that the other three also had similar designs. The recommendation went on to note that the four churches considered the CRC Home Mission Board to be a prime candidate for assuming responsibility for the Mission. By December of that same year, Home Missions did indeed accede and assumed control of the Mission.

Though not betrayed in the minutes, the debate over the Mission contained much vitriol. One layperson witnessed the dispute and recounted:

All four of the Roseland churches folded up. The terrible thing in my mind [about it] is that they wanted to drag this little dinky place down with them. They were determined that they were gonna shut down that facility. . . . Perhaps they thought it couldn't exist. I mean, I think they were putting the truth to the lie to what they were saying about that 'we can't witness to this community, we're so different.' [One local pastor] was adamant that the Pullman Church was gonna shut down. It couldn't survive because the CRC denomination and the black folks had nothing in common. They worked incredibly hard to shutdown Pullman and that was the churches that were folding. They were talking about closing the place.

[The consistories of the four churches] would not allow [white] members of the church [Pullman] to come to come and speak to them. [Some members] literally pounded on the doors and windows and they would not let them in to speak.[57]

In 1971 the control of the Pullman Gospel Center passed to the Home Mission Board. The next year Classis Chicago South, though, would not be able to meet its financial obligations to Pullman CRC. In a letter to Synod, the Classis noted two of its churches were "were burdened with costly building programs due to the necessity of relocating."[58] Another written history of Pullman CRC recounted that the larger established congregations "couldn't adapt themselves to the community."[59] Eventually, however, the problems of the community would be history for Fourth and the three other CRC congregations of Roseland. By 1972 all four had successfully relocated to the Chicago suburbs with no responsibility for their neighborhood Mission.

COMPLICATING RACE AND PLACE

The implications of place also resonate within the narrative of the CRC congregations exiting the Roseland neighborhood of Chicago. Intuitively, the assumption could be made that this case of white flight would fit nicely under the rubric established by Michael Emerson and Christian Smith in *Divided by Faith: Evangelical Religion and the Problem of Race in America.* They posited that the very nature of evangelical Christianity has prohibited it from being an effective agent in the process of racial reconciliation. Indeed, they asserted that in fact the very opposite remained true: evangelical Christianity actually contributed to the construction and maintenance of a racialized society. Though not necessarily intentional, the nature of white evangelical religion—with its inability to address fundamental and structural stratifications—has functioned to perpetuate racial barriers. The emphasis on "personal salvation" and "personal relationships" made it very difficult for evangelical Christians to recognize and understand the deleterious consequences of institutionalized racism.

Thus, white evangelicals have been (at times) vocally opposed to expressions of racial prejudice, while they failed to comprehend the structural and institutional manifestations of racism. Emerson and Smith argued that the social reality of many white evangelicals prohibited them from understanding and assessing the lack of equal opportunity in the United States based on race. Moreover, by denying the existence of a racialized system, the white evangelicals have actually fostered and perpetuated it.

On an initial assessment, it would seem that Emerson and Smith's thesis would have much to contribute to an analysis of the exodus of the CRC from the Englewood and Roseland neighborhoods. It would seem to be intuitively true that the members of these churches fell under the rubric of evangelical racial blindness—that is, they could not fully understand the devastating ramification of their institutions fleeing the city because they did not possess the cultural tool kit for such an appraisal. In essence, it would be easy to dismiss the episode as simply an early proof of Emerson and Smith's assertion.

However, a more careful exposition of the outward mobilization of these churches would seem to demand a consideration of role (or lack thereof) of place. It has already been established that place in all ranges of society can be engineered to both foster and disintegrate community. To simply leave the sub-urbanization of these churches at the feet of a special brand of evangelical racial-ization or as a micro-history within the macro-story of white flight from urban America fails to adequately evaluate the importance of place.

Maria Krysan complicated the literature of white flight with her article, "Whites Who Say They'd Flee: Who Are They, and Why Would They Leave?" She sought to answer the question whether white flight found impetus in racial, race-associated ("the desire to avoid neighborhoods with certain characteristics that whites associate with African American neighborhoods"), or neutral ethno-centric ("the desire to live near one's 'own kind,' out of a sense of neutral ethno-centrism") concerns.[60] Based on individual-level attitudinal data, Krysan found that personal negative stereotypes acted as a strong predictor of white-flight attitudes. Moreover, she asserted that the neutral ethnocentric interpretation found no support in the data. Finally, Krysan contended that the race-associated concerns of falling property values and the perception of a neighborhood in decline as a cause for white departure had functioned as whites' most common explanation. Ultimately, the motivations for white flight remain complicated and highly variable.

Though it may risk making a categorization of white-flight rationalizations even more problematic, the case of CRC mobilization out of Englewood and Roseland may add another dimension to the debate. Though their evangelical Christianity may have been complicit, though outright racism may have been implicated, though race-associated reasons could be indicted, and though neu-tral ethnocentrism may have played a role, these factors inadequately assess the entire situation.

Throughout the story of CRC congregational departure from Englewood and Roseland, the prevalence of place can be clearly delineated. The narrative reveals that place for the CRC congregations had a serious disconnect with the larger community. Though these churches had a conception of place, they often manipulated it to make it more comfortable for themselves. That disconnect and exploitation of place greatly eased the transfer of these congregations to the suburbs and subsequent solidification of residential segregation.

That trend began in Englewood when the CRC members first addressed the social transition of their community in an organized manner. The formation of the Church-School Committee clearly delineated the fact that these people had social networks very much removed from the larger community. Their initial reaction was not to hold a communitywide assembly in a public space, but, rather, they chose to immediately confront the issue within the private realm of the two institutions that dominated their social lives: the church and school. It seemed that they were so disconnected to the larger "place" of Englewood that they had no social capital resources from which to make a withdrawal. They had strong, cohesive in-group ties, but no bridging ties. To them, their place in Englewood had some extremely exclusive aspects.

That same pattern held true in Roseland. Already in 1964 when African Americans families started making an appearance in the community, the church immediately discussed what it meant for their place. They asked themselves whether they should seek integration or whether the church should relocate. The leaders of Fourth CRC explicitly discussed whether African Americans would be able to use their place—their church building. It should be highlighted that the notion that the church could take their place to another locale also meant that the congregation could effectively circumvent the possibility of allowing certain people from entering their facilities. Moreover, when the council decided to forgo any physical expansion, they also tacitly endorsed the idea that the place within the edifice of the church was closed to families currently within the congregation. The decision not to create more place implicitly assumed that African Americans would not be joining the church. Indeed, such an assertion becomes more compelling when the council had to reverse itself on an earlier decision to not evangelize a largely African American community near their neighborhood. It would seem that the initial instincts of Fourth CRC had been to not invite African Americans to their place.

Eventually, however, the church would begin to canvas the newly arriving African Americans. Yet even then the newcomers could only enter the place on the terms of the church. Late arrivals would not be allowed to interrupt the service; the place would be locked to disallow those persons' (i.e., African Americans') attendance. Such a manipulation of place took on a more militant aspect when the churches initially sought security guards and eventually requested police services. When the church employed security to protect its place, it sent a message that this was not the domain of the larger neighborhood community.

Finally, the debate over the Pullman Mission reveals much about the CRC congregations' disconnect with the larger place called the neighborhood. First, the notion that a "mission" would be established within the confines of the home community connotes much about a church's relationship with the neighborhood. Some dictionaries described missions as embassies—the headquarters of ambassadors to foreign lands. Such a conception intimates that there resided within the community an element that the CRC congregations deemed "foreign." This only works to further bolster the contention that these congregants functioned in a social world largely limited to the church and Christian school. Any place in the neighborhood beyond those confines took on aspects of the "other." Such an attitude and disconnect from place made relocation an easier proposition to accept.

CONCLUSION

In the end, racial residential segregation continues to be a prevalent source of social inequality. The sources of this division are many, but the complicity of the phenomenon of white flight is undeniable. An accurate assessment of white flight demands that dimensions of religion, race-associated concerns, and neutral ethnocentrism be included in the analysis. However, a vivid explication of the situation would also include an exploration of the meaning of place within religious practices. Place can engender, but also disintegrate community. Place can be manipulated to function as a gatekeeper: welcoming some, deterring others. Moreover, when an insular community such as the CRC congregations of Roseland and Englewood (tightly delineated by the exclusive nature of the Dutch ethnic/religious ethos), creates a narrow definition of place, mobility is highly feasible. Detachment remains less problematic when few bridging ties exist and the places of the community constitute two buildings (church and school) that can be sold. At the same time, those places can be replicated in new locations. It is that mobility that facilitated outward migrations en masse for the suburbs.

Most important, such a narrow view of church as place is not unusual. The church is the site where a particular view of the truth is presented. That presentation must be maintained and protected. When threatened from within, "schisms result and new or splinter churches form."[61] When threatened from without, defensive mechanisms and mobilization become viable strategies toward preservation. The CRC congregations of these Chicago neighborhoods clearly felt threatened. In response, they removed their families and places away from the ostensible peril of the changing neighborhoods.

8 · THE SIGNIFICANCE OF POLITY

The phenomenon of "white flight" beset U.S. cities throughout the twentieth century, and the pattern of African American movement into certain neighborhoods and subsequent white emigration from the same locus has been well documented.[1] Both historians and sociologists have studied these incidents and have come to varying conclusions. The consensus, however, seems to be that such patterns of residential relocation based on race have led to and, indeed, have been factors in the continuing American urban crisis. That is, present patterns of residential segregation have been shown to have antecedents in the so-called "white flight" of the 1950s, 1960s, and 1970s.

There were many complicated reasons for the departure of whites, which calls into question sweeping assumptions about white flight. I contend that white outmigration that occurred in the Chicago neighborhoods of Englewood and Roseland beginning in the late 1950s and concluding in the early 1970s remains especially instructive. Seven entire CRC congregations from one denomination left the city during this period. These congregations ranged in size from five hundred to well over a thousand members. The response of these congregations to the perceived crisis of neighborhood change exemplifies how the political structure (congregational polity) and social networks of a particular denomination could allow for an almost seamless process of white flight.

Over a one-hundred-year period, the ethnically Dutch denomination had slowly adopted a uniquely American mode of church political structure: congregationalism. But that evolution also involved the CRC behaving in ways that would be best described as evangelical. The manner in which these seven congregations responded to the arrival of African Americans tells a story that has much to reveal about the confluence of race, religious polity, and evangelical culture in the United States.

EVANGELICAL CULTURE AND RACE

In their book *Divided by Faith*, Michael O. Emerson and Christian Smith focused on the oft-quoted sentiment that "11 AM on Sunday is the most segregated hour in America."[2] They contended that white Christian evangelicalism has exacerbated problems in race relations in the United States. Moreover, white evangelicalism contributes more to the perpetuation of a racialized society in America than to its dismantling. It does so by maintaining a limited cultural tool kit rooted in theology that tends to "1) minimize and individualize the race problem, 2) assign blame to blacks themselves for racial inequality, 3) obscure inequality as part of racial division, and 4) suggest unidimensional solutions to racial division."[3] Moreover, and more pertinent to this study, Emerson and Smith asserted that another contributing factor continued to be the manner in which evangelicals tended to organize into "internally similar congregations." They argued that such similarity arises as congregations compete, attempt to develop niches, and seek internal strength. In fact, "individual congregations tend to be made up of people from similar geographic locations, similar socioeconomic statuses, similar ethnicities, and, perhaps first and foremost, predominantly the same race."[4] Emerson and Smith continued by insisting that evangelicals and religious groups in general have difficulty in effectively addressing race relations. The processes that remain vital for internal strength and growth in the evangelical marketplace almost necessarily demand homogeneity. In contrast, the processes that intentionally promote the inclusion of diverse people also tend to erode the all-important sense of identity.[5]

The analysis offered by Emerson and Smith has significance for this case study, first because the CRC fits within the rubric of "evangelical." Considering their Calvinist heritage and attachment to the doctrine of predestination (that the salvation of the "elect" has been foreordained by God), it would not be intuitive to label the CRC "evangelical." However, Emerson and Smith clearly delineate the doctrinal hallmarks of evangelicals, and the CRC does fit the profile: that is, they 1) self-identify as evangelical (a minority within the denomination might protest such a label, but the CRC claims membership in the National Association of Evangelicals); 2) claim that Jesus Christ remains the sole avenue to salvation; 3) view the Bible as the ultimate authority; 4) emphasize a conversion experience; and 5) actively engage in evangelism or give financial support for such purposes.[6] The bulk of the CRC would claim all these identifiers.[7]

Within the category of evangelicals, Emerson and Smith found some interesting results while conducting their interviews. First, they discovered that 40 percent of "strong evangelicals" did not think that integrating congregations and neighborhoods were reasonable methods for addressing racism and race-related problems.[8] Interestingly, one of the strongly evangelical respondents within that 40 percent is actually identified as a member of the CRC. Emerson and Smith quoted him: "I think the whole concept of blacks and whites worshipping together is great, but how can you do that when you feel so uncomfortable?"[9] Such a sentiment sounds like an echo from the debates in CRC council rooms all over Chicago during the 1950s, 1960s, and 1970s.

Moreover, their interviews revealed severe opposition to residential integration as a step toward racial reconciliation. Some, again, cited comfort as a factor. However, the most prevalent objection had to do with forcing people to do something against their will. Emerson and Smith related that many responses indicated an inability to understand integrated neighborhoods as a result of anything other than coercion. They quoted one respondent at length: "Any solution that doesn't come naturally is gonna cause a problem. No one, I don't care, no one wants to be told where to live, Christians or non-Christians. No one wants to be told by the government or some other authority who to associate with, so I don't think that forced issues are going to fundamentally solve the problem."[10] Ultimately, Emerson and Smith found that within the evangelical church, the integration of neighborhoods as a vehicle for working against racial inequality is "almost never discussed or advocated."

POLITY

The role of polity is seen in stark relief when comparing these seven CRC congregations to the six Reformed Church of America (RCA) congregations that resided in the same two Chicago South Side neighborhoods. From an outsider's perspective, these two denominations would be largely indistinguishable: both have Dutch roots, worship with similar liturgy, and espouse the same Reformed/Calvinist doctrine.[11] Upon closer inspection, however, it becomes clear that church polity functioned as a critical distinction between them. Although both denominations claim a Presbyterian polity, the CRC would be more accurately described as congregational. That is, the bulk of power rested at the local level—any hierarchical apparatuses wielded little or no influence on the decisions that these congregations made when their neighborhoods changed with the arrival of African Americans during the Great Migration. In contrast, the RCA congregations answered to authorities within the denomination regarding the selling of church buildings. In the end, this single contrast in church polity predisposed the CRC congregations to higher levels of mobility and suburbanization as the neighborhoods changed racially, and speeded the departure dates of these congregations.

Though the story of the expansion of the African American community in Chicago after World War II remains familiar, the situation in the Englewood and Roseland neighborhoods of Chicago stands as a significant case among all rust-belt cities that experienced a white migration to the suburbs. The rapidity of the transition and complicity of local churches combined to allow a case study of white relocation and suburbanization that reveals much about urban residential patterns and the role of evangelical Christianity in influencing those patterns.

Recent studies indicate that fully one-third of Americans are evangelicals by affiliation.[12] Thus, evangelicals as a population have weighty influence on the social world of the United States. Moreover, almost all forms of white evangelicalism lean toward a congregational polity. As people in the United States continue to cluster into ever more separate residential enclaves, the role of religious influence remains significant in the creation and perpetuation of segregated residential areas.[13] As we have seen, the congregational polity of the CRC denomination made it easier for members of the churches and the churches themselves to leave the city neighborhoods as African Americans moved in.

In addition, the timing of the moves of these CRC congregations on the South Side of Chicago further complicates the notion of "white flight." While in this instance it remains true that the white Dutch ethnic population by and large left for the suburbs, it should also be noted that congregations of the RCA persuasion left much later (in some cases more than a decade and half later) than those from the CRC. Thus even within a single ethnic (Dutch) and religious (Reformed) subculture, the term "white flight" fails to capture the shades and differences in white departure.

Thus the case of Dutch relocation from Chicago helps to bolster and offer nuances to the case presented by Emerson and Smith. They posited that the very nature of evangelical Christianity has prohibited it from being an effective agent in racial reconciliation. Indeed, they asserted that in fact the very opposite remained true: evangelical Christianity actually contributed to construction and maintenance of a racialized society. Though not necessarily intentional, the nature of white evangelical religion—with its inability to address fundamental and structural stratifications—has functioned to perpetuate racial barriers.

In essence, white evangelicals have been opposed to individual racial prejudice while failing to understand the structural/institutional character of American racism. Emerson and Smith argued that the social reality of many evangelicals prohibited them from understanding and assessing the lack of equal opportunity in America based on race. Moreover, by denying the existence of a racialized system, the white evangelicals have actually fostered and perpetuated it. The inhibiting factor seems to be the white evangelical understanding of spirituality: each person is responsible for his or her salvation through Christ and maintenance of that relationship. Such a vision hinders a more communal view of Christianity.

Numerous historians and sociologists have asserted that that individualistic religiosity has direct translation in the congregational nature—that is, with authority resting at the local church level—of evangelical denominations. Such a polity allows the congregations to own their own worship buildings, which contributes to an increased mobility of church bodies. In the CRC polity the congregations did indeed own their buildings. Thus the very nature of the organizational structure of the denomination precluded any major impediment to mobilization and subsequent suburbanization.

THE ROLE OF CHURCH POLITY IN MOBILITY

The range of church polity—from the extremely hierarchical and parish-based Roman Catholic model to the more congregational and highly mobile Orthodox Jewish model—manifested radically different strategies in the face of changing neighborhood demographics. Already in 1962 Winter Gibson, a student of Talcott Parsons, had noted that the member-oriented Protestant churches would be more apt to quickly leave undesirable situations than Roman Catholics because of mobility and little identification with the neighborhood.[14] Similarly, Gerald Gamm posited that the institutional infrastructure of religion had a determinative role in allowing Jews to move to the surrounding suburbs and keeping Catholics bound to Boston proper.[15]

Gamm also used the nexus of religious polity and residential change to problematize the term "white flight." Gamm contended that the term "presumed to solve the riddle of the urban exodus," but failed fully account for the white middle-class departure from cities. He went on to note that his research indicated that whites had fled mostly white neighborhoods. Only after those neighborhoods had largely emptied did property values and rents decrease to the point that African Americans could move in. Gamm concluded that to fully appreciate the complexities of urban change, it remained imperative to consider the role of local institutions—including churches and synagogues.[16]

More recently, Jordan Stanger-Ross addressed the issue of white flight in a case study of two North Philadelphia synagogues.[17] Stanger-Ross contended that these religious institutions did not engage in white flight, but rather practiced a flexibility that allowed them preserve their religious institutions within the city center. However, it should be noted that in both cases, the actions of both synagogues could still plausibly be best described as modifications of white flight. First, the decisions of the synagogues did nothing to discourage attendees' movement away from African American influx. Second, though the two synagogues remained in Philadelphia proper, their strategies also allowed attendees to worship in areas unaffected by the recent arrival of African Americans. The first synagogue moved to the historic center of the city and became part of a museum of Jewish history. The second synagogue did maintain the original building, but also opened suburban branches to serve members no longer in the city. Neither synagogue followed a more traditional route of simple wholesale removal to the suburbs. Consequently, this case underscores the necessity of carefully parsing discussions about white flight.

In a vein similar to that offered by Gamm, John McGreevy noted that because of the parish structure in which the Roman Catholic church divided each diocese into distinct geographic areas with discernible boundaries, urban Catholics in the North had a distinctly different social experience from that of Protestants and Jews.[18] The church structure demanded that Catholic parishioners have a much stronger connection to the local community or neighborhood. In large part, the parish did not simply constitute the local church and school; it also included the neighborhood. In fact, because of the pervasive nature of parish life, the neighborhood itself took on a sacred quality for the parishioners. Thus, Catholics tended to stay longer in urban neighborhoods than either their Protestant or Jewish counterparts.[19]

Much as Emerson and Smith explored how evangelicalism affected America's racialized cities, Nancy Ammerman and a host of researchers examined how congregations reacted to significant community change.[20] Ammerman stated that she wanted to know how the congregations fare, "what processes they adapt (when they do), and even what the process of decline and death looks like."[21] Ammerman and her team focused on understanding how congregations respond to fundamental social change such as suburbanization, local factory closings, and the influx of ethnic immigrants. Included under the rubric of "community changes" was racial integration.

Ammerman asserted that congregations function as an integral component of a community's institutional infrastructure. In fact, the congregation actually helps in allowing social life to be possible because of its structure and connections that operate as living networks of meaning and activity. Not only that, Ammerman continued by insisting that because of "concentration of social energy" congregations can actually "channel the energies of . . . citizens in ways that . . . affect the world."[22] In the case of CRC congregations in Englewood and Roseland, then, the churches functioned as significant organizations that had capacities at their disposal to influence the social and economic lives of those neighborhoods.

Ultimately, Ammerman found that congregations in changing neighborhoods that refuse to modify their identity will either die or will be forced move (e.g., Englewood and Roseland CRCs). Only congregations that have the vision to transform their identity will survive. In the end, Ammerman's sociological study of congregations as organizations suggested that, in light of the particularities of the population and its homogeneous nature, it should not be unforeseen—in fact, it should be expected—that congregations relocate in the face of neighborhood change. Congregations remain "collectively oriented." In other words, "they direct the participants' attention toward a group larger than themselves and their immediate kin in a way that avowedly asserts this groups difference from every other."[23] In that sense, congregations operate as vehicles for helping to define the "other," and scholars should not be surprised when these institutions fail to adapt adequately to a changing community.

In the end, this case study of CRC congregations in Chicago offers a vivid representation of churches that sought to move rather than transform their vision. The significance of the influence of these local institutions on members and attendees during the era of social and geographic transition deserves an extended analysis in that it demonstrates the significance of religious structures and, subsequently, complicates notions of white flight.

THE CRC'S UNIQUE POLITY

To fully understand the CRC context, it is important to comprehend the structure and polity of the denomination. The Church Order of the CRC was, in effect, an articulation of the historic Reformed position that all professing members are "saints" and consequently have leadership roles within the church. Such an interpretation has led Reformed and Presbyterian churches—most notably for our purposes, the CRC—to conclude that power should ultimately be vested in the individual congregations where the saints actually reside. The very nature of the CRC polity thus lent considerable autonomy to particular churches and allowed no denominational deliberation or influence on their relocation.

The CRC Order designated the existence of three assemblies: the councils, the Classes (pl. of Classis), and the General Synod. The local council of each congregation (including both elders and deacons) operates as the basic unit of government.[24] Each council then sends representatives to Classis: a meeting of local or regional congregations for general supervision, designed to deal only with matters that could not be concluded in councils or those that the congregations have in common. Finally, Classes send representatives to Synod, an annual meeting of the denomination. Council authority retains responsibility for matters such as disciplining ministers. The only restraining factors concern the advice of the Classis in question and Synodical consent—which has limited binding authority.[25] So although the CRC has ostensibly maintained a Presbyterian-style Church Order (whereby the church leadership resides with the elders—presbyters), in the end, the evolution of the Church Order of the CRC within the context of the American religious scene led the denomination toward congregationalism—that is, an ordering that allows tremendous local autonomy over property, ministerial, and budgetary matters.

The CRC has made no claim that its Church Order and polity have an exclusively Presbyterian character. In fact, the CRC departs from the Presbyterian polity in that the denomination does not view the Order as retaining authority over the status of the creeds—Heidelberg Catechism, Belgic Confession, and Canons of Dort. Thus, the Order has regulative rather than confessional properties. As such, the CRC allows that the Order may indeed be flawed, and necessary alterations indeed should be administered when convincingly presented. In other words, the polity does not function as an intractable system of rigid, systematic rules. There exists an "amount of flexibility in procedures and practices possible within the polity of the Christian Reformed Church."[26] Such "flexibility" would be crucial as the denomination evolved in the United States.

In fact, the CRC polity deliberately delegates primacy to the minor assemblies rather than the major. The major assemblies, Classis and Synod, are restricted to those matters that could not be adjudicated by the minor assemblies, councils. The authority of the major assemblies over the minor assemblies has been described as thus: "it is derived, and not original; limited, and not general; smaller in measure, and not higher in degree; ministering, and not compelling; conditional, and not unconditional."[27] The Classis and the Synod may make rulings concerning individual congregations; however, it cannot enforce the execution of the ruling. The Church Order supposes the individual congregation would either submit or appeal a ruling. If it chose the latter route and lost the appeal, the congregation then would be expected to finally submit. However, the Church Order also goes on to state "if the judgment on the appeal is negative, submission of the minor assembly should follow unless great conscientious objection should make withdrawal from the denomination preferable."[28] Within CRC circles, complaints have frequently been heard that congregations have often been lax in applying decisions of the Synod. Such predilections merely echo the independent and congregational nature of the church ancestry in 1834 in the Netherlands and in 1857 in western Michigan.

By allowing the congregations such autonomy, the CRC has been criticized for a poorly developed Church Order—as have other adherents of Presbyterian polity.[29] In fact, the evolution of the Church Order has led the denomination away from Presbyterian polity and toward congregationalism. In response, CRC apologists simply insist that they have much more concern over doctrine than over polity, liturgy, or history. In essence, the CRC has had two goals: adhering to the pattern of the Church as described by the Bible and the maintenance of traditional Reformed orthodox theology.[30]

Interestingly, the CRC is a denomination descended from a territorial polity in the Netherlands. There, parish-based congregations—even Reformed congregations—functioned as the norm. As such, the church authority demarked an area and assigned the members to specific congregations: "individual believers do not choose their congregation, but become, so to say, incorporated in the church."[31] However, in the United States, the CRC drifted from its territorial heritage. In fact, one CRC minister noted the differences in the late 1990s: "In the Netherlands a church is a church in a given geographical area regardless of how many buildings it has. So if that heritage, that European, Reformed heritage had prevailed here, there would have been one church in Roseland with four worship centers and maybe six or eight pastors, but there would be one congregation."[32]

In the United States, the erosion of Presbyterian polity and irrelevance of geography went hand in hand. Thus it could be argued that congregational nature of the CRC was actually a mutation of the original polity. This same minister also noted that the polity of the CRC fails to be "faithful to its own heritage" and that it had been "modified to fit the American scene, which is very independent."[33] Feeling no obligations to the community or larger assemblies, the CRC congregations of Englewood and Roseland exercised a sovereignty solely concerned with institutional self-preservation. With such a focus, the relocation of these churches to the suburbs seemed instinctive. As largely self-determining institutions, they had no predilection or resources for integration. Thus departure represented the only viable means of survival, in their view.

A COMPARISON TO ROMAN CATHOLIC POLITY AND PRACTICE

Roman Catholics, however, represented the other end of the polity spectrum.[34] The historian John McGreevy asserted that a monolithic understanding of white racism fails to detect the complexity of the situation. Often, it is assumed that tensions between whites and African Americans catalyzed around labor competition, and that white racism thus had a largely "working class" pattern. McGreevy countered that a thoughtful analysis instead reveals that white-versus-black antagonism centered on the home, not work. Indeed, he stated that "racial violence in the North centered on housing and not, for the most part, on access to public space, employment issues, or voting rights."[35] McGreevy ultimately concerned himself with the question of why housing remained such a conspicuously divisive entity in northern cities of the United States.

In response, he answered that the pervasiveness of American Catholic communities in northern cities and the manner in which they defined their surroundings in religious terms had profound consequences on the emerging residential patterns of the 1960s. While scholars tend to focus on matters of class, gender, and ethnicity; McGreevy insisted that in doing so they overlook matters of faith. For instance, McGreevy noted that it became difficult to deny the ramifications of religion when 20 to 70 percent of the total population in northern cities claimed a Catholic faith or identity. The role of the church in shaping the congregants' attitudes and perspectives toward neighborhood and community had to be significant. These Catholics responded to African Americans not simply as "workers" or "ethnics," but also as people directed and influenced by their religious institutions.[36]

As noted above, because the church divided each diocese into distinct geographic areas (parishes) with discernible boundaries, urban Catholics in the North had a very different social experience from that of Protestants and Jews. The church structure demanded that Catholic parishioners have a much stronger connection to the local community or neighborhood. Because of the pervasive nature of parish life, the parishioners' connections to religion and to neighborhood became intertwined to the point of indissolubility. The parish priests reinforced this confluence by encouraging their congregants to demonstrate a commitment to the neighborhood by buying instead of renting, as well as investing in the parish facilities, and that they form social organizations throughout the neighborhood parish.

McGreevy further noted the strength and profile of the parish—even non-Catholics recognized the boundaries placed by the church structure. He contended that even Protestants and Jews who lived within parish boundaries were aware that they lived in a particular territory delineated by the Catholic church. Moreover, many often reported where they lived by parish name rather than by a more secular identification of their neighborhood.

That strong identification with the neighborhood often manifested itself in violent outbursts when Catholic parishioners perceived a threat of African American in-migration. On the surface, such activities seemed to simply be the outgrowth of white racism. McGreevy, however, offered the compelling notion that an ecclesiastical and theological subtext permeated the activities of these white Catholics. In the end, the parish model of American Catholicism played a primary role in the persistent segregation of the urban North.

Indeed, the contentions of McGreevy have been affirmed in other volumes on residential segregation: Arnold Hirsch and Thomas Sugrue both indicted various institutions for creating residential inequality in the urban North. Though neither provided a detailed analysis of the role of churches and religion, they both noted some involvement in the process by local churches. Hirsch confined his discussion almost exclusively to the church's apparent complicity in racial disorders and the overrepresentation of Catholics involved. Similarly, Sugrue noted that the Catholic Church strictly ordered urban life and that many priests encouraged parishioners to join homeowners' associations "for fear that black 'invasions' would hurt parish life."[37]

Though McGreevy detailed the violence that sometimes erupted in defense of the Catholic parish, he also asserted that "for all their faults, the Catholic parish worlds" effectively "strengthened family, faith, and community." While parishes sometimes blurred the distinctions between "community and fortress," the parish system ultimately "sustained faith while structuring a genuine community life."[38]

THE OTHER END OF THE POLITY SPECTRUM: JEWISH SYNAGOGUES

Like McGreevy, Gerald Gamm argued that though Boston parishes experienced white departure, some of those same areas eventually became "stable, racially integrated neighborhoods."[39] Gamm explored the role of religion in Boston neighborhoods that rapidly altered racial composition in the 1960s and 1970s. He emphasized that religious polity, authority, and institutional rootedness allowed Catholics and Jews to take dramatically different strategies in response to African American in-migration. The importance of his work lies in his insistence that the institutional infrastructure (what he called "institutional rules") of religion had a determinative role in allowing Jews to move to the surrounding suburbs and keeping Catholics bound to Boston proper.

Gamm analyzed three categories: congregational membership, rootedness, and authority. He described these as rules of definition—they are important not because they are written down, but because they are obeyed. The first class of rules concerns membership. Institutional membership for Jews remains entirely voluntary and the synagogue recognizes no territorial boundaries. In contrast, the Catholic parish church "exercises monopoly jurisdiction, receiving the loyalty of all Catholics within the parish who identify with a territorial church."[40]

The second class of rules involves rootedness. U.S. Jewish congregations relocate freely because building and location do not play an integral role within the religion. Within Jewish law, the highly portable Torah is holy—not the synagogue. The Catholic church holds a distinctly different place. Gamm noted that "the Catholic church is a permanent structure, consecrated to God and built around a permanent altar, and the territorial parish's relationship to its neighborhood is inalienable."[41]

Finally, Gamm presented the third class of rules: authority. The synagogue and the Catholic church have contrasting rules of authority in at least five different instances: "creation and dissolution of an institution; acquisition, ownership, and disposal of funds and property; determination of policy and doctrinal questions; selection and dismissal of clergy; and prerequisites for congregational worship."[42] These distinctions in the rules of authority allowed Jewish congregations an autonomy foreign to Catholic churches. Gamm went so far as to note that the "American Jewish synagogue enjoys the purest form of congregational authority," while a priest and a hierarchy are intrinsic to the very existence of a Catholic parish.

Gamm asserted that because of the manner in which they understood what constituted their synagogue or temple, Jewish congregations could easily follow members out of the city and into the suburbs. The people constituted the temple, thus it existed where they lived. Synagogues may be organized by as few as ten men and receive governance from the congregation itself, not by rabbis. The Jewish place of worship has absolutely no territorial orientation— members may live anywhere of their choosing. Within the Jewish tradition, the synagogue structure itself lacks any symbolic importance. The presence of God finds constitution in highly mobile writings of faith (e.g., the Torah) that can be accommodated in a wide variety of settings. Gamm concluded that these portable structures of the religion created a predilection within these Jewish communities toward efficient mobility as neighborhood demographics began to change.

Catholics, on the other hand, belonged to a more hierarchically organized and territorially committed ecclesiastical institution. The parish operated as the fundamental unit of organization. Gamm argued that the orientation of the Roman Catholic Church toward maintaining a presence in neighborhoods functioned to force parishioners to stay in city proper neighborhoods even as they changed demographically. Thus different patterns of out-migration from the city between Jews and Catholics had less to do with varying capacities for racist behavior and more to do with a divergent sense of attachment to territory or place. Gamm stated that "Catholics have a strong sense of turf, regarding their neighborhoods as defended geographical communities . . . Jews, in contrast, are much less likely to defend a neighborhood against outsiders."[43]

Thus, the institutions of the two different religions fostered different attitudes toward the local community. These attitudes became manifest when African Americans began their in-migration. Gamm contended that the local Catholic church "reassured and anchored its surrounding Catholic neighborhood." In contrast, the local synagogue "undermined and exacerbated stresses in its surrounding Jewish neighborhood."[44]

In the end, Gamm—much like Diamond and Emerson and Smith—reinforced the notion that the nature of religion and faith has played a critical role in American urban residential patterns. The practices of faith and the structures of religious institutions have had a profound effect on white congregants' responses to the influx of African Americans into their neighborhoods. Though the phenomenon of white flight included many relevant factors, the variable of religion cannot be dismissed.

THE ASCENDENCY OF CONGREGATIONALISM

The congregational polity of the CRC functions in contrast to the territorial parish system practiced by the Catholic Church. Though the CRC took an atypical route to congregationalism, they ultimately found themselves a fully American style of church polity. Congregationalism as a model of church polity emphasizes "voluntary membership rather than ascription or geography, lay involvement in decision making, a professional clergy, [and] the declining significance of denominationalism."[45] In the United States, the "religious experience has been predominantly a congregational one in which leaders and members share authority in a varied and complicated fashion."[46] In the case of the CRC bodies in Englewood and Roseland, a study of the nature of the congregationalism of those churches illuminates how they so easily joined the larger social movement to the suburbs.

In practice, the CRC's congregationalism was not unique. The trend in American religion has been toward more localized and autonomous religious units. Historian Nathan Hatch identified the "rise of democratic Christianity" as the most dynamic element in the American religious situation.[47] A natural outgrowth of that democratization has been the dispersal of power to the local congregations. As such, the "primary extrafamilial form of community for much of the American population has been the religious congregation."[48]

Especially in Protestant Christianity, the importance of the denomination has declined for church members. As denominations have waned, congregations have proliferated. The declining hierarchical authority has been evidenced by the fact that increasingly congregations within the same denomination "vary wildly in theology, liturgy, and social values." In addition, Protestant denominations have responded to the "clamor over centralized bureaucracy" by reducing staff and overhead. Such cutbacks have limited the denominations' abilities to oversee and intervene in congregational-level affairs.[49]

Though Hatch described the tendency toward decentralization in American religion since the inception of the nation, others have noted that the trend has increased in intensity since World War II (coinciding with some of the mass movement of white families out of many American central cities). A major national study that was published in 1972 surveyed the members of fifteen denominations. The findings stated:

> Out of the inherited citizenry-versus-the-colossus mentality has grown a kind of schizoid image of the church, split between the intimate local congregation on the one side and the more remote impersonal denomination on the other. Sometimes, the implication almost has seemed that they are pitted against each other. There was a tendency to concentrate resources on the community level and downgrade the denomination.[50]

In light of the decreased hierarchical power and subsequent growth in local religious autonomy, Stephen Warner offered the concept of "de facto congregationalism." The implication has been that in American religions "congregations can chart their own religious course despite their denominational ties."[51] For instance, the prevalence of implementing popular hymns instead of those sanctioned in the denominational hymnbook, and the practice of calling pastors from independent seminaries instead of those with denominational affiliations have left labels such as "Presbyterian," "Lutheran," or "Methodist" unable to convey much information to first-time visitors to local congregations. In general, uniformity and central control of congregations have decreased markedly in the United States since World War II. Peter Berger accurately summarized the situation when he noted that "for most lay Christians the form of the Church that means anything to them personally is their own local congregation."[52]

The increase in congregational autonomy has, in turn, led to less sense of territorial responsibility:

De facto congregationalism also means that the local church is effectively constituted by its members, not by geography. In a city like Chicago, the mobility of congregations and stability of edifices are often evident in building cornerstones and carved inscriptions. A former synagogue in Greek revival style is now owned by a Puerto Rican Pentecostal church. Another synagogue is now a Greek Orthodox church. A German Lutheran church built at the turn of the century is now owned by Hispanic Seventh-day Adventists. What was built as an Anglo-Saxon Presbyterian church and was later sold to a Korean congregation now houses an Orthodox church for Arab Christians.[53]

Once again we see that the more congregational a church's hierarchical structure, the easier for the local institutions to mobilize.

In a study on parish autonomy and the differences by denomination, Randolph Cantrell, James Krile, and George Donohue ranked a number of American denominations based on the independence that local churches maintained.[54] They found that Roman Catholic congregations had the least autonomy, while their counterparts in the United Church of Christ (UCC) had the most—these two denominations represented the poles on the continuum of denominational structure.[55] The authors found that Methodists, Presbyterians, and Lutherans fell somewhere in between. The three variables the researchers utilized were legal status (the degree to which control of the local church property rested in the hands of the congregation), deployment of clergy (the degree to which the local pastor is considered an officer of the congregation or an officer of the denomination), and budgetary procedures (degree to which the local congregation has the power to allocate funds).[56] On the basis of their findings, Cantrell et al. categorize church polities as Episcopal, Presbyterian, and Congregational.[57]

Within the typologies established by Cantrell et al., the CRC clearly falls into the congregational camp. Local church property is solely under the control of the congregation. Within the CRC, pastors are called and dismissed by congregations; they are not appointed and reassigned by the denomination. Finally, CRC congregations do have denominational quotas to fulfill, but the majority of fiscal decisions reside with the local churches.[58]

The implications of de facto congregationalism would be borne out as the neighborhoods of Englewood and Roseland began to change. While the Presbyterian polity ensured a level of stasis among the RCA congregations, the congregational polity of the CRC allowed for quicker relocation. The ecology changed in parallel ways for congregations in both denominations, but the nature of their polity became a significant variable that helped determine the courses each church would take.

9 · SECOND ROSELAND (CRC) LEAVES THE CITY

The departures of the CRC congregations from Englewood and Roseland are separated by time (roughly ten years apart) and space (roughly forty city blocks). Three CRC congregations left Englewood 1962–1964, whereas the four in Roseland had departed by 1972. In contrast, the RCA's congregations in these same neighborhoods remained in their locations longer. The two RCA congregations in Englewood remained until 1973 and 1978, and the four in Roseland left in 1971, 1974, 1977, and 1989. The departures of the CRC congregations will be examined more closely in this chapter, and compared with the moves of the RCA congregations in the next.

In many ways the departures of the seven CRC congregations followed very similar templates. For that reason, I will offer a detailed discussion of the last to leave, Second CRC of Roseland, and its surrounding neighborhood as an exemplar of how a church operating within a congregational framework self-sanctioned a departure from the city. After seventy-nine years of existence in Chicago proper, Second Roseland left for the outlying suburb of Orland Park in 1972.

In an interesting epilogue to the transition, in 1982 Classis Chicago South celebrated the 125th anniversary of the denomination with a worship service and the publishing of a commemorative booklet. Congregations that had once previously been located in Englewood and Roseland discussed their relocations to the suburbs "due to sociological conditions" in the publication.[1] Such coded language carefully avoided the racial concerns that precipitated the congregational movement.

CASE STUDY: SECOND CRC OF ROSELAND

As with all CRC congregations, Second Roseland exercised complete control over their location and buildings. The year 1964 seems to have been when the future of Roseland became a concern for the congregation of Second Roseland. During the first half of the year, the council of the 845-member congregation debated the feasibility of modernizing the parsonage. Such an investment displayed an intention to remain.[2] However, only a few months later the council reversed course and instead began to consider purchasing a parsonage in "a better neighborhood"—a euphemism for a whiter neighborhood where housing values would presumably remain stable.[3] It seems that the leadership of the church had started to worry about the numerous African American arrivals to the community.[4]

The concern over the neighborhood continued to appear on the agenda of council meetings. In January 1965, the Worship Committee reported to the council their recommendation that all doors of the church be locked five minutes after the beginning of worship services to "safeguard the property of members."[5] Such a gross violation of fire code indicated a high level of alarm within the congregation. At the same time, the elders engaged in discussions about the future of the CRC in general in the Roseland area.[6] These conversations included overtures to the Classis Chicago South and the denomination's Home Missions Board (a denominational office dedicated to domestic evangelism) about bringing in a missionary to work in Roseland's "changing community."[7] Such a request underscored how ill-equipped the congregation felt in reaching out African Americans moving into the neighborhood.

In November of 1965, Second Roseland received Classical visitors to assess the state of the congregation. In the subsequent report, the writers described the congregation representing "one of the stronger congregations of [Classis] Chicago South."[8] The state of the neighborhood warranted no remark in the report. The representatives concluded, though, that congregation had exhibited "joyous anticipation" that Charles Terpstra of Paterson, New Jersey had accepted a call to the church and would begin his service there in a few weeks as their new minister.[9]

That anticipation turned to disenchantment rather quickly. Terpstra and the congregation would soon clash over the church's response to the changing neighborhood. Terpstra instigated programming to demonstrate that the congregation could continue to exist with vitality in Roseland. To that end, a cohort of eight women from the congregation tutored local African American children every Wednesday afternoon at the church. Terpstra described the effort as a demonstration that "at least the parents [of the African American children] would let their children be taught in a white church. And they came faithfully, and they came eagerly, and that was, we said as part of the argument that this was something we could do."[10] In other words, Terpstra saw the tutoring as a template for how the congregation could remain a crucial part of the changing neighborhood. Despite these efforts, however, rumors of the congregation's impending relocation seeped out into the larger community.

Because of what had previously occurred in Englewood and what seemed to be on the horizon in Roseland, the denomination's Synod held an Inner-Cities

Ministries Conference. The conference sought to help congregations think more strategically about how to respond to neighborhood change. In December 1968, Terpstra brought before the council a request from the conference participants that had been forwarded to him: The conference participants requested that the CRC Synod "declare that any church congregation considering relocation of its ministry shall inform the Classis of which it is a member, and shall determine upon a site for a new location with the advice of Classis."[11] It seemed that the conference participants recognized the level of panic within the congregations. By offering counsel, the conference hoped to forestall situations where churches sited themselves with a dearth of analysis in regard to demographic trends. However, such a change in polity would undoubtedly have caused a firestorm at Synod and never received formal adoption at any governmental level within the CRC.

Back in Roseland, in January 1969 the congregation formally began the relocation process when the council appointed a committee to "consider the future" of the church. The committee reported back to the council that the church would soon face serious financial problems due to a loss of members and that an immediate possibility to alleviate that pressure would be a merger with Fourth Roseland. At the same time, all four of the CRC congregations in Roseland established a "Committee of 12" (three representatives from each church) to discuss the future of the denomination in the community.[12] The Committee of 12 represented the apex of a corporate approach to addressing the demographic changes in Roseland for the four CRC congregations. Over its brief lifetime (about two years), the Committee of 12 concerned itself with discussions of merger and consolidation. The committee expended little or no effort in addressing the possibility of maintaining the current population base of the CRC or in strategically attempting to integrate the congregations. Eventually the Committee of 12 proved itself quite impotent as each of the four churches made separate decisions with little regard for the other three congregations or the larger community. In a later interview regarding the Committee of 12, Terpstra would note with dismay, "Nobody can tell an individual congregation what to do. You can teach. And you can preach. And you can propagandize. But you can't enforce."[13]

By April 1969, the council of Second Roseland began to seriously consider relocation outside of Roseland. They listed some reasons for being preemptive and exploring the matter: 1) If planned early, the move could be very orderly and result in a better-planned ministry in both the old and new neighborhood. 2) Early strategic planning would allow for developing and maintaining a relevant ministry in both the "new suburban and older city communities." 3) The planning would allow for improved stewardship in using the church's resources. 4) The Church Order allowed it, thus the congregation had the freedom to explore relocation.[14] While the council discussed the move, attendance numbers at Sunday worship services continued to dwindle.

At the same time, a noticeable rift between Reverend Terpstra and the council had begun to develop. As a minister called to the congregation in 1965, Terpstra demonstrated a commitment to Roseland largely absent in many of the life-long CRC residents. Terpstra described his attitude upon arrival in Roseland:

> I went there intentionally with my eyes open and knowing what the situation was and being committed. As an urban minister I was committed to bring an integrated ministry or a ministry in that community, or I was committed to not let racism rule. [Pause] I didn't go there suspicious, or with any kind of vendetta, or "I know better than you and I'll show you." . . . And I believed with my whole heart and mind that it was God's will that we should stay there and minister to this changing population.[15]

Terpstra firmly believed that a white ethnic congregation could remain a vital component of the Roseland community.

In 1968, the congregation celebrated their seventy-fifth anniversary. As part of the festivities, the church published a history booklet. The author of the history referred to "changes and crises" that Second Roseland presently faced in the community, obvious codes for the recent influx of African Americans. In the introduction, though, the Reverend Terpstra challenged the congregation as a whole. He noted that he had only been in the church for two and a half years, but that that did not preclude him from saying something "about the church's continuing service." Clearly, from Terpstra's language, discussions of relocation had reached the minister's ears. He utilized the occasion of the anniversary booklet to challenge the congregation to remain in Roseland. Terpstra alluded to the struggles of the congregation when he asserted that he was convinced "that God had sent [him] here 'for such a time as this.'" Moreover, the minister boldly argued that Second Roseland should remain: "HERE—NOW."[16]

The tension between the respective positions of Terpstra and the council apparently made its way into the Sunday sermons of the minister. At one point, the minutes of the council reveal an explicit request from the elders that Terpstra please "withhold critical comment from the pulpit regarding the work" of the council.[17] The pastor and the council continued to be at odds, however. Ultimately, the council would be victorious. In the end, the Reformed polity assured such an outcome because the elders operated as definitive unit of government. The minister brought business before the council that involved "anticipating the future" in the Roseland area. In that, Terpstra sought creative strategies for remaining firmly within the neighborhood. The council, on the other hand, established a Church Extension Committee to oversee a potential relocation to the "Illiana" (a nickname for the Illinois/Indiana border region just south of Chicago) area.[18] By 1970, the council was sending elders to the suburban Lansing,

Illinois, area to administer a separate worship service for congregants who had already moved to the vicinity. At the same juncture, Terpstra spent a week at the Urban Center for Training and Christian Missions.[19]

The oppositional actions of the council and the minister continued through the summer of 1970. The council continued to study the advisability of disposing of the Roseland properties and potential sites for relocation. Terpstra successfully lobbied for the council to approve a motion that allowed him to "field test a race relations primer in the Roseland area."[20] The minister also attempted to have the congregation hire a staff worker to run programs directed at the "new population" in Roseland. When put before the congregation for a vote, this proposal for a new position was soundly defeated by a two-to-one ratio. Terpstra described himself leaving that meeting in a "discombobulated" state. He went on to relate: "When we walked out of the building at the end of the meeting . . . the [council] vice president's wife said to me, 'Well, now you know what the will of God is,'" indicating that the vote proved that God sanctioned the departure from Roseland. Terpstra responded, "Indeed I do, and I also know what the will of man is," expressing his sense that the vote to leave the neighborhood and the city had been an "act of disobedience on the part of the church."[21] Because of the nature of the CRC's local authority, the leadership was effectively divided. It became a battle to decide whose vision would succeed. In the end, the momentum of suburbanization left Terpstra with little chance for success.

In early 1971, Terpstra accepted a call from another church within the denomination in the core city of Grand Rapids, Michigan. Terpstra described his acceptance of the call from another church as a "non-decision." He wryly noted that not one member of Second Roseland asked him to stay. Later that year, Second Roseland passed a motion to sell the church property and seek a merger by a vote of fifty-six to twenty-six. With that result in hand, the council appointed a Sale Committee and a Merger Committee.[22] The Sale Committee almost immediately fielded requests from both denominational and Classical Home Missions boards to sell their facilities at a reduced rate to the denomination to allow for a continued "reformed witness in the Roseland area."[23] In the waning months of 1971 the Home Missions Board and Classis Chicago South twice formally requested that Second Roseland remain in the neighborhood.[24]

THE CRC SYNOD ADDRESSES RACIAL ISSUES

In addition, the last few Synods had made racial injustice a significant aspect of the agenda at the meetings. In fact, the issue of race relations first received Synodical attention as early as 1957 in connection with the issue of segregation. From that point on, race relations appeared on the Synod docket in 1959, 1964, 1966, and 1968 through 1974. New committees were established by the Synod to study and assess how the denomination could be more just and integrated.

The formation of new committees required funding from local congregations. Demonstrating a palpable belligerence to the efforts of Synod, the council of Second Roseland passed a motion to accept an overture from First Roseland to "make no financial appropriation for the denominational race expenditures."[25] In other words, Second Roseland demonstrated a strong resistance to any of its money being utilized for denominational efforts addressing race and integration.

In early 1972, the Sale Committee had an acceptable offer from Tate Tabernacle Church of God in Christ (an African American church), and the Merger Committee had distilled the list of potential churches for merging with down to Orland Park CRC (formerly Fourth CRC of Roseland). In June, the congregation passed motions to accept Tate Tabernacle's offer of $100,000.00 and to merge with Orland Park CRC.[26]

In a lot of ways, the exodus of Second Roseland, along with First, Third, and Fourth, represented a major defeat for the denomination. The Synod of the CRC had recently found itself faced with having to make some definitive statements about the church and race. When the Synod first addressed the issue of race relations in 1957, the delegates agreed that "the problem of race segregation is not confined to a single congregation or Classis, but it is an issue on which many congregations in many places have need of guidance."[27] Later in the week, the Synod declared that the

> deprivation of equal rights and opportunities in society on the basis of race or color is contrary to the will of God. . . . Negroes have been deprived of rights and opportunities equal to those given whites, have been relegated to a position inferior to that of whites in social respectability. Racial prejudice leading to such social injustice is a tragic blot on our society. It is the duty of the members of the church of Christ to be active in removing this stain. The church is called upon to heal that which is broken and raise up that which is fallen. Therefore, it is called to give special help and nurture to those against whom a social injustice has been committed.[28]

By 1958, the CRC Synod adopted a twelve-point declaration on race relations written by the Reformed Ecumenical Synod (a loose affiliation of Reformed churches in North America, Great Britain, South Africa, and the Netherlands), demonstrating that the denomination understood the church to have a significant responsibility in addressing social injustice based on race. Point Nine in the declaration seemed especially applicable to the churches in Roseland: "The practical implication for the ministry of the Church is that in common congregational meetings and in admitting members of another race to our own gatherings, we should guard against any impression of discrimination that would imply the inferiority of another race the members of which should be made to feel that are being regarded as fellow-members in the body of Christ, bound to us by the closest of ties."[29] The Synod grounded the adoption on the basis that "racial tensions and the flagrant violation of the Scriptural principle of equality" had been occurring in both society and in the church.

In 1964 the Synod reaffirmed its stance on race relations when it recommended that CRC congregations particularly note Reformed Ecumenical Synod's statement when persons of different ethnicities or races live in proximity, that all individuals and groups should be afforded "God-given rights."[30] Four years later, Synod made perhaps its boldest statement on race relations and the integration of CRC and CRC-affiliated institutions:

> Fear of persecution or of disadvantage to self or our institutions arising out of obedience to Christ does not warrant denial to anyone, for reasons of race or color, of full Christian fellowship and privilege in the church or related organizations, such as Christian colleges and schools, institutions of mercy and recreational associations; and that if members of the Christian Reformed Church advocate such denial, by whatever means, they must be reckoned as disobedient to Christ and dealt with according to the provisions of the Church Order regarding Admonition and Discipline.[31]

A Cicero, Illinois, congregation (Warren Park CRC), which was struggling with its own race-related issues (probably the Timothy Christian School issue), responded to the statement by noting that it was inadvisable for Synod to "adjudicate on a local matter concerning which the church at large has only a limited knowledge of the situation and the circumstances involved."[32]

Undeterred by the snub from Warren Park CRC, the 1969 Synod strongly urged all CRC congregations to examine themselves for instances of racism and to hold regional conferences for discussing and combating the subject. Moreover, the Synod urged all member churches to reject every form of racism and the subtle forms of racial discrimination found in housing, employment, education, and law enforcement.[33] Though they did not use the language, the statements from Synod indicated a progressive notion that the church needed to understand racism as something more than an individual sin. In fact, by invoking housing, employment, education, and law enforcement, they signaled that racism could also be structural and institutional in nature. In order to more effectively combat insidious structural racism within the denomination, the Synod directed the Home Missions Board to create a Race Commission. Home Missions responded by creating a subcommittee of its Urban Fields Committee. The 1970 Synod charged the Race Commission with creating a "concerted denominational effort . . . to welcome black Christians in our churches, that they be given a voice, and that qualified black men are encouraged to enter the ministry of our denomination."[34] Beyond that, the Synod also expressed a desire for all denominational periodicals to emphasize "brotherhood between all races."[35]

THE CRC'S SYNODICAL COMMITTEE ON RACE RELATIONS

The issue of racial injustice remained prominent within the denomination at large. At Synod 1971, the Race Commission reported its recommendation that Synod create an entirely separate committee—directly answerable to and directly funded by Synod. The Commission argued that they had been hampered by the bureaucracy of being a "subcommittee of a subcommittee" and that a new committee with a higher degree of autonomy would be more effective. Synod adopted the recommendation from the Race Commission and created the Synodical Committee on Race Relations (SCORR). Synod charged SCORR with the mandate "to design, organize, and implement programs through which the denomination, individual churches, and members, can effectively use all available resources to eliminate racism, both causes and effects, within the body of believers, and throughout the world in which we live."[36] More explicitly, SCORR had responsibilities to produce materials regarding race relations, alert the denomination to existing racial problems, engage in research, serve as agents of reconciliation, provide scholarships to minority groups, and assist in providing legal aid where specific racial problems required it.

Even with the creation of SCORR, the Home Missions Board of the CRC remained highly active in the area of race relations. At Synod 1971, the board recommended that the denomination become a participant in Project Equality, which promoted equal opportunity in employment. Interestingly, Classis Chicago South—which included the Englewood, Roseland, and descendent churches—quickly registered a recommendation that Synod not become a participant in Project Equality. With this recommendation on the table, the Home Missions board presented a report entitled "The Christian Reformed Church's Participation in Project Equality." The report delineated the activities of Project Equality and offered a rationale for CRC involvement.[37]

Originally conceived by the National Catholic Conference for Interracial Justice as an equal opportunity employment program, Project Equality had grown since its inception in 1969 into an inter-religious program. By 1971, Project Equality operated in twenty-three states, included seventeen local chapters, and had an annual budget of over one million dollars. Twenty-seven religious denominations supported Project Equality, and the report to Synod described it as "probably [receiving] more financial support on a broad inter-religious base than any other program ever launched in the United States."[38] The report described Project Equality as a coherent system that allowed religious institutions to leverage their purchasing power to promote equal opportunity employment practices by their suppliers.

The Home Missions Board articulated that the CRC ought to participate in Project Equality because it constructively combined "economic muscle" with a "moral persuasion" that resonated with the Christian principles of the CRC.

Moreover, membership in Project Equality would assist the denomination in fostering racial justice. In the end, membership in the program would lend integrity to much of the race reconciliation rhetoric that the CRC, as a denomination, espoused. The Home Missions Board concluded their remarks with an "enthusiastic recommendation" to participate in Project Equality:

> By membership we are adding our voice to the voices of many other religious institutions saying that we intend to make our buying practices as consistent with our beliefs and preaching as possible. . . . We are joining a project that will help us become aware of some of the underlying causes of economic injustice and poverty to which we are frequently insensitive.[39]

The congregational delegates at Synod took the recommendation under advisement, but declined to participate immediately. Synod justified tabling the issue by noting that although they "endorsed employment policies that affirmatively promote equality of opportunity for all people," Project Equality needed "more elucidation."[40]

By 1972, SCORR had increased college scholarships for minority students and conducted research on institutionalized racism. At that year's Synod, SCORR reiterated the assertion that joining Project Equality would indicate a "meaningful action" on the part of the CRC. Perhaps most radically, SCORR also proposed that Synod create a committee on Central City Parish Problems "to give strong and necessary support to local churches in their attempts to facilitate better housing conditions and programs attuned to other major parish problems such as public safety and consumerism."[41] SCORR offered three points of rationale. First, the inner-city locations of many CRC congregations maintained a strategic importance in economic and social value to their inhabitants. Subsequently, those areas functioned as "'home' and should be prevented from becoming completely unlivable." Second, SCORR asserted that the "local church . . . has a responsibility to its parish, to stabilize it and to facilitate its spiritual and physical development." Such a statement clearly indicted the behavior of CRC congregations in Roseland and Englewood. Finally, the immensity of the task demanded more resources than those typically available to the local church.[42] Synod 1972 accepted the recommendation as information but made no formal attempt to implement it immediately. However, the activities and overtures of SCORR would continue to appear on the agenda of the Synodical meetings throughout the 1970s.

A DENOMINATIONAL TENSION OVER RACE

Thus, beginning in the 1950s and continuing through the 1970s, the CRC operated as a denomination full of contradictions. While the leaders at the Synodical level clearly understood the damage that racial injustice wreaked on the urban United States, those at the congregational level steadfastly failed either to see or acknowledge the same phenomenon. The crux of the matter, however, remained the fact that the Synods had virtually no established means for coercing or even cajoling individual congregations to adhere to the denominational statements on racism and institutional racial injustice. In fact, in some instances the congregations the Synod attempted to censure reacted with more disdain than contrition to its admonitions.

The impotence of the Synod in matters of racial justice resided in the design of the CRC polity. With limited hierarchical authority, neither Classis nor Synod had a basis to interfere with the relocation of a congregation. Local CRC pastor Derke Bergsma observed that the only parameters that would have predicated Classical involvement would have been an appeal from congregants within a church body who objected to a council decision, or if the congregation specifically solicited advice from the Classis. In all other circumstances, the relocation of a church remained solely the prerogative of majority approval at a congregational meeting. The local congregation reserved total autonomy for financing and administering the physical properties to which it held the title. Bergsma went on to note that, in the end, "a congregation may do what it wills with its physical resources, move when and where it decides to, and simply inform the Classical Stated Clerk of its change of address."[43] In fact, a CRC congregation could theoretically relocate to a lot immediately adjacent to an existing CRC congregation, if they so desired.

Synodical- and Classical-level minutes during the late 1960s and early 1970s frequently referred to the overarching question of race. Beyond that, it seems vividly clear that within the denominational leadership there were palpable concerns about white flight and the consequent fallout for these neighborhoods or parishes. However, both the Synod and Classis Chicago South remained without recourse. Three decades later, Terpstra lamented: "neither Classis nor Synod ever addressed the question of white flight and how all those churches were picking up and going west and southwest. But they all did."[44] Neither assembly had any delegated power to intervene in the process of congregational relocation.

In fact, the deliberations of Second Roseland's council revealed a conspicuous absence: absolutely no dialogue with Synod or Classis Chicago South. Moreover, the congregation sought no professional advice from existing bodies such as the Church Federation of Greater Chicago (CFGC). They seemed to possess little vision for the future of the community. Bergsma argued that CFGC "could have told them that their community was residentially mature and, from their particular point of view, had reached its peak. If they had been patient the pressure on the capacity of those two churches would have been eased in no time. But they didn't look beyond their own walls."[45] In a similar circumstance, when Third Roseland discerned in 1964 the block-by-block advance of African

American families, they purchased land and built a new sanctuary less than one mile west of their previous location. The congregation worshiped at the new site little more than seven years before the encroaching Black Belt caused them to sell and relocate once more.[46] In both cases, the congregations demonstrated the outcomes for a church that does all planning based solely on internal information. With no input from denominational or interdenominational bodies, the congregations made decisions with little sense of context. Third Roseland's decision was especially shortsighted. Bergsma, witness of the quick movements of Third Roseland, ascribed the relocations to extreme "congregational thinking. If they had consulted the Church Federation of Greater Chicago they could've been told what was happening. Their only viewpoint was 'congregationally.' They couldn't even think 'Classically.'"[47] Such de facto congregationalism allowed for highly individualized organizational decisions that failed to take into account authority, expertise, or community.

In sum, the inability to ally effectively with congregations from the same denomination plagued the churches of Roseland. Reverend Terpstra specifically created the Committee of 12 in an effort to honestly discuss the intentions of all the congregations concerned. Terpstra later described the proceedings: "And we promised each other at those meetings that we would all keep each other exactly informed of what was happening. But it did happen that someone rented Chicago Christian High School in suburban Palos Heights for worship services and didn't tell the rest of us. . . . It didn't take long at those committee meetings that it was understood that everyone was going to leave."[48] The conspirator that had undermined the Committee of 12 by sanctioning worship services in the suburbs turned out to be Fourth Roseland, the first congregation to depart from the neighborhood.

CRC POLITY AND LUTHERAN POLITY: A COMPARISON

Historians Gerald Gamm and John McGreevy have clearly demonstrated that the Roman Catholic parish-style polity tied families to the local church and, thus, to the local community. Such an organizational structure gave great pause to parishioners as African Americans began arriving in their neighborhood. Gamm especially delineated how the Roman Catholics responded differently, because of church political structure, from the more congregational Jews.

However, it would also be useful to compare the activities of the CRC to fellow Protestant denominations.[49] The scale of congregational autonomy produced by Cantrell et al. places Lutheran churches firmly between the extremes of Roman Catholicism and United Church of Christ (most similar to CRC). Though they did experience a loss of inner city congregations during the 1950s, 1960s, and 1970s, the Lutheran denominations as a whole demonstrated a much more concerted effort to avoid closures and relocations due to white exodus.

In other words, the Lutheran denominations' central authorities employed strategies of cooperation that were available to them because of their hierarchical structure. In stark contrast to the CRC, whose Synod made obvious but unsuccessful efforts to combat racial inequality and injustice, the Lutheran denominations exercised their authority to ensure that congregations participated in these efforts more robustly.[50]

The most notable of Lutheran efforts to remain involved in changing communities was the National Lutheran Council (NLC). The NLC was an example of intra-Lutheran planning that sought to foster cooperation in urban ministry. The NLC conducted in-depth studies of urban areas in an effort to make churches aware of the need for greater cooperation with each other. Moreover, specific attempts were "made to get urban and suburban congregations to cooperate."[51]

In addition, Lutheran churches formed citywide cooperative ministries. The judicatories and denominational offices not only approved such endeavors, they also offered financial support. In fact, "the general principle for organizing the cooperative ministry was either, 'We will do together what none of us can do alone' or 'As Lutherans we need to build strength upon strength to have a voice in a changing society.'"[52] That sentiment clearly indicated a proclivity toward inter-congregational efforts that did not exist in the CRC.

In Chicago in 1954, Lutheran churches met to discuss their "special responsibility and challenge in their relations to minority groups."[53] The twenty-one churches of the Southern Chicago District of Augustana Churches adopted a statement wherein they announced that "no local church has any more right to decide to be racially or culturally exclusive than it has to modify or abandon any articles of faith" and that it was wrong for churches to "abandon fields simply because the racial or cultural composition has changed." With such language, the District condemned those who would leave because of racial change. Most forcefully, the twenty-one churches of the Southern Chicago District asserted that it was "spiritually dangerous and inconsistent with the Christian faith and the decision of our Church" to be "unwilling to pay the spiritual price of adjusting to a situation where minority races are involved." Moreover, the District encouraged "any member who wishes to disassociate himself from a congregation where minority groups are likely to be received" to "rethink his motivation." The statement concluded with the acknowledgement that "a true church of Jesus Christ does not make racial differences a disqualification for membership."[54] In essence, the District thus declared that congregations bore the burden of adaptation and integration.

Beyond congregations collaborating in Chicago to inhibit members from leaving the city, Lutheran churches also allied themselves with other denominations in creating entities such as the Joint Action and Strategy Committee, an endeavor to coordinate resources nationally and regionally. These efforts raised the consciousness of the church "regarding urban issues."[55] Remarkably, some of the cooperative ministries formed during the 1960s and 1970s still existed well into the 1990s, demonstrating institutional longevity.

These assorted actions on the denominational level functioned as the impetus for individual urban congregations that made concerted efforts to root themselves in their neighborhoods during the 1960s. The churches became more integrated: "The racial, economic, and social makeup of the neighborhood was increasingly reflected in the membership, worship, and leadership of the congregation. The church became a part of the neighborhood. . . . The pastor and the congregation became the Lutheran church for that place."[56] The process of rooting within the neighborhood became especially structured in Philadelphia with the formation of the Center City Lutheran Parish in 1964. The coalition sought to support Lutheran congregations as they "rerooted themselves in their neighborhoods."[57]

The broader efforts of the less congregational Lutheran denominations manifested themselves in Englewood. In October 1963 (more than a year after three CRC congregations had left for the suburbs), Bethel Lutheran Church not only remained at their location in Englewood, but they also hosted a conference of local clergy. The meeting had the stated purpose of addressing the "current problems in Englewood" and discussing "what responsibility the clergy have and what role they might take in developing a strong community organization."[58] The meeting notably lacked language pertaining to congregational survival. The meeting also demonstrated the Lutherans' ability to develop interfaith partnerships, as the conference included the local Catholic churches.

In the end, the fact that the Lutheran denominations had a less congregational polity produced more effective and concerted efforts to keep Lutheran congregations within cities and within diverse communities. The congregational nature of the CRC precluded any similar measures within that denomination. Evidence demonstrated that there existed elements within the CRC who desired to confront the mass relocation of the urban congregations in Chicago. However, they had no options at their disposal within the confines of the church polity to consider a strategy for responding to the changes in Englewood and Roseland.

10 · THE CONTRAST BETWEEN SISTER DENOMINATIONS

As we have seen, comparison of the CRC (a thoroughly congregational denomination) with Catholics and Lutherans (less congregational in polity) reveals that religious polity had a role in changing urban and suburban residential patterns and helps to complicate notions of white flight. Under the Americanized polity of the CRC, the congregations in Englewood and Roseland stood in stark contrast to the Catholic parishes. There existed no authority structure to ensure that the congregations remained responsible for and involved in their local communities. The CRC polity allowed congregations to act only in terms of self-preservation. The survival impulse seemed to permeate every decision of the churches. Moreover, while the denominational leaders of the CRC demonstrated an understanding of the insidious nature of institutionalized racism, the congregations in question remained unpersuaded. The Synod consistently addressed racism within the denomination, created an organization solely to deal with racial injustice, and even thoughtfully considered joining an interreligious organization, Project Equality—a radical step for a denomination wary of formal associations with Roman Catholics and mainline Protestant denominations. At the same time, the Roseland congregations of the same CRC denomination undermined much of what the Synod attempted. Within the CRC polity, however, these congregations effectively answered to no other authority in these instances.

Feeling no obligations to the community or larger assemblies, the CRC congregations of Englewood and Roseland exercised a sovereignty solely concerned with institutional self-preservation. As largely independent institutions, they had no predilection or resources for integration. Thus departure represented the only viable means of survival, in their view. In contrast, the polities of neighboring Lutheran congregations forced those churches to at least deliberate and seek some hierarchical sanction to leave the city. In the end, the style of congregational polity allowed the churches in Englewood and Roseland a high level of mobility compared to fellow Protestants. Such distinctions ultimately demonstrate the role of religious polity in the variegated nature of white departure from the city. Although the comparison of CRC to Lutheran remains instructive, the evaluation is complicated, however, because of doctrinal and ethnic distinctions. But where the CRC-Lutheran comparison might falter, the CRC-RCA comparison becomes more robust. The denominations shared more characteristics than not; in addition to ethnic connections, both denominations endorsed the same three confessions as foundational to their doctrine.[1] And the fact that CRC and RCA congregations inhabited the same neighborhoods in Chicago allows for a vivid analysis of how seemingly small differences in religious life have implications for broader social movements.

Differences certainly did exist between the two denominations. When comparing CRC and RCA youth in urban contexts, Robert Swierenga in one study examined outmarriage rates and conversion to non-Dutch churches. He argued that the RCA exposure to public education accelerated the assimilation process of those particular Dutch-Americans by "at least a generation or two." Whereas the CRC identified closely with their Christian schools, the RCA Synod gave "ringing endorsements" to public education as being foundational to a democratic society. The RCA understood the Christian schools as un-American.[2]

These contrasting opinions regarding education are fairly easily discernible. The polity distinction between the two denominations regarding control of congregational property, though, is a bit more elusive. Both claim a Presbyterian polity. Whereas the CRC Church Orders allow complete autonomy for local congregations in this regard, the RCA reserves authority over property for the respective Classis. In other words, the RCA Classes may limit the mobility of congregations, while the CRC has no such mechanism. For the CRC and RCA congregations on the South Side of Chicago, that difference would prove crucial.

THE CASE OF AN RCA CONGREGATION IN ROSELAND

Emmanuel Reformed in Roseland experienced the same neighborhood change as the CRC congregations, all four of which had left Chicago by 1972. Emmanuel would remain in Roseland until 1989. Those seventeen years did not see Emmanuel exactly thrive, and by 1987 worship services averaged little more than two dozen attenders.[3] However, the congregation endured and demonstrated how variegated white flight could be, even within religio-ethnic cultures. Emmanuel was not terribly dissimilar to the CRC congregations with which they shared a neighborhood. In fact, in the early 1960s the leadership actually monetarily supported the National Association of Evangelicals, which CRC had joined in 1942 (see Chapter 2).[4] Beyond that, the congregation demonstrated a modicum of appreciation for isolation from other denominations when in 1964 they decided against joining the Church Federation of Chicago.[5] Yet, despite these types of convergences in their identity, CRC and RCA congregations reacted differently as the Black Belt approached. The history of Emmanuel Reformed compared to Second CRC delineates those disparities well.

The first indication that Emmanuel Reformed had concerns related to neighborhood change appeared in the minutes of a Special Consistory Meeting in late July 1963. The minister of the congregation had participated in a meeting of pastors and real estate agents from Roseland. An African American family had recently moved into the neighborhood, causing anxiety: "The discussion at this meeting concerned the Colored family that recently moved into the neighborhood . . . and the resulting unwelcome behavior."[6] Though the minutes failed to elaborate upon who engaged in the "unwelcome behavior," the clerk noted, "It was pointed out that we should work together as Christians with no bitterness or ill feelings. We should work toward maintaining a good community and do it in a Christian way."[7] More than likely, the in-migration of an African American family had instigated some form of white hostility. In that regard, the minutes conveyed a sense of fear and anxiety: "We best serve by trying to keep people from becoming panicky."[8] That the movement of one African American family into the neighborhood caused ministers to meet with realtors and churches to call special meetings offers evidence that the residents had a strong sense that the deliberate movement of the Black Belt could eventually incorporate Roseland. Despite that, Emmanuel exuded a level of confidence. Later that same year, the congregation approved a construction project for the church that would cost between $21,000 and $25,000. Such an investment indicated a congregation that saw Roseland as a viable home for a while.

The issue of neighborhood change reappeared on the congregation's agenda in 1966, when the consistory defeated a motion to "appoint a committee to formulate a policy of procedure in regards to the Negro situation in our community."[9] Although the consistory failed to create a new committee, a motion indicating the leadership's intention to "maintain Emmanuel Reformed Church" in Roseland "even though there may be some Negro membership" carried. However, in rare demonstration of disagreement, five members of the council requested that names be put on record as dissenting. Later, at the same meeting, the consistory approved the formation of a committee to craft a plan for evangelism of African Americans in Roseland.[10]

The next month the consistory continued to wrestle with divisiveness regarding the stated intention of the church to remain. Some wanted to formally communicate the sentiments of the consistory. Others claimed that it would be unconstitutional for the consistory to approve the intention to stay.[11] It would seem that the latter argument had legal weight within the polity of the RCA: instead of outlining a plan for remaining, the consistory passed a motion to "request the congregation's opinion on canvassing the neighborhood, inviting Negroes to our worship services."[12] Though the results of that survey never appeared within the consistory meeting minutes, a petition in 1970 signed by eighty-six individuals "urging the church to remain in the community" indicated that a significant proportion of the congregation preferred to remain in Roseland.[13]

The petition seemed necessary when the attenders of Emmanuel Reformed in Roseland saw that the pace of neighborhood change had accelerated in Roseland in the late 1960s. Classis Chicago demonstrated a concern for the future of Emmanuel in Roseland, as well. In June of 1967, the consistory received a letter from Classis Chicago, written by the Reverend Douglas van Gessel, chair of the Extension Committee, established to plant new RCA congregations in the greater Chicago area. Van Gessel wrote to indicate that Classis Chicago recognized the challenges confronting Emmanuel Reformed in Roseland. Moreover, he offered encouragement for the congregation to engage "in the full ministry of Christ in the community in which you find yourselves."[14] In an effort to better understand the changing demography of Chicago, the consistory screened a film entitled *Inner City* at a meeting in 1968.[15] Despite some anxiety, Emmanuel Reformed continued to demonstrate a level of commitment to Roseland. At the autumn meeting of Classis Chicago, the assembly noted that all congregations should "evangelize and serve their communities," and went on record to note the "Christian witness of the Emmanuel Reformed Church" in their particular circumstances.[16]

Perhaps most significantly, in September of 1968, the church leadership of Emmanuel Reformed approved a motion to hire a woman with a social work background "to work in [the church's] community."[17] Demonstrating a level of cooperation on the part of the denomination, the salary of the social worker would be paid in thirds by the RCA Board of Domestic Missions, Classis Chicago, and Emmanuel Reformed Church. Classis Chicago had also discussed the hiring of personnel "by the older churches in racially changing neighborhoods" and establishing a fund of $30,000 to support those efforts. They seemed especially pleased that Emmanuel RCA had already employed someone whose "background gives her an understanding of both theology and social work" and moved to support the effort with a $2,500 subsidy.[18]

At the next convening of Classis Chicago, Emmanuel reported that their social worker had been working with twenty-five families who had shown "a measure of interest" and that Sunday school attendance had been "increasing sharply." Moreover, the minister of Emmanuel RCA reported a list of queries they had received from African Americans: "Questions being asked by our black people are: 'How do you really feel toward us?' 'Why do your people continue to leave?' Why should we get in the boat if you're all getting out?' 'Rev, what are your plans?'"[19] The pastor went to indicate that "the questions make us thoughtful" and that the church concurred with the social worker's assessment that "her work in the community has just begun."[20] The questions also demonstrated the level of distrust that existed between African Americans and whites in Roseland.

The minister's response, though, seemed to intimate that the congregation anticipated fully engaging with the African Americans in the neighborhood.

Just a few months later, Emmanuel RCA offered a decidedly different report to Classis Chicago. Though the congregation expressed gratitude for Classical support of the church's neighborhood social worker and reported on her work (including personal visits, Bible studies, remedial reading classes, and vacation Bible school), they also intimated a sense of dismay: "Weakening under community pressure, decimated in membership because of the constant moving out of our people, Emmanuel is, at the moment, not contemplating any definitive action program in the black community."[21] The difficulties of remaining in the neighborhood caused anxiety regarding the congregation's capacity to engage in any new programming.

That doubt abated somewhat, it seems, as in a 1971 report to the Particular Synod of Chicago the field secretary reported "exciting things are happening at Emmanuel Reformed Church in Chicago where on Decision Sunday in early March seventy young people responded to the call to commitment."[22] Beyond that, the congregation reported an Easter Sunday church and Sunday school combined attendance of over 825.[23] The next year, Emmanuel RCA indicated that while still facing a transitional context, the congregation, with strong assistance from Classis Chicago, had been steadily increasing African American participation in the life of the congregation.[24] Later in 1972, Classis Chicago noted that Emmanuel retained a "dedicated core of persons who desire to continue to accept the challenge of that area."[25] Moreover, the congregation called an African American minister and Classis Chicago recommended $9,000 in support from Synod for his salary. Again, in 1973 the Synod of Chicago heard that "Emmanuel Church is happy and experiencing growth."[26]

Surprisingly, the church leadership documents during the early 1970s revealed that the consistory of Emmanuel Reformed discussed little regarding the church's neighborhood. In December of 1970, the consistory discussed having men watch the parking lot for security purposes during evening events and placed a notice in the bulletin urging attenders to not leave packages or other objects exposed on the seats of cars. Such discussions indicated a level of consternation regarding the security of the neighborhood.[27] However, the fact that discussions about relocation failed to dominate meetings during these years is significant. Such an omission stood in stark relief to the CRC congregations of Roseland, who had all left by 1972.

By the late 1970s, Emmanuel Reformed exhibited continued commitment to Roseland. In August of 1977, the consistory approved hiring a person dedicated to urban ministry. In a demonstration of support, Classis Chicago agreed to be responsible for all expenses related to the position.[28] Early the next year, the consistory responded to a standardized query from Classis Chicago. To the question, what are your "feelings about church locality?" the consistory responded, "overall feeling positive." They went on to indicate that they felt "very optimistic" about community outreach.[29] At the same meeting, the consistory lamented that the church had "been very 'lax' about zeroing in on community needs."[30] Of course, the church had few monetary resources by this juncture. Classis Chicago had been subsidizing the operation of the congregation since 1976.[31] In early 1979, the consistory concluded that they would commit to community evangelism once a month: "passing out literature and conversing about . . . our beliefs, programs, sermons . . . youth group could assist with passing out literature."[32] The leadership of Emmanuel continued to be committed to Roseland. Moreover, they demonstrated the depth of commitment by enlisting the youth of the congregation in the endeavor.

Emmanuel Reformed, with active support and assistance from Classis Chicago, remained in Roseland until 1989. That endurance, though, should not necessarily be confused with a successful adaptation to the changes in the neighborhood. In fact, a divinity student conducted a study on Emmanuel Reformed in 1987 and offered a withering critique of the church: "Often racial change gets the blame for the failure of the church. But if the situation was fully known, the church's failure to properly respond to many transitional factors over the years is really the fault. A church cannot afford to be static while the rest of the community is shifting and changing."[33] In all likelihood, the student had been swayed by the fact that all six of the individuals he approached in the streets near the church to interview regarding perceptions of the congregation responded with intense anger and cursing. The student offered an example: "Another man said, 'I've lived three blocks from that [expletive] church for fourteen years and nobody has come yet!. . . . I have yet to hear somebody say something good about *that* church.'"[34] Emmanuel Reformed certainly found itself in dire straits at the time of the divinity student's study: Sunday morning worship averaged twenty-five attenders.[35] At the time of Emmanuel's dissolution, however, all CRC congregations had been relocated from Roseland for at least fifteen years, and one had left twenty years earlier.

SIMILAR SYNODS

The differences in how CRC and RCA congregations responded to neighborhood change cannot be traced to the Synodical level of church polity. Both Synods consistently dealt with racial injustice and condemned it. Indeed, the hierarchical leadership of both denominations had similar opinions regarding racial injustice. In other words, the different manners in these congregations left cannot be traced to attitudinal differences within the denominations regarding race.

Throughout their entangled history, the CRC and RCA intelligentsia engaged in vigorous debate. In one instance, a religious nonprofit composed of ministers and lay people from the RCA and CRC called Reformed Fellowship published a periodical, *Torch and Trumpet*. The journal sought to stimulate discussion regarding Reformed Calvinist faith and doctrine, church practice, and social issues. In the April 1961 issue, writer Peter Y. DeJong, a well-known CRC minister, wrote an article in which he considered the movement of churches from cities to suburbs: "Should the Church Follow Its Members?" Although DeJong somewhat clumsily noted that "huge concentrations of negroes and Puerto Ricans are found where once the native-born lived," he counseled that congregations in these areas should reconsider leaving the city. In fact, he cautioned that departing churches needed to reflect upon their possible disobedience to God and that they may have calloused themselves to the "heavenly vision." DeJong also questioned whether such a movement to the suburbs could be indicted for evidence of poor stewardship: "Is it justified to sell these properties at a loss and invest much more money [in a suburban edifice] simply to keep a congregation intact?" He went on to posit that these churches should ask whether they were "interested only in those who have always been members of our [CRC and RCA] churches." De Jong's perspective, to be sure, represented the leadership of both denominations more than it did the attenders sitting in the pews on Sunday.[36]

The RCA, it should be noted, had seen some measure of successful integration of congregations in New York during the 1950s. Churches in both Brooklyn and the Bronx were described as having become "bi-racial." A history of African Americans in the RCA noted that the Mott Haven Church in the RCA initially responded with fear as African Americans began moving into the Bronx neighborhood of the congregation. However, "Negroes moving into the community were welcomed into the Mott Haven Church. Wilbur Washington, a Negro student attending New Brunswick Theological Seminary, was secured for part time work, and now he and the regular Pastor, Rev. F. Buttenbaum, are striving to win souls regardless of race or color."[37]

Later that decade, the RCA's Board of Domestic Missions noted, "the Inner-City is a constantly-expanding work and challenges us to face it realistically. Changing neighborhoods in some of our Reformed Church areas provide a great opportunity to reach out in many ways."[38] The board went on to identify Elmendorf Reformed Church in New York City as providing an exemplary model: "Here is an old Reformed Church that might have closed its doors because of the changing complexion of the community. But it now seeks to minister to the many nationalities and races moving into the area seeking to integrate them into the life of the Church through its many avenues of service."[39]

At the same Synodical meeting in the late 1950s, the Board of Domestic Missions recommended that in light of increased activity in "Church Extension in recent years," an overture be approved that noted "the formal organization of new churches is the exclusive prerogative of the several Classes" and that "no Classis shall organize a new church outside its accepted boundaries without the formal consent of the Particular Synod to which it belongs."[40] In essence, the board asked the Synod to ensure an orderly and somewhat hierarchical approach to church extension activities. Synod approved the overture.[41]

In 1957, the RCA General Synod adopted a "Credo on Race Relations." The statement asserted the following responsibilities for congregations: "the racially inclusive and culturally integrated church represents the highest demonstration of the transforming fellowship of reconciliation which characterizes the Christian fellowship at its best. We believe that where opportunities for such churches to exist, conscientious efforts be made to realize this ideal." In other words, the leaders of the RCA saw urban congregations in the midst of demographic transition as having distinctive opportunities and obligations. The credo went on to discuss residential segregation:

> Racially restricted housing covenants, real or implied, are inconsistent with Christian integrity. We believe that according to scripture, the rights of property are subservient to the rights of people. . . . We believe that restrictive pressures and flight-in-panic on the part of dominant groups often lead to unnecessary real estate declines and contribute to the establishment and perpetuation of ghetto existence.[42]

Lynn Japinga, a professor of religion who has studied the denomination, described the credo as "remarkably progressive."[43]

Following up at the 1959 convening of the RCA General Synod, the Board of Domestic Missions expressed concern over "the failure of many Churches to minister to the changing neighborhoods about them." The board also described the apparent lack of interest on the part of these congregations in the racial minorities now in their respective neighborhoods as a "flagrant sin." From the report of the board, it seemed apparent that some of these congregations had defended themselves by asserting that the newcomers to the neighborhood found the RCA theology and worship style unattractive. The board summarily dismissed the argument as undermining all missionary activity.[44]

That same year the Synod would adopt the Board of Domestic Missions recommendation that it "express its moral indignation over the fact that hundreds of people are being left without functioning Churches in great cities, and instruct the Board of Domestic Missions to alert Classes to point out the moral dereliction involved in this neglect."[45] The Synod clearly demonstrated here the authority that individual RCA Classes held in regard to how congregations responded to racial change. Later at the same meeting, the Christian Action Commission reported their conviction that "residential segregation is contrary to God's will."[46] The commission, similar to the Board of Domestic Missions, recommended that the individual Classes consider this matter very seriously.

A year later, the Board of Domestic Missions asserted that the Classes had been requesting funds designated for assisting churches with "inner city problems."[47] The board noted that the denomination required many more "adequately trained ordained and lay personnel" to address the "vacancies" in core city work. That same year, the Christian Action Commission argued that "our basic American dilemma is discrimination in housing. Discrimination in housing promotes segregated schools, inhibits urban redevelopment in that minorities of our slum areas cannot be rehoused elsewhere, produces slums which destroy property and human beings, and we become a scandal before the world's non-white population."[48] Astutely, the commission identified "white panic" as causing and exacerbating the problem. In response, they indicated plans for next Synodical meeting: "Next year we would like to present a housing covenant in which individuals of our communion could unite in a Christian position of action and determination to end the panic, hatred, and flight which now attend real estate in its relationship to the Negro population it our cities."[49] Two years later the General Synod would take a step further and approved a motion that encouraged individual congregations to ensure that housing in their neighborhoods was not racially restricted.[50]

Just as the CRC Synod consistently crafted progressive documents that lamented racial injustice, the RCA Synod also took aggressive steps to address inequality based on race. In some cases, outsiders would force their hand: as the RCA Synod was about to get under way in 1969, members of the Black Economic Development Conference moved into the Reformed Church offices in New York City. The representatives of the conference indicated that they intended to occupy the offices until given the opportunity to speak to the assembled RCA delegates. In response, Synod tabled the anticipated agenda and gave the floor on the opening night to James Forman, who spoke for the conference. Forman "spoke at length, describing centuries of abuse of black people by white people and criticizing the complicity of many churches in such abuse."[51] Assuming the gathered wealth of white churches because of their role in exploiting African Americans, Forman finally presented a list of demands in which the RCA should share financial resources. The next morning the Synod appointed an ad hoc committee to consider a suitable response to the Black Economic Development Conference's assertions.

A few days later the ad hoc committee reported to General Synod. Although the document expressed dissatisfaction with Forman's method, it also offered gratitude that he forced the denomination to consider more explicitly its sinful role in racism and racial discrimination. The committee then offered twelve recommendations to directly address the denomination's "decision-making structures . . . so dominated by the presence, attitudes, values, and traditions of white people" in order to give more authority to racial minorities.[52] Two of the recommendations included the formation of a "Black Caucus" within the denomination to share in both program and investment decisions and the creation of a fund of $100,000 to be disbursed by that same Black Caucus.[53] The proposal passed without a dissenting vote. Later that year, *Christianity Today* described the approval of the twelve recommendations by the RCA General Synod "as perhaps the most significant racial action of any church during the year."[54]

In the end, both CRC and RCA Synods demonstrated keen sensitivity to racial injustice. Both offered admirable documents that exposed racism as a form of sin. Both understood racism as not simply individual thoughts and actions but institutional and structural phenomena as well. The denominational understandings of attitudes toward racism did not influence the timing of departure of core city congregations for the suburbs. Instead, the cultural practices and polity at more local levels proved pivotal in determining how churches reacted to their changing neighborhoods.

DISSIMILAR CLASSES

The CRC and RCA congregations in Englewood and Roseland belonged to Classes, the regional assemblies of the churches from the respective denominations. The CRC congregations belonged to Classis Chicago South; the RCA congregations belonged to Classis Chicago. Classis Chicago South reported directly to the General Synod of the CRC. In the RCA, however, Classis Chicago had an intermediary level of church polity, the Particular Synod. Within RCA church government, contiguous Classes were united into these district Synods. Particular Synods were designed to nurture combined action among the Classes since they would have "common interests" and could offer "mutual helpfulness." One commenter on church government noted that "as the churches are no longer separate units, because of the Classis, so the Classes are no longer separate units, because of the Particular Synod."[55] Always a bit more suspicious of hierarchy, the CRC had no parallel organization. An analysis of the respective Classes and the RCA's Particular Synod Chicago reveals how the apparatus of church government shaded the decisions of congregations regarding the possibility of relocation to the suburbs. Whereas the CRC's Classis Chicago South remained detached, the RCA's Classis Chicago actively sought to engage the difficult questions of neighborhood change and residential segregation.

Interestingly, though, both Classes under scrutiny here reacted negatively to the idea of using economic pressure to pursue racial justice. In fact, when Classis Chicago South deliberated about denominational support for Project Equality, they determined that they would petition the Synod not to become a participant in the organization. The approved motion cited two reasons: 1) the church would be infringing on the tasks of the federal government by "policing" economic policies, and 2) the Reformed confessional integrity of the CRC would be jeopardized by cooperating with "such bodies as the Unitarian Universalist Church, Jewish Synagogues of both Orthodox and Reformed persuasion, etc."[56]

In a similar fashion, both Classis Chicago and the Particular Synod of Chicago sent overtures to the RCA General Synod asking that the denomination's Christian Action Commission be instructed to "exercise extreme caution when it considers endorsing or recommending economic boycotts," as both assemblies saw the precedent of denominational boycotts as dangerous.[57] The consternation from the Classis and Particular Synod arose when in 1968 the Christian Action Committee had proposed that General Synod approve a statement on "Withholding Consumer Patronage to Secure Justice"—a concerted effort by the denomination to exert economic pressure on businesses "who practiced . . . exploitation or discrimination."[58] The CRC and RCA Chicago Classes thus demonstrated a similar hesitancy for the church to engage in what they deemed as radical economic protests. The difference in congregational endurance between the two denominations cannot be traced to disparate political agendas.

Classis Chicago South (CRC)

The assemblies of the two denominations addressed the issue of changing neighborhoods in markedly different manners. Whereas the RCA Classis actively addressed and managed the activities of individual congregations, the CRC typically received "items for information" from the congregations regarding the future of the churches. They demonstrated little inclination to involve themselves in matters they understood as congregational.

A typical CRC Classis had numerous committees. To address the "race problem" in Roseland, the Classical Home Missions Committee in 1968 recommended that Classis Chicago South call and supervise a "Home Missionary" specifically to work in the neighborhoods of racial transition surrounding the Roseland congregations. However, the next year, because of the uncertainty regarding the long-range intentions of the congregations, the same committee reversed course and advised Classis Chicago South to postpone the calling of the missionary to work in the neighborhood.[59]

As it became clear that Roseland would eventually be left without an established CRC congregation, the Classical Home Missions Committee recommended that the Second Roseland properties be purchased by Classis Chicago South to continue evangelistic work in the neighborhood. The committee offered the following grounds:

1) It appears to the Committee that black communicant families from the Englewood mission area are moving to the Roseland area, 2) There are a number of families from Lawndale CRC who have moved into the south side of Chicago near Roseland, and 3) A group of white CRC members, purporting to represent 35 families, has appeared before the committee and pledged their moral, financial, and personal support to such a venture.[60]

The assembly defeated the motion, which some interpreted to indicate a desire to prove that a CRC congregation could not survive in Roseland.[61]

The battle over a continued CRC presence in Roseland spilled into the next Classical meeting. In January of 1972, the Classical Home Missions Committee recommended that a new CRC congregation be organized in Roseland. The motion was defeated. Later at the same meeting, the Classis directed all consistories to announce in their respective bulletins "the request for permission to organize on the part of the families desiring a church in Roseland was not granted."[62]

Classis Chicago South, at times, demonstrated antipathy toward attempts for racial justice that it deemed too radical. In fact, at a May meeting in 1968 the assembly received a letter from the Social Action Committee of Calvin Seminary (the denomination's only seminary) that alluded to an overture that Ebenezar CRC in Chicago had sent to Synod in 1968. In the midst of the Timothy Christian School controversy, the consistory of Ebenezar had made overtures to Synod to make a declaration that any member of the denomination judged to be participating in racially exclusive activities be admonished and disciplined. Furthermore, the letter asked Synod "to declare that fear of persecution or any other adversity arising out of obedience to Christ does not warrant the denial of full Christian fellowship and privilege in the church or in related organizations, such as Christian colleges and schools."[63] Moreover, the committee insisted on the need to eliminate "racism from the body of Christ."[64] The Classis refused to hear it: "It was moved, supported, and adopted that the letter be not read."[65] The following year, Classis Chicago South voted against having an editorial from Calvin College's *Chimes* regarding racial issues read aloud at the meeting.[66] With these decisions, the Classis demonstrated a belligerence toward any who would condemn them on issues related to race. Such matters cut too close as the congregations contemplated leaving the city because of racial demographic transition. They would not be admonished or disciplined in any manner by a hierarchical structure.

At that same January meeting, the Classis received the previously mentioned overture from Second Roseland that attempted to establish a measure of responsibility and oversight for congregations deciding to relocate (Chapter 9). The overture requested "That Synod declare that any congregation considering relocation of its ministry shall inform the Classis of which it is a member, and shall determine upon a site for a new location with the advice of Classis."[67] The impetus for such a letter clearly came from the minister of Second Roseland, the Reverend Terpstra. At any rate, the Classis referred the request back to the congregation for more precision and further rationale.[68] It would take much more than an overture to attempt to limit congregational authority over church location.

As a case in point, Fourth Roseland quickly attempted to forestall any similar attempt toward Classical oversight of relocation. At the May 1969 Classis Chicago South assembly, the congregation informed the body that it would be moving to Orland Park. With no recourse, Classis Chicago South received the communiqué for information.[69] Later at the same meeting, the Classis considered Second Roseland's revised overture regarding oversight of relocation. As instructed at the last meeting, Second Roseland submitted a new letter that delineated the rationale for the overture. The letter argued that the overture allowed for 1) "more orderly movement and better planned ministry in both the old and new areas"; 2) "a better opportunity to develop and maintain a relevant ministry" for urban and suburban communities; 3) "an improved stewardship and coordination of resources"; and 4) "a highly desirable extension of the basic principles of [CRC] Church Order to the new problems created by urbanization and the mobility of society."[70] Largely unconvinced, Classis passed an amended and denuded version of the overture. The original overture, "That Synod declare that any congregation considering relocation of its ministry shall inform the Classis of which it is a member . . ." was amended so that the following phrase, "and shall determine upon a site for a new location with the advice of Classis" was deleted. Thus, the new overture read, "That any congregation considering relocation of its ministry shall consult officially with the neighboring congregations and the Classis of which it is a member."[71] The end result undermined the intent of Terpstra and Second Roseland. Instead of forcing congregations to be accountable and to at least seek the advice of Classis, the revised overture ensured that the de facto congregationalism of the CRC would continue to be practiced. "Consult," of course, functioned as an abstract word that could be interpreted in numerous ways by the congregations. Notice too that the amended overture dispersed some of the consultation among the congregations.

In the end, though, not even that stripped-down overture from Classis Chicago South could find support at the 1969 General Synod of the CRC. The overture would go down to defeat after the committee chartered to study it recommended that it not be adopted "at all events" and because "delegates felt [the overture] would intrude on the autonomy of the local church."[72] In 1971, both First and Third Roseland followed the lead of Fourth Roseland and practiced their congregational independence by communicating to Classis Chicago South that both churches intended to sell their buildings and relocate to the suburbs. At the same meeting, a Classical representative reported as well that Fourth Roseland "did feel that they experienced the leading of God in making the decision they did to move out to Orland Park."[73] With no church polity oversight, there existed little opportunity for the relocation choices of congregations to be seriously interrogated.

Classis Chicago (RCA)

While the CRC's Classis Chicago South watched congregations depart for the suburbs, the RCA's Classis Chicago assumed a higher level of authority over and involvement in relocation plans. The Classis reported as early as 1958 their cognizance of demographic changes afoot. After noting the growth of some suburban congregations, the Classis lamented,

> If only we could successfully establish some new Reformed churches that are distinctly urban in character and thus keep pace with the more gradual and less spectacular growth of Chicago's inner-city population, we shall the more effectively demonstrate not only our capacity to survive as a Reformed Church with our distinctly Reformed Church heritage, but will be able to strike a new stride that may mean for our two metropolitan Classes in particular and for the Particular Synod of Chicago as a whole, a distinctive place of trail-blazing leadership in the total life of our denomination.[74]

Such a note indicated the leadership role that RCA Classes assumed in the realm of congregational facilities and location.

A few years later, Classis Chicago lamented the loss of three hundred members within their congregations over the 1950s and signs of "diminishing effectiveness" of the RCA in Chicago proper. The Classis found it especially troubling that the neighborhoods around the congregations either maintained or expanded in total population, so the loss of membership could not simply be attributed to a more general population loss. The author of a report from Classis Chicago to Chicago Synod noted, "A diminishing church in the midst of a growing population is a sad commentary on our sense of mission. . . . Though a number of churches can report a decrease of the Dutch element in their area, no church can report a decrease of population in their area."[75] The Classis did not see neighborhood change as a legitimate excuse for declining membership.

Both Classis Chicago and the Particular Synod of Chicago demonstrated a keen interest in the physical location of the congregations included within their respective assemblies. At a 1968 meeting, Classis Chicago recommended that all churches thoughtfully consider the role that their church buildings played in their communities and how they might make the structures more available to serve the needs of the wider community. The Classis also reiterated the denominational policy regarding church facilities:

> Specifically each congregation which devotes a considerable portion of its human and financial resources to building and maintaining its physical property thereby expresses its Christian concern for the community as a whole and the people within it as much as it does through its activities and programs. Moreover, in so far as churches receive very real aid in maintaining their buildings and grounds from their communities at large through tax exemption, they are under an additional moral obligation to make their properties serve the total community as well as the internal needs of the congregation.[76]

In other words, the congregation had a responsibility to the community beyond self-preservation.

The next year, the Classis revealed that "the level of stewardship within changing neighborhoods is beginning to decline."[77] It seemed that Classis Chicago had concerns about the solvency of some its congregations. In response, the assembly began to discuss whether congregations should be willing to consistently donate money to churches with financial need in changing neighborhoods. At the same meeting, Classis Chicago discussed a "Classis-wide approach" to the difficulties faced by the individual churches.[78]

The assembly applied that methodical, Classis-wide approach further along in the agenda, When First RCA of Roseland requested permission from Classis Chicago to purchase land for relocating in South Holland, the Classis allowed the congregation to make the purchase, but with the stipulation that they neither build on the new property nor sell their current property in Roseland until meeting the Church Extension Subcommittee and receiving permission from Classis Chicago after further consultation and deliberation.[79]

Later in 1969, Classis Chicago adopted a policy regarding church relocation. The Classical Mission Committee offered guidelines that sought to establish a protocol for churches that found themselves in the midst of neighborhood change: "In the midst of pervasive social change and racial antagonism, it is quite probable that we will retain no continuing ministries in the city at our present church locations unless we make some hard and clear decisions to retain ministries in certain locations."[80] The Mission Committee also recommended that Emmanuel RCA and Hope RCA be the foci of energy to maintain RCA congregations in the city. They went on to note, however, that by identifying these two churches they had no intention of encouraging other congregations to relocate: "on the contrary, we encourage all of our churches to continue to minister in the city if at all possible."[81] To that end, the committee also indicated that any congregation that sought relocation had to first conduct a study that would be reported to Classis. Beyond identifying the goals and needs of the congregation itself, the study also would have to consider "the goals and needs of the two communities involved; both the one the congregation seeks to leave and the one the congregation seeks to enter" and "goals and needs of other Christian congregations, both in the community being left and in the community being entered, including both the Reformed Churches now in existence and in churches of other Christian denominations."[82]

Classis Chicago also assumed control of "our city ministry" as the neighborhoods around RCA congregations integrated.[83] Part of the rationale for Classical involvement was to be as minimally disruptive to the involved neighborhoods as possible. In addition, Classis Chicago would be responsible for providing a roster of ministry professionals to help churches better minister to changing neighborhoods. The report even provided a threshold for Classical involvement: the subcommittee would supply the "help by the time the neighborhood is one-third black."[84] Any congregation that instead sought to relocate out of the city had to satisfactorily respond to a set of questions that included:

1. Is another congregation needed in the area of proposed location?
2. Could members of the requesting church find suitable church homes in their new communities apart from church relocation?
3. Has the congregation attempted to follow the Classis directive of 1967, "to seek to minister to the communities in which their buildings are located, making no distinction between people, but manifesting a willingness to minister to all in the name of Jesus Christ"?
4. Is the requesting church such as could successfully make the move? Does it have enough internal strength in terms of membership and finances? Is the constituency of the congregation such as will make it likely to be able to evangelize the new community successfully? Is there enough youth in the congregation to make the move feasible? What provisions are being made for older members who may be left behind in the old community when the relocation takes place?[85]

Thus, the Mission Committee insisted that the burden of proof rested with the individual congregations that desired to relocate. With that in mind, any relocating congregation had to prepare a report that stated why its goals as a body of faith would be better achieved in the new neighborhood as opposed to the old and demonstrate a willingness to accept Classis Chicago's recommendation "concerning the further use, sale, or trade of its old building facilities."[86] Finally, the Mission Committee noted that the Classis retained final authority regarding "dissolution, consolidation, or relocation" and concluded that "the subjectivity of the local church is needed when evaluating its own program and the objectivity of Classis is needed when determining major courses of action moves."[87] The polity of the RCA recognized an inherent self-preservation tendency in the actions of congregations. Moreover, those activities could have deleterious consequences for communities and other churches. Thus, within the RCA polity the Classis reserved the authority to limit relocation.

CRC AND RCA CONGREGATIONS ON THE SOUTH SIDE OF CHICAGO: A COMPARISON

The congregationalism of the CRC, as we have noted, allowed for no such supervision. A denomination known for its Dutch ethnicity, the CRC oddly enough evolved into a denomination that practiced a virile form of congregationalism—a distinctly American manifestation of religion. In contrast, the RCA, a denomination that had a much longer history in the United States, practiced a more centralized polity. In the RCA, the authority to purchase and sell property was not solely under the control of the local congregation but fell under the auspices of the appropriate Classis: "The consistory [of the local congregation] shall not sell, transfer, lease, mortgage or otherwise alienate or encumber any real property of the church on which there stands a building designed for worship or religious instruction, or as a residence for the minister, unless the approval of the Classis of which that church is a member has been secured."[88] Such a statement within the Church Order allowed the Classis in question the opportunity to deliberate upon and even prohibit the relocation of congregations. In essence, the Classis in the RCA had the jurisdiction to assess the effect of movement on the Classis as a whole and the community within which the congregation currently existed.

In contrast, the de facto congregationalism of the CRC ensured that higher deliberative bodies could not impinge on the freedoms of the local church body. The limited allusion within the CRC Church Order regarding the congregational mobility merely stated: "Each assembly shall provide for the safeguarding of its property through incorporation."[89] A commentary on the Church Order elucidated that such an article should be interpreted to allow congregations "the right to buy and build; to serve God unmolested; to retain their properties; etc."[90] Moreover, this statement on property was designed "to assure the churches against the unfair infringement upon their property rights, both on the part of individuals and groups—the latter especially."[91]

The divergent language in the church orders of the CRC and RCA indicating a significant difference in polity theory for the two denominations had a discernible influence on the reaction of congregations in Englewood and Roseland to the presence of African Americans in their communities. To recapitulate, in Englewood, First CRC left in 1961, Second CRC in 1962, and Auburn Park CRC in 1964. In contrast, with mobility limited by classis, Hope RCA remained until 1973 and First RCA until 1978. Similar to the sequence of events in Englewood, in Roseland two RCA congregations remained for years after the CRC churches had left the neighborhood. All four CRC congregations in Roseland left for the suburbs between 1969 and 1971. Conversely, Gano RCA and Emmanuel RCA remained until 1977 and 1989, respectively.[92]

In the language of congregational ecology, an approach mentioned as possibly appropriate to this study in Chapter 1, Classis Chicago of the RCA seemed intent on Emmanuel attempting a niche switch.[93] That is, rather than simply following familiar resources to the suburbs, the church would survive with a different identity that would attract the newly arrived African Americans and any remaining white holdovers.[94] The CRC congregations, however, had no similar structures. This crucial polity difference permitted the CRC congregations to depart more easily and more quickly, demonstrating that the responses of these

CRC and RCA congregations cannot simply be explained by changing ecology. Instead, the disparate frameworks of church government and culture within the denominations caused different responses from the affiliated congregations. The structures (or lack thereof) within the polity of a denomination may limit the ability of congregational ecology to fully explain church responses to environmental modification.

11 · CONCLUSION

The Continuing Resonance of Religion in Race and Urban Patterns

Residential segregation has, inarguably, been a vital factor in engendering multiple platforms of inequality in U.S. cities. The failure to integrate continues to haunt the urban United States, and as populations continue to shift around metropolitan regions, careful attention needs to be given to the social practices that influence residential choices. Thus the relevance of the experience of CRC and RCA congregations in the neighborhoods of Englewood and Roseland and how they responded to African American in-migration in Chicago endures.

Scholars have been consistently searching for the answers as to how racial residential segregation became so institutionalized and entrenched. In some social science accounts, it seems to be interpreted as inevitable. However, poor government policy, predatory lending practices, unscrupulous real estate agents, and white racial animus all surely played a role. In short, the shape of the current U.S. city "is the result of political and economic decisions, of choices made and not made by various institutions, groups, and individuals."[1] Moreover, I contend that because of its dominant role in U.S. social history, religion must also be considered as a contributing factor. The historical identity and culture of congregations, the practices of faith, the role of the church within families, and the structure of religious polity have had dramatic influences on the social structure of the nation.

Cities and suburbs continue in a dynamic relationship of population flow in the twenty-first century. Although largely speculative to this point, there are studies that indicate that the dominant urban demographic trend of the post–World War II United States (white departure from core cities to outlying suburbs) may have ebbed. In fact, some authors have concluded that the country stands on the precipice of a demographic inversion. That is, we might be seeing a return of middle- and upper-class whites back into cities proper—a movement that may push the poor and racial minorities into the adjacent older, inner-ring suburbs. In fact, many studies have already noted that concentrated poverty has indeed begun a migration to these suburbs.

If we are to better understand and anticipate urban and suburban population movement and its consequences, it remains important to appreciate how the metropolitan United States came to look as it does today. Questions regarding the role of religion in the "white flight" of the 1950s, 1960s, and 1970s remain critically significant: some observers are asserting that that the demographic inversion of the early twenty-first century might again be linked to religion, and have described a burgeoning phenomenon of middle-class white evangelicals re-urbanizing.[2] In that case, questions loom about how that trend might affect urban residential patterns. Will contemporary evangelicals and their congregations follow the lead of their predecessors and make residential decisions with little regard for neighbors or input from authorities and experts?

The intersection of race and religion in Englewood and Roseland in the middle of the twentieth century remains relevant in this regard. Chicago has been a city long recognized as having a high level of residential segregation, and the families of the CRC functioned as a subculture strongly influenced and motivated by their faith and their church. Thus, the mass exodus from Chicago of families belonging to the Christian Reformed Church reveals compelling insights into how religion (in this case, an evangelical strain) has fostered residential segregation.

COMPLICATING WHITE FLIGHT AND SEGREGATION

Again, the city of Chicago has consistently registered in various studies as one of the most segregated cities in the United States. In fact, by the mid 1990s experts proclaimed Chicago "the most segregated." Moreover, Douglas Massey asserted in 1996: "[Segregation] is worse than we imagined. Racial segregation in this country is deeper and more profound than previous attempts to study it had indicated." He went on to posit that segregation in Chicago had become so intense that the usual categories did not adequately describe the situation. Instead, mere segregation in Chicago had mutated into something called "hypersegregation." Scholars employed this new term because "segregation" alone understated the severity and multidimensional layering of racial residential separation.[3] And we know that segregation has proved foundational to profound socioeconomic inequities.[4] This level of extreme segregation had origins decades earlier, when institutional practices made it desirable for white families to leave areas where African American families were arriving.

Other observers have demonstrated interest in the role of religion in the systematic creation of residential segregation. However, none of the previous studies adequately delineate how particular contours of a conservative Protestant subculture could actually function to sanction and encourage suburban migration in the face of the African American influx. Michael O. Emerson and Christian Smith elucidated how the nature of evangelical Christianity handicaps adherents' ability to understand the structural nature of racism because of its emphasis on personal salvation and personal relationships as antidotes to society's ills.[5] Beyond that, Gerald Gamm and John McGreevy clearly demonstrated how the model Catholic parish structure ultimately produced different responses from Catholics compared to Jews and Protestants when faced with African American in-migration. Moreover, Nancy Tatom Ammerman vividly articulated how different congregations responded to racial change in their communities.

None of these studies, though, explicitly examined how various Protestant denominations and congregations have actively functioned as co-conspirators as individual members and families left the city for the suburb en masse. Thus when authors attempt to explicate the nature and reasons for white mass suburbanization and ignore religious affiliations, they fail to sufficiently assess the social phenomenon. It is not enough to categorize why whites fled the inner city in terms of racial, race-associated, or neutral ethnocentric concerns. The story of Englewood and Roseland displayed that these "concerns" failed to illuminate why virtually all the CRC-affiliated residents left in such a relatively short period of time and why, for instance, Lutheran and RCA congregations tended to remain longer. Considering its continuing pervasive significance in U.S. society, observers must regard religion as a significant element of the mid-century white exodus for the suburbs in the urban north.

PRECEDENCE, PLACE, POLITY

The features of the CRC history, culture, polity, and conception of place created among its members a predilection for high mobility. Within the CRC, three influences ultimately allowed the congregants to leave their Englewood and Roseland home neighborhoods relatively easily. These three can be succinctly described as precedence, place, and polity. First, the CRC had a long and pronounced history of fissure and mobility that led to the rise of closed networks. Second, the CRC operated as such a closed society that they maintained little investment in any "place," that is, location, beyond their churches and schools. With such narrow definitions of place, they could easily move and transport themselves elsewhere. Finally, the congregational nature of the CRC polity made the elders of each individual church the ultimate authority. Subsequently, when the larger deliberative bodies of the CRC demonstrated particular concern about racism and its fallout, they could not persuade or force the individual congregations to remain in the neighborhoods in which they had been originally established. These three elements, precedence, place, and polity, allowed the members and congregations the ability to easily mobilize and depart for the suburbs as their communities began to change.

Precedence

The history and ancestry of these CRC congregations in Englewood and Roseland was replete with stories of schism and mobility. The members of these particular congregations were the descendants of cross-Atlantic immigrants, and some were immigrants themselves. In essence, the denomination had antecedents of secession that stretched back to 1834 in the Netherlands and 1857 in the United States. The pattern of mobility and fissure continued into the twentieth century as several congregations left and established the Protestant Reformed Churches in 1925. In the early 1990s, the pattern repeated. Synod debated the issue of women's ordination and decided to allow individual Classes to make policy in that regard. By not condemning women's ordination, Synod raised the ire of an ultra-conservative element of the denomination and watched as thirty-six congregations and thousands of members left the CRC. These new seceders would ultimately establish the United Reformed Churches in North America.

The wholesale departure of these CRC congregations from Englewood and Roseland functions as an example of contingent history. Those who left these two communities came from a long line of people prone to schisms and mobility. For well over a century, the tribe who eventually became known as the CRC had been on a path toward maintaining isolation. Having gone from members of the National Church to persecuted outcasts who belonged to a sect had dramatic consequences for them and their posterity. Patterns and precedents were established within this line of Dutch Reformed Protestant history that predisposed the congregations toward activities that fostered removal and isolation.

Place

Because the CRC families found almost all social fulfillment within the institutional rubric of the church and school, they had few bridging ties to the wider community and, subsequently, a very narrow conception of place. The CRC became so isolated that it nurtured a closed network. Out of necessity, CRC members could conduct business with persons not belonging to the denomination. However, for all other social activities the members of the CRC generally only endured limited interaction with the non-CRC population. To ascertain the level of social seclusion, one has only to note the CRC idea that matrimony with individuals from the RCA should be labeled as "intermarriage."[6]

The CRC churches in Englewood and Roseland remained so detached that they lacked the ability to unite with other faith bodies to address the changing demographics on the South Side of Chicago. The first response was to create a particular CRC organization that allied the churches and the schools. When that failed, they took the formidable step (for them) of joining a broader community organization: Organization for the Southwest Community (OSC). However, their social separatism revealed itself again when the congregations quibbled over some of the organization's activities. Because the CRC congregations had principally functioned in a manner disconnected from the larger community, when a crisis arose they had no social capital from which they could draw to address the situation. Indeed, the strong emphasis on the in-group social ties handicapped their ability to respond with any strategy other than relocation.

As narrow social circles, the CRC had only two places: the church and the school. When African Americans first moved into Englewood and Roseland, the CRC congregations responded by reconfiguring and manipulating their places so that any new "visitors" would be keenly aware that the original congregants controlled the place. Some of the churches had even been considering physical expansion. When they ended all further discussion of building additions, they implicitly stated that they never expected the newly arriving African Americans to join their congregations—in essence, this place was not for them. Moreover, when the congregations began to perceive safety and security issues, they became more militant in the protection of their places. They initially utilized church ushers as security guards, but eventually went as far as requesting police presence.

In the end, however, the insularity and constricted sense of place allowed the seven congregations of Englewood and Roseland easy mobility out of the city and into the suburbs. They had little investment in the old city neighborhoods beyond the two primary institutions of church and school. They could sell these physical structures easily.

Polity

Precedent and the historical theme of insularity also manifested itself in the polity of the CRC. In the Chicago area the CRC congregations ultimately answered to no higher authority when confronted by issues of race. Beyond that, as I have argued, the CRC practiced a de facto congregationalism.

Though the lineage of the CRC traces back to a parish or territorial model of church structure in the Netherlands, the denomination in America resolutely refused to tether itself to place. Instead, the members explicitly considered themselves as largely a spiritual community. Thus, they had no social responsibility to the broader community or neighborhood. With such a disposition, they could justifiably remove their church at any time and for any reason. In contrast to the Roman Catholic parishioners who remained intrinsically tied to their locale, the CRC congregants had little binding them to the community when the racial composition began to change.

In addition to its non-territorial nature, the Church Order of the CRC abetted the departure of the congregations by establishing a congregational polity in which authority rested ultimately with the local Council. On the Synodical level, the denomination persistently sought to address the issue of race and racial injustice adequately. However, because of the polity, those higher efforts had little impact in Englewood and Roseland. Though much of the rest of the denomination could discern what was happening in the neighborhoods of Chicago, the church hierarchy had no power to coerce the individual churches to stay and integrate.

The Timothy/Lawndale episode vividly revealed the individual authority of the congregations. While the Synod attempted to censure the congregations that supported Timothy Christian School, those same congregations responded almost spitefully. Indeed, the suspicion of church authority continued to manifest within the denomination into the twenty-first century. When the *Banner* published a retrospective on the Timothy Christian School controversy in 2013, a letter to the editor in the next issue applauded the polity that had rendered the denomination without recourse. The letter writer noted that the federal court had declined to rule on the issue, citing the autonomy of private schools. She went on to assert: "Synod should have done the same thing."[7] Such a notion is indicative of the congregationalism that courses through the denomination. In the case of Englewood and Roseland, the denomination had no established protocol for addressing the mass exodus of these two neighborhoods. That surely engendered racial alienation.

IMPLICATIONS

In sum, the relocation of seven CRC churches from Chicago proper to the surrounding suburbs complicates the larger national story of white flight. The nature of the faith of these CRC congregants afforded them an almost unfettered departure. First, the precedent of fissure and mobility was a strong theme within their religious identity. Second, the insular nature of their religious community engendered little attachment to the places and structures of the broader community that they inhabited. Third, the congregational nature of the CRC polity made it possible for the local congregation to make decisions solely in their own best interests and self-survival—the council did not have to answer to higher church authorities regarding location.

More generally, the import of the CRC relocation from Englewood and Roseland lies in the fact that any study of the departure of white families from Rust Belt cities in the middle of the twentieth century would do well to include the variable of religion and religious structures. Outright racism, concern over property values, poor policy, and economic avarice surely remain important factors. However, any assessment of why and how people left the cities for the suburbs must include an appraisal of religious faith. In this case, the success of evangelical congregations had negative effects for the urban neighborhood. It remains somewhat remarkable that they reconstituted both the Christian schools and the congregations in outlying suburbs. That achievement, though, contributed to and exacerbated racial segregation.

Though there are some unique features of the CRC departures from Englewood and Roseland, there also exist strong elements within the narrative that transcend this microhistory and link it to broader elements within the U.S. religious scene. That more encompassing feature is the individualism and congregationalism that existed within the CRC, American evangelicalism as a whole, and even with groups as disparate as Orthodox Jews (whom Gamm referred to as having the "purest form of congregational authority").[8] A dominant theme of general U.S. social life has been individualism and independence. Likewise, a dominant theme within U.S. religion has been congregationalism. Recent studies have indicated the continued pertinence of congregations in American lives. Scholars estimate that between 50 and 60 percent of the U.S. population has a congregational affiliation—compared with less than 30 percent of the population at the beginning of the nineteenth. In addition, when one ascertains that there exist over 340,000 congregations in America, it becomes very difficult to study social patterns without taking these institutions into account.[9]

Moreover, the consequence of that congregationalism has had a direct effect on urban residential patterns. The autonomy of the CRC congregations was not unique. Their history demonstrated a predisposition to fissure, mobility, and insularity. These traits allowed the denomination to eventually become part of a broader religious pattern taking place in the United States: "de facto congregationalism." In other words, scholars have noted a trend in American religion whereby groups as dissimilar as Mormons and Muslims have converged toward "the model of the reformed Protestant tradition of the congregation as a (local) voluntary gathered community."[10] The congregational polity embraced by the CRC has also become a significant feature of U.S. religion in general.

In the end, the linchpin of the ability of the churches to leave the city was the congregational hierarchy of the denomination. Though H. Richard Niebuhr bemoaned the "denominationalism" of American Christianity and its consequent divisiveness, perhaps he would have been more correct to consider the "congregationalism."[11] It was congregationalism that allowed CRC churches and members to freely leave the city as African Americans moved into the neighborhoods. Such a model of church polity surely had culpability in the rapid relocation of so many white families.

Of course, if we consider this line of events under the rubric of the voluntary nature of religion in the U.S. marketplace, perhaps the congregations leaving for the suburbs could simply be interpreted as churches following their congregant customers. However, a critical examination undermines that notion. First, at least one of the churches chose a spot in the suburbs to which they directed attenders to relocate. That effort demonstrated that the congregations had agency in the relocation to the suburbs. Second, the different responses from CRC as opposed to RCA congregations revealed that some churches remained constrained under authority structures that inhibited a market niche strategy.

While CRC congregations followed their customer market to better-resourced areas, the RCA hierarchy ensured that churches within that denomination at the very least would attempt to persist in their current market.

The established RCA congregations remained in Englewood and Roseland longer not because they maintained access to resources, but because of a distinctive church polity. In order to foster an enduring presence in Roseland in particular, higher assemblies within the RCA gave financial support. In the end, organizations not only respond to environment, they shape it. Again, the fact that in the CRC, one congregation even offered a recommendation for the residential relocation of its attending families is instructive. The nature of the closed community and the manner in which the CRC attenders relied on in-group networks assured that the church's directive would find a suggestible audience. On the other hand, the responsibilities that the RCA as denomination felt for changing neighborhoods translated into a limitation in the movement of its congregations. The freedom of the market, in this case, fails to fully account for the agency that might exist within congregational leadership and church political structures.

Similarly, the frame of congregational ecology helps explain the relocation of churches only to a point. In the congregational ecology model, the changing environment of the neighborhoods naturally selected which congregations would remain viable. In that way, congregations are vulnerable to the shifting demographics of a city. They need attenders to survive and thrive. Therefore, it would be logical for these churches to follow traditional resources to the nutrient-rich suburbs. For both sets of congregations, CRC and RCA, the habitat in which they found themselves rapidly altered the resource (people) offerings. However, in response, they followed different patterns because of internal denominational structures. In other words, internal institutional factors can limit the ability of congregational ecology to explain church movement or stasis. Thus, the case of CRC and RCA congregations demonstrates the limitations of congregational ecology to fully explain the lives of churches.

On the surface, the CRC families in question here could be summarily dismissed as an insignificant component of a larger social phenomenon. A closer examination reveals that elements and practices of their faith actually predisposed them to leaving when things became unstable. The successes of these white evangelicals and their congregations allowed them to relocate—contributing to the exacerbation of racial segregation. In other words, the strength of the CRC congregations as institutions led to weakness in the potential for cross-racial relationships with the newly arrived African Americans and contributed to the economic decline of Englewood and Roseland. Though it remains easy to make sweeping statements regarding the culpable structures, institutions, and agents, to assess the reasons and motives of white flight adequately, religion and faith practices and cultures must be included. Only in that way can we fully ascertain the intertwined roots of the segregation that plagues the urban United States.

NOTES

CHAPTER 1 INTRODUCTION

1. I in no way intend to reduce the race issue in the United States to a simple white versus African American dichotomy. There is no doubt that other minority groups suffer inordinate segregation, especially Latino and immigrant communities; however, I would contend that the dominant story of the twentieth century involved the residential tensions that flared up between whites and African Americans. Though the following pages feature that narrative, it should not be misinterpreted as a dismissal of the both historical and contemporary struggles of other racial minorities for residential integration in the United States.

2. Mary Patillo, *Black Picket Fences: Privilege and Peril among the Black Middle Class* (Chicago: University of Chicago Press, 1999) and *Black on the Block: The Politics of Race and Class in the City* (Chicago: University of Chicago Press, 2007); William Julius Wilson, *The Declining Significance of Race: Blacks and Changing American Institutions* (Chicago: University of Chicago Press, 1978) and *When Work Disappears: The World of the New Urban Poor* (New York: Vintage, 1996); Stephen Steinberg, *The Ethnic Myth: Race, Ethnicity, and Class in America* (Boston: Beacon, 1981) and *Turning Back: The Retreat from Racial Justice in American Thought* (Boston: Beacon, 1995); Douglas S. Massey and Nancy A. Denton, *American Apartheid: Segregation and the Making of the Underclass* (Cambridge, MA: Harvard University Press, 1993).

3. Massey and Denton, *American Apartheid*, 10.

4. Alan Ehrenhalt, *The Great Inversion and the Future of the American City* (New York: Alfred A. Knopf, 2012).

5. Corwin Smidt, Donald Luidens, James Penning, and Roger Nemeth, *Divided by a Common Heritage: The Christian Reformed Church and the Reformed Church in America at the Beginning of a New Millennium* (Grand Rapids, MI: Eerdmans, 2006), 19.

6. For a detailed analysis of how closed communities might contribute to segregation, see Troy C. Blanchard, "Conservative Protestant Congregations and Racial Residential Segregation: Evaluating the Closed Community Thesis in Metropolitan and Nonmetropolitan Counties," *American Sociological Review* 72 (June 2007): 416–433.

7. Amanda I. Seligman, *Block by Block: Neighborhoods, Public Policy, and "White Flight" in Richard J. Daley's Chicago* (Chicago: University of Chicago Press, 2005).

8. Rachael Woldoff, *White Flight/Black Flight: The Dynamics of Racial Change in an American Neighborhood* (Ithaca, NY: Cornell University Press, 2011).

9. Kevin Kruse, *White Flight: Atlanta and the Making of Modern Conservatism* (Princeton, NJ: Princeton University Press, 2007).

10. For an insightful study of a fundamentalist congregation departing another rust belt locale, see Darren Dochuk, "'Praying for a Wicked City': Congregation, Community, and the Suburbanization of Fundamentalism," *Religion and Culture: An Interpretative Journal* 13 (Summer 2003): 167–203. Dochuk finds that the transformation of the Highland Park Baptist Church to a premillenialist fundamentalism gave sanction to its relocation after ten years of consideration. In short, theological orientation mattered.

11. Nancy Tatom Ammerman, *Congregation and Community* (New Brunswick, NJ: Rutgers University Press, 1997).

12. Michael O. Emerson and Christian Smith, *Divided by Faith: Evangelical Religion and the Problem of Race in America* (New York: Oxford University Press, 2000).

13. Jason E. Shelton and Michael O. Emerson, *Blacks and Whites in Christian America: How Racial Discrimination Shapes Religious Convictions* (New York: New York University Press, 2012).

14. See R. Stephen Warner, "A Work in Progress toward a New Paradigm for the Sociological Study of Religion in the United States," *American Journal of Sociology* 98 (March 1993): 1044–1093.

15. Robert Wuthnow, *Producing the Sacred: An Essay on Public Religion* (Chicago: University of Chicago Press, 1994), 43, and Robert D. Putnam and David E. Campbell, *American Grace: How Religion Divides and Unites Us* (New York: Simon and Schuster, 2010), 8.

16. Ammerman, *Congregation and Community*; Nancy Eisland, *A Particular Place: Urban Restructuring and Religious Ecology in a Southern Exurb* (New Brunswick, NJ: Rutgers University Press, 1999); Omar M. McRoberts, *Streets of Glory: Church and Community in a Black Urban Neighborhood* (Chicago: University of Chicago Press, 2003); Kevin D. Dougherty and Mark T. Mulder, "Congregational Responses to Growing Urban Diversity in a White Ethnic Denomination," *Social Problems* 56 (May 2009): 335–356; and Katie Day, *Faith on the Avenue: Religion on a City Street* (New York: Oxford University Press, 2014).

17. McRoberts, *Streets of Glory*, 10. The creation of grinding residential segregation in the urban United States did not occur naturally or though happenstance. Instead, according to urban political economy theory, a nexus of white animus, government policy, and economic exclusion conspired to foster racial segregation.

18. Wade Clark Roof and William McKinney, *American Mainline Religion* (New Brunswick, NJ: Rutgers University Press, 1987); Laurence R. Iannaconne, "The Consequences of Religious Market Structure: Adam Smith and the Economics of Religion," *Rationality and Society* 3 (April 1991): 156–177; and Warner, "Work in Progress."

19. Patrick Sharkey, *Stuck in Place: Urban Neighborhoods and the End of Progress toward Racial Equality* (Chicago: University of Chicago Press, 2013).

20. Ibid., 50. Italics in original.

21. Robert J. Sampson, *Great American City: Chicago and the Enduring Neighborhood Effect* (Chicago: University of Chicago Press, 2012), 396 and 401.

22. Ibid., 398.

23. Ehrenhalt, *The Great Inversion*.

24. James S. Bielo, "City of God, City of Man: The Re-urbanization of American Evangelicals," *City and Society* 23 (2011): 2–23.

25. James Joyce, *Portrait of the Artist as a Young Man* (New York: Viking, 1971), 251.

26. Gerald Gamm, *Urban Exodus: Why the Jews Left Boston and the Catholics Stayed* (Cambridge, MA: Harvard University Press, 1999), 19.

27. Ammerman, *Congregation and Community*, 2.

28. Ibid.

CHAPTER 2 MOBILITY AND INSULARITY

1. See Kevin D. Dougherty and Mark T. Mulder, "Congregational Responses to Growing Urban Diversity in a White Ethnic Denomination," *Social Problems* 56 (2009): 335–356.

2. The Great Migration is the northward movement of African Americans from the South to the booming industrial areas of cities such as Chicago. The phenomenon began with World War I and continued through and after World War II. Chapter 5 will offer more detail on the particulars of the Great Migration to Chicago.

3. For more on the issue of race in the United States, see William Julius Wilson, *The Declining Significance of Race: Blacks and Changing American Institutions* (Chicago: University of Chicago Press, 1978) and *When Work Disappears: The World of the New Urban Poor* (New York: Vintage, 1996); Stephen Steinberg, *Turning Back: The Retreat from Racial Justice in American Thought* (Boston: Beacon, 1995); Howard Winant, *Racial Conditions: Politics, Theory, Comparisons* (Minneapolis: University of Minnesota Press, 1994); Thomas D. Boston, *Race, Class, and Conservatism* (Boston: Allen and Unwin, 1988). For more on the development of a "white identity," see David R. Roediger, *The Wages of Whiteness: Race and the Making of the American Working Class*, 2nd ed. (New York: Verso, 1999); Matthew Jacobson, *Whiteness of a Different Color: European Immigrants and the Alchemy of Race* (Cambridge, MA: Harvard University Press, 1999); Noel Ignatiev, *How the Irish Became White* (New York: Routledge, 1995); and Theodore W. Allen, *The Invention of the White Race, Volume 1: Racial Oppression and Social Control*, 2nd ed.(London: Verso, 2012).

4. Etan Diamond, *And I Will Dwell in Their Midst: Orthodox Jews in Suburbia* (Chapel Hill: University of North Carolina Press, 2000).

5. Gerald F. De Jong, *The Dutch in America, 1609–1974* (Boston: Twayne, 1975), 92.

6. *The 1618 Formula of Subscription*, reprinted in Hendrik De Cock's "Secession in the Netherlands," 1866. Heritage Hall Archives, Calvin College, Grand Rapids, MI (hereafter cited as HHA), 3–4.

7. Hendrik De Cock, "Secession in the Netherlands," 1866. Translated by John C. Verbrugge. HHA, 5–6.

8. Albertus Pieters, "Historical Introduction," *Classis Holland: Minutes 1848–1858*. Translated by the Joint Committee of the Christian Reformed Church and the Reformed Church in America (Grand Rapids, MI: Grand Rapids Printing, 1943), 9–10.

9. Ibid.

10. Isaac N. Wyckoff to Albertus C. Van Raalte, 18 October 1846. HHA, 1.

11. Thomas DeWitt, an untitled article that appeared in *The Christian Intelligencer*, 8 October 1846, in *Dutch Immigrant Memoirs and Related Writings*, comp. and ed. Henry Lucas (Grand Rapids, MI: Eerdmans, 1997), 1:24–25.

12. Robert Swierenga, "Dutch Immigrant Patterns in the Nineteenth and Twentieth Centuries," in *The Dutch in America: Immigration, Settlement, and Cultural Change*, ed. Robert Swierenga (New Brunswick, NJ: Rutgers University Press, 1985), 20 and 35.

13. Engbertus Van Der Veen, "Life Reminiscences" (1915), in *Dutch Immigrant Memoirs and Related Writings*, comp. and ed. Henry Lucas, 1:504; and Frans Van Driele, "First Experiences" (1897), in *Dutch Immigrant Memoirs and Related Writings*, comp. and ed. Henry Lucas, 1:335.

14. *Classis Holland: Minutes 1848–1858*. Translated by the Joint Committee of the CRC and RCA (Grand Rapids, MI: Grand Rapids Printing, 1943), 36–37.

15. Ibid., 53.

16. Van Der Veen, "Life Reminiscences," 507–508.

17. *Classis Holland*, 58–60 and 179.

18. Ibid., 241–243.

19. Door W. P. De Jonge, "A Voice from the RCA: Contribution to the History of the Church Struggle: A Recommendation toward a Further and Impartial Research" (1872). Translated by Dirk Mellema (1978). HHA, 3.

20. *Classis Holland*, 144.

21. Jacobus Brandt to unknown cousin, February 1885. Jacobus Brandt Papers, HHA, 2–3.

22. *Acts of the General Synod of the RCA* (New York: Board of Publication of the Reformed Church in America, 1882), 80. For a succinct description of the Freemasonary controversy and the CRC and RCA, see Robert P. Swierenga, "Walls or Bridges? Acculturation Processes in the Reformed and Christian Reformed Churches in North America," in *Morsels in the Melting Pot: The Persistence of Dutch Immigrant Communities in North*

America, ed. George Harinck and Hans Krabbendam (Amersterdam: VU University Press, 2006), 37.

23. D. H. Kromminga, *The Christian Reformed Tradition* (Grand Rapids, MI: Eerdmans, 1943), 120.

24. Paul Conkin, *The Uneasy Center: Reformed Christianity in Antebellum America* (Chapel Hill: University of North Carolina Press, 1995), 177.

25. Ibid., 182.

26. John Van Lonkhuyzen, *Billy Sunday: Een Beeld uit het Tegenwoordige Amerikaanische Godsdienstige Leven* (Grand Rapids, MI: Eerdmans, 1916), 153, quoted by James D. Bratt in *Dutch Calvinism in Modern America: A History of a Conservative Subculture* (Grand Rapids, MI: Eerdmans, 1984), 61.

27. Bratt, *Dutch Calvinism,* 59.

28. Darryl G. Hart, *The Lost Soul of American Protestantism* (New York: Rowman & Littlefield, 2002), 124.

29. Ibid., 40.

30. James Bratt, *Abraham Kuyper: Modern Calvinist, Christian Democrat* (Grand Rapids, MI: Eerdmans, 2013), 195.

31. Herman Hoeksema, *The Protestant Reformed Churches in America: Their Origin, Early History, and Doctrine* (Grand Rapids, MI: First Protestant Reformed Church, 1936), 16, 314.

32. The CRC polity includes three levels of assembly: Councils, Classes, and the General Synod. The local Council operates as the basic unit of government. Each Council then sends representatives to Classis: a meeting of local congregations for general supervision (designed to deal only with matters that could not be concluded in Councils or those that the congregations have in common). Finally, Classes send representatives to Synod, an annual meeting of the denomination. See John Kromminga, *The Christian Reformed Church: A Study in Orthodoxy* (Grand Rapids, MI: Baker Book House, 1949).

33. Richard Mouw, *He Shines in All That's Fair: Culture and Common Grace* (Grand Rapids, MI: Eerdmans, 2001), 9.

34. John H. Bratt, "Dutch Calvinism in America," in *John Calvin: His Influence in the Western World,* ed. W. Stanford Reid (Grand Rapids, MI: Zondervan, 1982), 299.

35. Henry Beets, "Not Ashamed of the Basis of 1857," *Banner,* 11 April 1907, 184–185, quoted by Bratt, *Dutch Calvinism,* 41.

36. Bratt, *Dutch Calvinism,* 300.

37. Ibid., 83–86.

38. Ibid., 90.

39. *Agenda of the Christian Reformed Church, 1928,* 4–56, and James D. Bratt, "The Dutch Schools," in *Reformed Theology in America: A History of Its Modern Development,* ed. David F. Wells (Grand Rapids, MI: Baker Book House, 1997), 119.

40. Bratt, "The Dutch Schools," 114–119.

41. Henry J. Kuiper, "Our Church in the Last Forty Years," *Banner* 12 (January 1940): 28–29.

42. Bratt, *Dutch Calvinism,* 134–141.

43. CRC, *Acts of Synod* (1945), p. 272.

44. Hart, *Old-Time Religion,* 128.

45. Ibid., 131–132.

46. These five elements of Calvinist doctrine are also known as the Five Canons and are derived from the Canons of Dort. Though originally conceived of as a response to the Arminian Controversy (a debate within Reformed churches in the Netherlands in the early seventeenth century concerning predestination and free will), TULIP—the acronym—was

often utilized in CRC circles as a succinct statement of the tenets of Reformed doctrine. More recently, Reformed theologians have claimed that TULIP functions as an insufficient and stereotypical encapsulation of Calvinism. See Richard Mouw, *Calvinism in a Las Vegas Airport: Making Connections in Today's World* (Grand Rapids, MI: Zondervan, 2004).

47. CRC, *Acts of Synod* (1948), 410–411.

48. CRC, *Acts of Synod* (1949), 300.

49. Bratt, *Dutch Calvinism*, 187–198.

50. Ibid., 200.

51. Ibid., 202.

52. Ibid., 220.

53. Ibid., 43–54.

CHAPTER 3 SHUTTERED IN CHICAGO

1. Marie K. Rowlands, "Down an Indian Trail: The Story of Roseland," *Calumet Index* (June 1949) (Reprinted for The Dutch Heritage Center, Palos Heights, Illinois), 1–42.

2. Henry S. Lucas, *Netherlanders in America: Dutch Immigration to the United States, 1879–1850* (Ann Arbor: University of Michigan Press, 1955), 231.

3. Ibid., 323–324.

4. A. T. Andreas, *History of Cook County, Illinois from the Earliest Period to the Present Time* (Chicago, 1884), 607–609. Quoted in Amry Vanden Bosch, *Dutch Communities of Chicago* (Chicago: Knickerbocker Society of Chicago, 1927), 14–15.

5. Lucas, *Netherlanders in America*, 327.

6. Ibid., 328.

7. Vanden Bosch, *Dutch Communities of Chicago*, 2.

8. Robert Swierenga, *Faith and Family: Dutch Immigration and Settlement in the United States, 1820–1920* (New York: Holmes and Meier, 2000), 214. The results of this meeting are typically referred to as the Canons of Dort. The Canons strongly articulate five points of Calvinism regarding unconditional election, limited atonement, total depravity, irresistible grace, and the perseverance of the saints. For more, see *Ecumenical Creeds and Reformed Confessions* (Grand Rapids, MI: CRC Publications, 1988).

9. Robert Putnam and David Campbell, *American Grace: How Religion Divides and Unites Us* (New York: Simon & Schuster, 2010).

10. Swierenga, *Faith and Family*, 5.

11. Vanden Bosch, *Dutch Communities of Chicago*, 5.

12. Swierenga, *Faith and Family*, 220.

13. Ibid.

14. Ibid., 226.

15. Ibid., 223, and Swierenga, "The Dutch Urban Experience," in *The Dutch in Urban America*, ed. Robert Swierenga, Donald Sinnema, and Hans Krabbendam, 1–12 (Holland, MI: Joint Archives of Holland [hereafter JAH], 2004).

16. Vanden Bosch, *Dutch Communities of Chicago*, 35–37.

17. Ibid., 38.

18. Ibid., 59.

19. Quoted by Swierenga, *Faith and Family*, 225.

20. Swierenga, *Faith and Family*, 225–226.

21. Ibid., 225.

22. Swierenga, "The Dutch Urban Experience," 7. For more discussion of the differences in CRC and RCA acculturation see Robert P. Swierenga, "Walls or Bridges? Acculturation

Processes in the Reformed and Christian Reformed Churches in North America," in *Morsels in the Melting Pot: The Persistence of Dutch Immigrant Communities in North America,* ed. George Harinck and Hans Krabbendam (Amersterdam: VU University Press, 2006), 33–42. Swierenga creates a "cultural continuum" in which he demonstrates the "bridging" or "walling" nature of eleven Dutch Reformed denominations in North America. Pages 34–37 describe the Dutch Reformed milieu in Chicago.

23. Vanden Bosch, *Dutch Communities of Chicago,* 79–80.

24. Robert Swierenga, *Dutch Chicago: A History of Hollanders in the Windy City* (Grand Rapids, MI: Eerdmans, 2002), 450.

25. *Heidelberg Catechism,* Lord's Day 30, Question and Answer 80 found in *Ecumenical Creeds and Reformed Confessions* (Grand Rapids, MI: CRC Publications, 1988), 49.

26. Quoted in Swierenga, *Dutch Chicago,* 493.

27. Swierenga, *Faith and Family,* 224.

28. *Acts of Synod,* 1928, 88.

29. Swierenga, *Dutch Chicago,* 458.

30. Ibid., 467–468.

31. Correspondence in the Minutes of Classis Chicago South, January 18, 1966, HHA.

32. Herbert J. Brinks, "Johanna (Gelderloos) LaMaire: Notes for and about the Past," *Origins* 2, no 1 (1993): 32, quoted by Swierenga, *Dutch Chicago,* 450–451.

33. Richard R. Tiemersma, "Growing Up in Roseland in the Twenties and Thirties," *Origins* 5, no 1 (1987): 15.

34. Author's interview with Charles Terpstra, 18 June 2003, Grand Rapids, MI.

CHAPTER 4   A CASE STUDY OF THE CLOSED COMMUNITY

1. Robert Swierenga, *Dutch Chicago: A History of the Hollanders in the Windy City* (Grand Rapids, MI: Eerdmans, 2002), 351.

2. Ebenezar Christian School Semi-Centennial Celebration booklet, 1933. Dutch Heritage Archives, Trinity Christian College, Palos Heights, IL (hereafter DHA).

3. Swierenga, *Dutch Chicago,* 351.

4. Ibid., 354.

5. Ibid., 355.

6. Gerald F. De Jong, "125 Years of the Synod of Chicago, Reformed Church in America: History of the Synod of Chicago, 1856–1981," 1981, 24. DHA.

7. Ibid., quoting the 1926 RCA Committee on Education, 27.

8. Swierenga, *Dutch Chicago,* 42.

9. Ibid., 357.

10. Quoted ibid., 447.

11. *Acts of Synod,* 1936, 35–37.

12. Richard R. Tiemersma, "Growing Up in Roseland in the Twenties and Thirties," *Origins* 5 (1987), 15.

13. Swierenga, *Dutch Chicago,* 448.

14. Scott Hoezee and Christopher H. Meehan, *Flourishing in the Land: A Hundred-Year History of Christian Reformed Missions in North America* (Grand Rapids, MI: Eerdmans, 1996), 135–137.

15. "Timothy: Crisis in Christian Education," Calvin College *Chimes* 64 (3 October 1969), 6.

16. "By Their Fruits Shall Ye Know Them," *Chimes* 64 (3 October 1969), 6.

17. Ibid.

18. Reverend John Rozendal, quoted in the 3 October 1969 *Chimes* article, "By Their Fruits Shall Ye Know Them."

19. *Cicero Life*, August 18, 1968, quoted in "By Their Fruits Shall Ye Know Them."

20. "By Their Fruits Shall Ye Know Them."

21. Timothy Christian School Board Minutes, quoted by Hoezee and Meehan, *Flourishing in the Land*, 137.

22. *Chicago Tribune*, 11 November 1969, quoted by Hoezee and Meehan, *Flourishing in the Land*, 138.

23. Letter of Dorothy Roberts to the editor, *Banner*, August 29, 1969.

24. Lester DeKoster, "The Other Side of the Coin," *Banner*, October 10, 1969, 9.

25. *Acts of Synod 1968* (Grand Rapids, MI: CRC Board of Publications, 1968), 562.

26. Classis is a meeting of local or regional congregations for general supervision; see Chapter 2, note 31.

27. "Voices," *Chimes*, 3 October 1969.

28. Ibid.

29. Chris Meehan, "Learning from Timothy," *Banner* 148 (July 2013): 50–53

30. "And Behold, There Came Wise Men from the East," *Chimes*, 3 October 1969.

31. Classical Advisory Committee on the Lawndale Educational Needs report to Classis Chicago North, 17 September 1969, quoted by Martin LaMaire, "Compliance in Cicero," *Reformed Journal*, March 1970, 8.

32. Ibid.

33. Nicholas Wolterstorff, "Is the Christian Reformed Church Serious?" and Henry Stob, "Let Us Repent," *Reformed Journal*, March 1970, 2–15.

34. *Acts of Synod*, 1970, 64.

35. Hoezee and Meehan, *Flourishing in the Land*, 139.

36. Martin LaMaire, "Acts of a Minor Assembly: A Report on Classis Chicago North's Response to Synod 1970," *Reformed Journal*, January 1971, 14.

37. Quoted by Lester DeKoster in "God Was Not Wasting His Time," *Banner* 107 (14 January 1972): 8.

38. Meehan, "Learning from Timothy," 51.

39. LaMaire, "Acts of a Minor Assembly," 17.

40. James D. Bratt, *Dutch Calvinism in Modern America: A History of a Conservative Subculture* (Grand Rapids, MI: Eerdmans, 1984), 51.

41. Emile Durkheim, *The Division of Labor in Society* (New York: Free Press, 1984).

CHAPTER 5 CHICAGO

1. James R. Grossman, *Land of Hope: Chicago, Black Southerners, and the Great Migration* (Chicago: University of Chicago Press, 1989), 3.

2. Thomas Sugrue, *The Origins of the Urban Crisis: Race and Inequality in Postwar Detroit* (Princeton, NJ: Princeton University Press, 1996). For information on racial change in New York, Washington, DC, and St. Louis, respectively. see Harold X. Connolly, *A Ghetto Grows in Brooklyn* (New York: New York University Press, 1977); Constance Green, *The Secret City: A History of Race Relations in the Nation's Capital* (Princeton, NJ: Princeton University Press, 1967); and James T. Little, Hugh O. Nourse, R. B. Read, and Charles L. Leven, *The Contemporary Neighborhood Succession Process: Lessons in the Dynamic of Decay from the St. Louis Experience* (St. Louis: Institute for Urban and Regional Studies, 1975).

3. Sugrue, *Origins of the Urban Crisis*, 8.

4. Ibid.

5. Arnold Hirsch, *Making the Second Ghetto: Race and Housing in Chicago, 1940–1960* (New York: Cambridge University Press, 1998), x. For more on Chicago specifically, see Chapter 6.

6. Ibid., vii. For more on the development of ghettos, see Wendell Pritchett, *Brownsville, Brooklyn: Blacks Jews, and the Changing Face of the Ghetto* (Chicago: University of Chicago Press, 2002). Pritchett traced the history of Brownsville as it was transformed from a white, predominantly Jewish neighborhood, to 75 percent African American and 20 percent Puerto Rican. He carefully emphasized the important role of local communities as they responded to seemingly inevitable postwar urban decline.

7. Carole Marks, *Farewell—We're Good and Gone: The Great Black Migration* (Bloomington: Indiana University Press, 1989), 165.

8. In addition to Grossman and Marks, these authors have also made valuable contributions to the study of the Great Migration to Chicago: Allan H. Spear, *Black Chicago: The Making of a Negro Ghetto, 1890–1920* (Chicago: University of Chicago Press, 1967); William M. Tuttle, *Race Riot: Chicago in the Red Summer of 1919* (New York: Atheneum, 1970); and Thomas Philpott, *The Slum and the Ghetto: Immigrants, Blacks, and Reformers in Chicago, 1880–1930* (New York: Oxford University Press, 1978). Moreover, these authors relied heavily on the Chicago Commission on Race Relations, *The Negro in Chicago: A Study of Race Relations and a Race Riot* (Chicago: University of Chicago Press, 1922).

9. Marks, *Farewell—We're Good and Gone,* 14.

10. Grossman, *Land of Hope,* 13–14.

11. See also Kenneth Jackson, *Crabgrass Frontier: The Suburbanization of the United States* (New York: Oxford University Press, 1985); Charles Abrams, *Forbidden Neighbors: A Study of Prejudice in Housing* (New York: Harper, 1955); Rose Helper, *Racial Policies and Practices of Real Estate Brokers* (Minneapolis: University of Minnesota Press, 1969); Brian J. L. Berry, *The Open Housing Question: Race and Housing in Chicago, 1966–1976* (Cambridge, UK: Ballinger, 1979); Harvey Molotch, *Managed Integration: Dilemmas of Doing Good in the City* (Berkeley: University of California Press, 1972); and Clement Vose, *Caucasians Only: The Supreme Court, the NAACP, and the Restrictive Covenant Cases* (Berkeley: University of California Press, 1959).

12. Spear, *Black Chicago,* 209.

13. Grossman, *Land of Hope,* 174.

14. Marks, *Farewell—We're Good and Gone,* 162–164.

15. Ibid., 164.

16. Ibid.

17. Philpott, *The Slum and the Ghetto,* 119.

18. Ibid., 142.

19. Grossman, *Land of Hope,* 174.

20. Philpott, *The Slum and the Ghetto,* 167–168.

21. Tuttle, *Race Riot,* 119.

22. Chicago Commission on Race Relations, *The Negro in Chicago,* 1.

23. St. Clair Drake and Horace R. Cayton, *Black Metropolis: A Study of Negro Life in a Northern City* (New York: Harcourt, Brace, and Company, 1945), 77.

24. Gregory D. Squires, Larry Bennett, Kathleen McCourt, and Philip Nyden, *Chicago: Race, Class, and the Response to Urban Decline* (Philadelphia: Temple University Press, 1987), 100.

25. Drake and Cayton, *Black Metropolis,* 80–83.

26. Ibid., 88.

27. Ibid., 90.

28. Ibid., 90–91.

29. Squires et al., *Chicago,* 101.

30. Drake and Cayton, *Black Metropolis,* 90–91.

31. Squires et al., *Chicago,* 102.

32. Hirsch, *Making the Second Ghetto,* 41.

33. "Elements in the South Side Problem" (1939), Church Federation of Greater Chicago Collection, Chicago History Museum, Chicago.

34. Nicholas Lemann, *The Promised Land: The Great Black Migration and How It Changed America* (New York, New York: Alfred A. Knopf, 1991), 63. Another popular account, Louis Rosen's *The South Side: The Racial Transformation of an American Neighborhood* (Chicago: Ivan R. Dee, 1998), utilizes interviews to document the racial transformation of Chicago's South Shore Garden and South Shore Valley in the late 1960s.

35. John Fish, Gordon Nelson, Walter Stuhr, and Lawrence Witmer, *The Edge of the Ghetto: A Study of Church Involvement in Community Organization* (New York: Seabury, 1966), 2.

36. Drake and Cayton, *Black Metropolis*, 113.

37. Ibid., 268.

38. Hirsch, *Making the Second Ghetto*, p. 41.

39. Mark Santow, "Saul Alinsky and the Dilemmas of Race in the Post-war City" (Ph.D. dissertation, University of Pennsylvania, 2000), 101.

40. Commission on Religion and Race, Presbytery of Chicago, *Residential Desegregation in Suburban Chicago: 1963–1965* (1967), cited by Santow, "Saul Alinsky," 104.

41. Squires et al., *Chicago*, 101; and Santow, "Saul Alinsky," 103.

42. An early assessment of the dual housing market was written by Charles Abrams, *Forbidden Neighbors* (New York: Harper and Brothers, 1955). The phenomenon has also been studied in specific cities. On Boston, see Harriet Lee Taggart and Kevin W. Smith, "Redlining: An Assessment of the Evidence of Disinvestment in Metropolitan Boston," *Urban Affairs Quarterly* 17 (September 1981): 91–107 and Hillel Levine and Lawrence Harmon, *The Death of an American Jewish Community: A Tragedy of Good Intentions* (New York: Free Press, 1992). On Baltimore, see Garret Power, "'Apartheid Baltimore Style': The Residential Segregation Ordinances of 1910–1913," *Maryland Law Review* 2 (1983): 289–328.

43. "Elements in the South Side Problem."

44. Santow, "Saul Alinsky," 106–109.

45. Hirsch, *Making the Second Ghetto*, 10.

46. Sudhir Alladi Venkatesh, *American Project: The Rise and Fall of a Modern Ghetto* (Cambridge, MA: Harvard University Press, 2000), 8.

47. Carl Condit, *Chicago: 1930–1970* (Chicago: University of Chicago Press, 1974), 159.

48. Venkatesh, *American Project*, 17.

49. Squires et al., *Chicago*, 103.

50. *Chicago Housing Authority Times* (Chicago: Chicago Housing Authority, April 1962), quoted by Venkatesh, *American Project*, 19.

51. Venkatesh, *American Project*, 19.

52. Ibid. A biography, *American Pharaoh: Mayor Richard J. Daley: His Battle for Chicago and the Nation* (Boston: Little, Brown, 2000), by Adam Cohen and Elizabeth Taylor, discusses Daley's relationship to the African Americans in Chicago. The authors posited that Daley's plans for integrating the newly arrived African Americans from the South into his "machine" failed due to the overwhelming numbers involved in the Migration. The manifestation of Daley's plan for handling the influx of African Americans was the "State Street Corridor" south of the Loop business district. Within the corridor lived 40,000 African Americans in high-rise housing projects that included the Robert Taylor Homes. These projects were perceived as such a dismal failure that they have been torn down. It also important to note in the discussion of Daley and his relationship to the housing projects that no less an author than Arnold Hirsch described the mayor as less the "architect" and more the "keeper" of "Chicago's latest racial accommodation"; *Making the Second Ghetto*, 257. See also Roger Biles,

Richard J. Daley: Politics, Race, and the Governing of Chicago (DeKalb: Northern Illinois University Press, 1995) and Mike Royko, *Boss: Richard J. Daley of Chicago* (New York: Dutton, 1971).

53. Squires et al., *Chicago*, 103–104.

CHAPTER 6   THE BLACK BELT REACHES ENGLEWOOD AND ROSELAND

1. Ebenezar Christian Reformed Church, *Centennial Booklet, 1867–1967* (1967) Dutch Heritage Archives at Trinity Christian College, Palos Heights, IL (hereafter DHA), 11; Gerald E. Sullivan, *The Story of Englewood, 1835–1923* (Chicago: Englewood Business Men's Association, 1923), 16–37; and Robert P. Swierenga, *Dutch Chicago: A History of the Hollanders in the Windy City* (Grand Rapids, MI: Eerdmans, 2002), 32–35.

2. Study Committee of the Englewood Committee for Community Action, "Goals for Community Organization in Englewood" (1960), Church Federation of Greater Chicago Collection, Chicago History Museum.

3. Mark Santow, "Saul Alinsky and the Dilemmas of Race in the Post-war City" (Ph.D. dissertation, University of Pennsylvania, 2000), 19.

4. *Englewood Study Area*, Bureau of Research, Church Federation of Greater Chicago (Chicago: Church Federation of Greater Chicago, 1963), 7–9.

5. *Chicago Local Community Fact Book* (Chicago: Chicago Review Press, 1984), 151.

6. Arnold Hirsch, *The Making of the Second Ghetto: Race and Housing in Chicago, 1940–1960* (New York: Cambridge University Press, 1983), 37.

7. Ibid.

8. Santow, "Saul Alinsky," 117–120.

9. Hirsch, *The Making of the Second Ghetto*, 65.

10. Santow, "Saul Alinsky," 120.

11. Derke Bergsma, "A Tale of Two Churches: An Analysis and Critique of the Process of Decision Leading to Relocation from City to Suburb" (seminar paper, University of Chicago, 1968, DHA), 3. Bergsma, a CRC pastor in Chicago at the time, nicely delineated the history of the CRC congregations in Englewood. Much of the narrative here about the Englewood and the churches is based on his assessment in the paper and in an interview conducted with the author, July 24, 2002, Palos Heights, IL.

12. Hirsch, *The Making of the Second Ghetto*, 89.

13. Ibid., 55.

14. Study Committee of the Englewood Committee for Community Action.

15. H. Kris Ronnow, "The Englewood Community Organization Proposal" (1963), Church Federation of Greater Chicago Collection, Chicago History Museum.

16. *Local Community Fact Book* (1984), 129.

17. Charles H. Gallion, "Seeing Pullman-Roseland: A Quick Trip through an Interesting Section of Chicago—Ideal Home-Owning and Manufacturing Community" (n.d.), Church Federation of Greater Chicago Collection, Chicago History Museum, 4.

18. *Local Community Fact Book* (1984), 129.

19. Gallion, "Seeing Pullman-Roseland," 6.

20. One resident had described the earlier houses of Roseland as "box-like, single-gabled, 1 ½ -story originals with dirt basements and nickel-plated heaters." See Richard R. Tiemersma, "Growing Up in Roseland in the Twenties and Thirties," *Origins* 5, no. 1 (1987): 3.

21. Ibid., 4.

22. Hirsch, *The Making of the Second Ghetto*, 84.

23. *Local Community Fact Book* (1984), 129.

24. Hirsch, *The Making of the Second Ghetto*, 131.

25. Ibid.

26. Ronald G. Patterson, "The Historical Geography of 300 Block West on 110th Place, Roseland Community, Chicago, Illinois" (Paper written for Historical Geography 302 at Chicago State College, March 1964), Church Federation of Greater Chicago Collection, Chicago History Museum.

27. The Far South Side comprised the southeast corner of Chicago proper, which included the communities of Roseland, Pullman, South Deering, East Side, West Pullman, Riverdale, and Hegewisch. The area centered on Lake Calumet, which had become a harbor and port for national and international freight. The total population of the Far South Side in 1960 was 164,951. For more information on this area, see James C. Downs Jr., "Zones of Analysis: City of Chicago" (Report prepared for the Real Estate Research Corporation, March 1963), Church Federation of Greater Chicago, Chicago History Museum, 119–128.

28. *Local Community Fact Book* (1990), 152.

29. Downs, "Zones of Analysis: City of Chicago," 121 and 128.

30. *Local Community Fact Book* (1990), 152.

31. *Local Community Fact Book* (1984), 129–130.

32. Ibid., 129.

33. Ibid.

34. Edward Orser, *Blockbusting in Baltimore: The Edmondson Village Story* (Lexington: University of Kentucky Press, 1994). Raymond A. Mohl's "The Second Ghetto and 'Infiltration Theory' in Urban Real Estate," in *Urban Planning and the African American Community: In the Shadows*, ed. June Manning Thomas and Marsha Ritzdorf, 58–74 (Thousand Oaks, CA: Sage Publications, 1997), described the Great Migration and resulting urban violence. He also closely delineated the reactionary response of the real estate industry to the newly arrived African Americans through an examination of real estate journals and trade magazines. Mohl found that "infiltration theory" (the thought that "unharmonious" racial groups within the same neighborhood should be avoided at all costs in order to protect property values) supported and perpetuated residential racial segregation. Also see Raymond A. Mohl, "Making the Second Ghetto in Metropolitan Miami, 1940–1960," *Journal of Urban History* 21 (March 1995): 395–427. In *Race, Real Estate, and Uneven Development: The Kansas City Experience, 1900–2000* (Albany: State University of New York Press, 2002), Kevin Fox Gotham also specifically studied the real estate industry and the Federal Housing Administration and their influence on the racial construction of Kansas City. Gotham contended that both institutions promulgated racial residential segregation and, consequently, uneven development (the shifting of population, wealth, jobs, and resources from the inner city to the suburbs). Finally, Stephen Grant Meyer's *As Long as They Don't Move Next Door: Segregation and Racial Conflict in American Neighborhoods* (Lanham, MD: Rowman & Littlefield, 2000) also noted the persistence of segregation throughout the twentieth century and the role of the government and real estate industry as co-conspirators working on behalf of a white unwillingness to integrate.

35. Orser, *Blockbusting in Baltimore*, 4.

36. Also see Rose Helper, *Racial Policies and Practices of Real Estate Brokers* (Minneapolis: University of Minnesota Press, 1969); Gary Tobin, ed., *Divided Neighborhoods: Changing Patterns of Racial Segregation* (Newbury Park, CA: Sage, 1987).

37. Minutes of Classis Chicago South, January 18, 1966, Document 23, Heritage Hall Archives at Calvin College, Grand Rapids, Michigan (hereafter HHA).

38. Correspondence in Minutes of Classis Chicago South, January 18, 1966, HHA.

39. Minutes of Classis Chicago South, September 19, 1967, Document 9, HHA.

CHAPTER 7 THE INSIGNIFICANCE OF PLACE

1. See Robert Wuthnow, "Mobilizing Civic Engagement: The Changing Impact of Religious Involvement," in *Civic Engagement in American Democracy*, ed. Theda Skocpol and Morris P. Fiorina (Washington, DC: Brookings Institute, 1999), 331–363; John Wilson and Thomas Janoski, "The Contribution of Religion to Volunteer Work," *Sociology of Religion* 56 (Summer 1995): 137–152; Bob Altemeyer, "Why Do Religious Fundamentalists Tend to Be Prejudiced?" *International Journal for the Psychology of Religion* 13 (November 2003): 17–28; and Laurence Iannaccone, "Why Strict Churches Are Strong," *American Journal of Sociology* 99 (March 1994): 1180–1211.

2. Alejandro Portes, "Social Capital: Its Origins and Applications in Modern Sociology," *Annual Review of Sociology* 24 (August 1998): 1–24.

3. Englewood Cliffs, NJ: Prentice-Hall, 1974. Bennet Harrison also discussed place in terms of "community proximity" and its importance for relationship building. See Harrison, "Industrial Districts: Old Wine in New Bottles?" *Regional Studies* 26 (1992): 469–483. In *The Consequences of Modernity* (Stanford, CA: Stanford University Press, 1990), A. Giddens asserted that time and space within the concept of place are central to understanding the way social reality is constructed. Moreover, A. H. Raedeke and J. S. Rikoon contended that places operated as mediums of social relations and as material products that have an effect on social relations: "Temporal and Spatial Dimensions of Knowledge," *Agriculture and Human Values* 14 (1997): 145–158.

4. David Lowenthal, book review in *Geographical Review* 3 (July 1975): 423–424.

5. Robert David Sack, *Homo Geographicus: A Framework for Action, Awareness, and Moral Concern* (Baltimore: Johns Hopkins Press, 1997), 61. See also Richard Hartshorne, *The Nature of Geography: A Critical Survey of Current Thought in Light of the Past* (Lancaster, PA: Annals of the Association of American Geographers, 1939).

6. Sack, *Homo Geographicus*, 61.

7. Derke Bergsma, "A Tale of Two Churches: An Analysis and Critique of the Process Leading to Relocation from City to Suburb" (seminar paper, University of Chicago, 1963), Dutch Heritage Archives, Trinity Christian College, Palos Heights, IL (hereafter DHA), 1. Bergsma focused on the decision-making processes of the Englewood CRC. His distillation of the events in the seminar paper and decades later interview with the author offered rich insights in analyzing how these churches chose to leave Chicago.

8. See Nancy Tatom Ammerman, *Congregation and Community* (New Brunswick, NJ: Rutgers University Press, 1997); and Michael Emerson, *People of the Dream: Multiracial Congregations in the United States* (Princeton, NJ: Princeton University Press, 2006).

9. Council Minutes, Second CRC of Englewood, October 3, 1960, Article 12, Heritage Hall Archives, Calvin College, Grand Rapids, MI (hereafter HHA).

10. Bergsma, "A Tale of Two Churches," 6.

11. Ibid.

12. Ibid., 9.

13. Council Minutes, First CRC of Englewood, September 19, 1960, Article 8, HHA.

14. Ibid., October 23, 1960, Article 6.

15. Ibid., January 6, 1961, Article 4.

16. Council Minutes, Second CRC of Englewood, October 10, 1960, Article 11.

17. Bergsma, "A Tale of Two Churches," 9.

18. *Yearbook of the Christian Reformed Church* (Grand Rapids, MI: Christian Reformed Publishing House, 1959), p. 18. Previous membership totals for First CRC: 1954–1033; 1955–1062; 1956–1031; 1957–1000; and 1958–799. Post-1959 rolls stated the following: 1960–939

and 1961–864. Previous membership totals for Second CRC: 1954–999; 1955–950; 1956–879; 1957–830; and 1958–770. Post-1959 rolls stated the following: 1960–697 and 1961–678.

19. Bergsma, "A Tale of Two Churches," 4.

20. John Fish, Gordon Nelson, Walter Stuhr, and Lawrence Witmer, *The Edge of the Ghetto: A Study of Church Involvement in Community Engagement* (New York: Seabury Press), 1.

21. Bergsma, "A Tale of Two Churches," 5–6.

22. Ibid., 4.

23. Ibid., 4–5.

24. Council Minutes, Fourth CRC of Roseland, February 5, 1964, Article 12, Orland Park CRC, Orland Park, IL (hereafter OPCRC).

25. Ibid., May 19, 1965, Article 8.

26. Evangelism Committee Minutes, Fourth CRC of Roseland, October 4, 1966, n.p.

27. Ibid., December 1, 1967.

28. Ibid., July 12, 1968.

29. Building Study and Report Recommendations, Fourth CRC of Roseland, May 5, 1965, n.p.

30. Council Minutes, Fourth CRC of Roseland, April 6, 1966, Article 6.

31. Ibid., July 12, 1967, attached document.

32. Ibid.

33. Ibid., November 1, 1967, Article 11.

34. Ibid., April 17, 1968, Article 3.

35. Ibid. May 1, 1968, Article 18.

36. Ibid., May 15, 1968, Article 2. Article 2 also notes that a tract being distributed by the Pullman Gospel Center was being complained about because of its "Hippie-type language" and had ultimately been rejected by other committees.

37. For more on niches and CRC congregations, see Kevin D. Dougherty and Mark T. Mulder, "Congregational Responses to Growing Urban Diversity in a White Ethnic Denomination," *Social Problems* 56 (2009): 335–356.

38. Council Minutes, Fourth CRC of Roseland, October 2, 1968, Article 8; October 16, 1968, Article 10; October 30, 1968, Article 7; and November 6, 1968, Article 11.

39. Ibid., November 6, 1968, Article 11.

40. Ibid., December 11, 1968, Article 13 and February 5, 1969, Article 9.

41. Ibid., January 8, 1969, Article 8.

42. Ibid., March 4, 1969, Article 8.

43. Congregational Meeting Minutes, Fourth CRC of Roseland, May 7, 1969, Article 5.

44. "Fiftieth Anniversary of Fourth CRC of Roseland, 1969: The History" 1969, n.p., (OPCRC).

45. Robert S. Lecky and H. Elliot Wright, eds. *Black Manifesto: Religion, Racism, and Reparations* (New York: Sheed and Ward, 1969), 3.

46. Council Minutes, Fourth CRC of Roseland, July 2, 1969, Articles 8 and 15.

47. Ibid., December 3, 1969, Article 9.

48. Council Minutes, Second CRC of Roseland, July 7, 1970, Article 5.

49. Ibid., August 4, 1970, Article 5.

50. Ibid., Article 11.

51. Ibid., Article 13.

52. Ibid., Article 3.

53. Ibid., March 20, 1971, Article 5.

54. Council Minutes, Fourth CRC of Roseland, October 19, 1971, Article 3.

55. The 125th Anniversary Committee of Classis Chicago South, "Precious Heritage, Precious Future: Classis Chicago South Celebrates the 125th Anniversary of the Christian Reformed Church," 1982, HHA.

56. Special Congregational Meeting Minutes, Fourth CRC of Roseland, April 21, 1971, Article 4.

57. Author interview, B. Jordan (alias), July 25, 2002, Chicago, IL.

58. Letter to Synod of 1972, Minutes of Classis Chicago South, September 20, 1972, HHA.

59. "Pullman Christian Reformed Church: History," no date, no page. HHA.

60. Maria Krysan, "Whites Who Say They'd Flee: Who Are They, and Why Would They Leave?" *Demography* 39 (November 2002): 675–696.

61. Sack, *Homo Geographicus*, 69.

CHAPTER 8   THE SIGNIFICANCE OF POLITY

1. See Douglas S. Massey and Nancy A. Denton, *American Apartheid: Segregation and the Making of the Underclass* (Cambridge, MA: Harvard University Press, 1993); William Julius Wilson, *The Declining Significance of Race: Blacks and Changing American Institutions* (Chicago: University of Chicago Press, 1978) and *When Work Disappears: The World of the New Urban Poor* (New York: Vintage Books, 1996); Edward Orser, *Blockbusting in Baltimore: The Edmondson Village Story* (Lexington: University of Kentucky Press, 1994); Thomas Sugrue, *The Origins of the Urban Crisis: Race and Inequality in Postwar Detroit* (Princeton, NJ: Princeton University Press, 1996); and Arnold Hirsch, *Making the Second Ghetto: Race and Housing in Chicago, 1940–1960* (New York: Cambridge University Press, 1998).

2. Michael Emerson and Christian Smith, *Divided by Faith: Evangelical Religion and the Problem of Race in America* (New York: Oxford University Press, 2000). On the subject of race and religion, also see Eric C. Lincoln, *Race, Religion, and the Continuing American Dilemma* (New York: Hill and Wang, 1984); Frank Loescher, *The Protestant Church and the Negro: A Pattern of Segregation* (Westport, CT: Negro Universities Press, 1948); James R. Wood and Mayer N. Zald, "Aspects of Racial Integration in the Methodist Church: Sources of Resistance to Organizational Policy," *Social Forces* 45 (1966): 255–264. More broadly on the subject of the city and the church, see Harvie M. Conn, *The American City and the Evangelical Church: A Historical Overview* (Grand Rapids, MI: Baker Books, 1994); Loyde Hartley, *Cities and Churches: An International Bibliography, 1800–1991*, vols. 1–3 (Metuchen, NJ: American Theological Library Association and Scarecrow Press, 1992); Diane Winston, "Babylon by the Hudson; Jerusalem on the Charles: Religion and the American City," *Journal of Urban History* 25 (November 1998): 122–129; and James W. Lewis, *The Protestant Experience in Gary, Indiana, 1905–1975: At Home in the City* (Knoxville: University of Tennessee Press, 1992).

3. Emerson and Smith, *Divided by Faith*, 170.

4. Ibid.

5. For more on evangelicals specifically, see Randall Balmer, *Mine Eyes Have Seen the Glory: A Journey into the Evangelical Subculture in America* (New York: Oxford University Press, 1989); Darryl G. Hart, *That Old-Time Religion in Modern America: Evangelical Protestantism in the Twentieth Century* (Chicago: Ivan R. Dee, 2002); Mark A. Noll, *American Evangelical Christianity: An Introduction* (Malden, MA: Blackwell, 2001); and George M. Marsden, *Understanding Fundamentalism and Evangelicalism* (Grand Rapids, MI: Eerdmans, 1991).

6. Emerson and Smith, *Divided by Faith*, 3.

7. Moreover, the RELTRAD taxonomy categorizes the CRC as "Evangelical Protestant" as well. See Brian Steensland, Jerry Z. Park, Mark D. Regnerus, Lynn D. Robinson, W. Bradford Wilcox, and Robert D. Woodberry, "The Measure of American Religion: Toward Improving the State of the Art," *Social Forces* 79 (September 2000): 291–318.

8. Emerson and Smith, *Divided by Faith*, 121. The authors described "strong evangelicals" as those who agreed with the aforementioned hallmarks of evangelicalism and maintained a conscious evangelical religious identity.

9. Ibid., 122.

10. Ibid., 123.

11. In fact, the two denominations have been so closely linked that recent discussions have even broached the feasibility of a merger. See Corwin Smidt, Donald Luidens, James Penning, and Roger Nemeth, *Divided by a Common Heritage: The Christian Reformed Church and the Reformed Church in America at the Beginning of the New Millennium* (Grand Rapids, MI: Eerdmans, 2006).

12. Christopher Bader, Kevin Dougherty, Paul Froese, Byron Johnson, F. Carson Mencken, Jerry Z. Park, and Rodney Stark, *American Piety in the 21st Century: New Insights to the Depth and Complexity of Religion in the US* (Waco, TX: Baylor Institute for Studies of Religion, 2006), 8.

13. Bill Bishop, *The Big Sort: Why the Clustering of Like-Minded America Is Tearing Us Apart* (Boston: Houghton Mifflin Company, 2008).

14. Winter Gibson, *The Suburban Captivity of the Churches: An Analysis of Protestant Responsibility in the Expanding Metropolis* (New York: Macmillan, 1962).

15. Gerald Gamm, *Urban Exodus: Why the Jews Left Boston and the Catholics Stayed* (Cambridge, MA: Harvard University Press, 1999).

16. Ibid., 16–17.

17. Jordan Stanger-Ross, "Neither Fight nor Flight: Urban Synagogues in Postwar Philadelphia," *Journal of Urban History* 32 (September 2006): 791–812.

18. For an assessment of a more recent Roman Catholic attempt to reaffirm the relationship and synthesized identity of parish and neighborhood in Chicago, see Elfriede Wedam, "If We Let the Market Prevail, We Won't Have a Neighborhood Left: Religious Agency and Urban Restructuring on Chicago's Southwest Side," *City and Society* 17 (June 2005): 211–233.

19. John T. McGreevy, *Parish Boundaries: The Catholic Encounter with Race in the Twentieth Century Urban North* (Chicago: University of Chicago Press, 1996).

20. Nancy Tatom Ammerman, *Congregation and Community* (New Brunswick, NJ: Rutgers University Press, 2001). An excellent study on congregations is edited by James P. Wind and James W. Lewis: *American Congregations*, vol. 1, *Portraits of Twelve Religious Communities*, and vol. 2, *New Perspectives in the Study of Congregations* (Chicago: University of Chicago Press, 1994). In addition, R. Stephen Warner's *New Wine in Old Wineskins: Evangelicals and Liberals in a Small-Town Church* (Berkeley: University of California Press, 1988) offers insight on a Presbyterian congregation experiencing change.

21. Ammerman, *Congregation and Community*, 346.

22. Ibid., 354–355. For more on congregations, see William McKinney and Dean R. Hoge, "Community and Congregational Factors in the Growth and Decline of Protestant Churches," *Journal for the Scientific Study of Religion* 22 (1983): 51–66; James Hopewell, *Congregation: Stories and Structures* (Philadelphia: Fortress, 1987); Carroll Jackson and David R. Roozen, "Congregational Identities in the Presbyterian Church," *Review of Religious Research* 31 (1990): 351–369; and Barbara Wheeler, "Uncharted Territory: Congregational Identity and Mainline Protestantism," in *The Presbyterian Predicament: Six Perspectives*, ed. Milton J. Coalter, John M. Mulder, and Louis B. Weeks, 67–89 (Louisville, KY: Westminster/John Knox, 1990).

23. Ammerman, *Congregation and Community*, 355.

24. In the original language, "consistory" would have used in place of "council." More recently, "consistory" has been reserved in the CRC for the meetings of the elders and ministers. Consistories are tasked with pastoral care and discipline while the council functions as the governing body.

25. John Kromminga, *The Christian Reformed Church: A Study in Orthodoxy* (Grand Rapids, MI: Baker Book House, 1949), 207–208.

26. William P. Brink and Richard R. De Ridder, *Manual of Christian Reformed Church Government* (Grand Rapids, MI: CRC Publications, 1987), 1.

27. I. Van Dellen and M. Monsma, *The Church Order Commentary* (Grand Rapids, MI: Zondervan, 1941), 162.

28. Kromminga, *The Christian Reformed Church*, 209.

29. J. L. Schaver, *The Polity of Churches* (Chicago: Chicago Polity Press, 1947), 61. For more on this criticism, see Darryl G. Hart, *The Lost Soul of American Protestantism* (New York: Rowman & Littlefield, 2002). Especially relevant is chapter 5, "The Sectarianism of Reformed Polity" (113–140). Hart contended that the isolation of the CRC was a byproduct of their strict adherence to Reformed confessionalism.

30. Kromminga, *The Christian Reformed Church*, 210.

31. Gerard Dekker, "A Changing World Asks for Changing Congregations" (paper presented at the Fourth Triennial Conference of the International Society for the Study of Reformed Communities, Edinburgh, Scotland, June 28–July 2, 2003).

32. Bergsma interview by author, Palos Heights, IL, 24 July 2002.

33. Ibid.

34. In a vein similar to McGreevy, Eileen M. McMahon explored how religion and the Catholic Church bonded the Irish in Chicago in *What Parish Are You From? A Chicago Irish Community and Race Relations* (Lexington: University Press of Kentucky, 1995). McMahon argued that parish boundaries were integral in reinforcing religious, ethnic, and class boundaries. Examining specifically the Saint Sabina parish, she noted that the Catholic clergy took a leading role in attempting to both stabilize and integrate the neighborhood as African Americans began moving into the community. For more on the Catholic experience in Chicago, see Steven Avella, *This Confident Church: Catholic Leadership in the Life of Chicago* (South Bend, IN: University of Notre Dame Press, 1993); Charles Dahm and Robert Ghelardi, *Power and Authority in the Catholic Church: Cardinal Cody in Chicago* (South Bend, IN: University of Notre Dame Press, 1982). An earlier, more general monograph is William A. Osborne's *The Segregated Covenant: Race Relations and American Catholics* (New York: Herder and Herder, 1967). Also see Mark Santow, "Saul Alinsky and the Dilemmas of Race in the Post-war City" (Ph.D. dissertation, University of Pennsylvania, 2000).

35. McGreevy, *Parish Boundaries*, 4.

36. Ibid., 5.

37. Thomas Sugrue, *The Origins of the Urban Crisis: Race and Inequality in Postwar Detroit* (Princeton, NJ: Princeton University Press, 1996), 214; and Hirsch, *Making the Second Ghetto*, 86.

38. McGreevy, *Parish Boundaries*, 264.

39. Gamm, *Urban Exodus*, 278.

40. Ibid., 18.

41. Ibid.

42. Ibid., 19.

43. Ibid., 15–16.

44. Ibid., 17.

45. Helen Rose Ebaugh and Janet Saltzman Chafetz, "Structural Adaptations in Immigrant Congregations," *Sociology of Religion* 61 (Summer 2000): 136.

46. Wind and Lewis, *American Congregations: Portraits of Twelve Religious Communities*, 9.

47. Nathan O. Hatch, *The Democratization of American Christianity* (New Haven, CT: Yale University Press, 1989), 16.

48. E. Brooks Holifield, "Toward a History of American Congregations," in *American Congregations: New Perspectives in the Study of Congregations*, vol. 2, ed. James P. Wind and James W. Lewis (Chicago: University of Chicago Press, 1994), 23.

49. R. Stephen Warner, "The Place of the Congregation in Contemporary American Religious Configuration," in *American Congregations: New Perspectives in the Study of Congregations*, vol. 2, ed. James P. Wind and James W. Lewis (Chicago: University of Chicago Press, 1994), 74.

50. Douglas W. Johnson and George W. Cornell, *Puncture Preconceptions: What North American Christians Think about the Church* (New York: Friendship Press, 1972), 14.

51. Warner, "The Place of the Congregation," 76.

52. Ibid., and Peter L. Berger, *The Noise of Solemn Assemblies: Christian Commitment and the Religious Establishment in America* (Garden City, NY: Doubleday, 1961), 158.

53. Warner, "The Place of the Congregation," 76.

54. Randolph L. Cantrell, James F. Krile, and George A. Donohue, "Parish Autonomy: Measuring Denominational Differences," *Journal for the Scientific Study of Religion* 22 (Summer 1983): 276–287.

55. The scale offered by Cantrell, Krile, and Donohue has been replicated, most notably, by Mike McMullen, "Religious Polities as Institutions," *Social Forces* 73 (December 1994): 709–728. On p. 710 McMullen noted that the Roman Catholic Church and the United Church of Christ "have very different institutional structures, called 'polities,' in the sociology of religion literature, where a polity refers to denomination's form of government. The Catholic church is an episcopal polity that has a hierarchical structure invested with formal authority; the UCC is a congregational polity with a decentralized structure, where all formal authority is situated in the local church."

56. McMullen made similar definitions of episcopal and congregational polity. He noted that a congregational polity included a "decentralized structure" that gave the "autonomous local congregation the authority to hire or fire ministers, discipline its members, control its finances" (ibid., 712).

57. This tripartite typology of Episcopal, Presbyterian, and Congregational has been used by other authors as well—most notably, D. Moberg. See *The Church as a Social Institution* (Englewood Cliffs, NJ: Prentice Hall, 1962) and "Theological Position and Institutional Characteristics of Protestant Institutions," *Journal for the Scientific Study of Religion* 9 (1970): 53–58.

58. Cantrell, Krile, and Donohue, "Parish Autonomy," 280.

CHAPTER 9   SECOND ROSELAND (CRC) LEAVES THE CITY

1. The 125th Anniversary Committee of Classis Chicago South, "Precious Heritage, Precious Future: Classis Chicago South Celebrates the 125th Anniversary of the Christian Reformed Church," 1982, Heritage Hall Archives at Calvin College, Grand Rapids, Michigan (hereafter HHA), 13.

2. Council Minutes, Second CRC of Roseland, 15 May 1964, Article 14, HHA.

3. Council Minutes, Second CRC of Roseland, 13 October 1964, Article 20.

4. *Yearbook of the Christian Reformed Church* (Grand Rapids, MI: Christian Reformed Publishing House, 1965), 28. Post-1965 membership rolls for Second CRC: 1966—812, 1967—802, 1968—733, 1969—631, 1970—489, 1971—379, and 1972—249. During the same period the membership of First CRC of Roseland went from 960 to 546, Third CRC of Roseland went from 571 to 350, and Fourth went from 496 to 330. For earlier membership figures, see Chapter 7 note 8.

5. Council Minutes, Second CRC of Roseland, 5 January 1965, Article 9 and 7 November 1967, Article 5a.

6. Ibid., 19 December 1958, Article 8.

7. Ibid., 5 December 1968, Article 11e.

8. "Minutes of Classis Chicago South," January 18, 1966, Letter, HHA.

9. Ibid.

10. Author's interview with Charles Terpstra, June 18, 2003, Grand Rapids, MI.

11. Council Minutes, Second CRC of Roseland, Letter from Inner-cities Ministry Conference. Crossed out in the minutes are the words "and approval" after "advice." Such editing might indicate some controversy about whether classes should be given authority on the question of relocation.

12. Ibid., 11 February 1969, Article 17; 18 February 1969, Article 13; and 4 March 1969, Article 6.

13. Terpstra interview.

14. Council Minutes, Second CRC of Roseland, 1 April 1969, Article 9.

15. Terpstra interview.

16. Second CRC of Roseland, Seventy-Fifth Anniversary, "Our Pastor Speaks" (Charles Terpstra) and "We Remember . . ." (Jean DeBoer); Dutch Heritage Archives (hereafter DHA), Trinity Christian College, Palos Heights, IL. The capitalizations are Charles Terpstra's.

17. Council Minutes, Second CRC of Roseland, 18 October 1969, Article 7.

18. Appended church bulletin, 17 March 1970, 4 November 1969, Article 6d and Congregational Meeting Minutes, 4 December 1969, Article 10.

19. Council Minutes, Second CRC of Roseland, 6 January 1970, Articles 9 and 13.

20. Ibid., 4 August 1970, Articles 8 and 9b.

21. Terpstra interview.

22. Congregational Meeting Minutes, Second CRC of Roseland, 14 June 1971, Article 6.

23. Council Minutes, Second CRC of Roseland, 27 June 1971, Article 4 and 17 August 1971, Article 9.

24. Ibid., 24 October 1971, Article 1 and 14 December 1971, Article 6.

25. Ibid., 5 April 1971, Article 11.

26. Ibid., 4 April 1972, Article 8; 16 May 1972, Article 9; and Congregational Meeting Minutes, 19 June 1972.

27. *Acts of Synod, 1957* (Grand Rapids, MI: CRC Board of Publications), 20.

28. Ibid., p. 128.

29. *Acts of Synod*, 1959, 82–84.

30. *Acts of Synod*, 1964, 74.

31. *Acts of Synod*, 1968, 19.

32. Ibid., 589–590.

33. *Acts of Synod*, 1969, 210–211.

34. The denomination would not ordain women until the 1990s.

35. *Acts of Synod*, 1970, 101.

36. *Acts of Synod*, 1971, 113–117.

37. Ibid., 117 and 303–315.

38. Ibid., 305.

39. Ibid., 310–311.

40. *Acts of Synod*, 1972, 317.

41. Ibid., 321.

42. Ibid.

43. Derke Bergsma, "A Tale of Two Churches: An Analysis and Critique of the Process Leading to Relocation from City to Suburb" (seminar paper, University of Chicago, 1963), DHA, 10.

44. Terpstra interview.

45. Author's interview with Derke Bergsma, July 24, 2002, Palos Heights, IL.

46. Council Minutes, Third CRC of Roseland, 1961–1971, HHA, and Robert Swierenga, *Dutch Chicago: A History of the Hollanders in the Windy City* (Grand Rapids, MI: Eerdmans, 2002), 337.

47. Bergsma interview.

48. Terpstra interview.

49. For another comparative study of Protestant suburbanization, see Etan Diamond, *Souls of the City: Religion and the Search for Community in Postwar America* (Bloomington: Indiana University Press, 2003). Diamond outlines how mainline congregations in Indianapolis used demographic research to follow attenders to the suburbs. The analysis included "neighborhood surveys, coordination with nearby congregations, and the participation of denominational officials" (34). Diamond also notes that a mainline Protestant consultant complained about how comparatively aggressively ("warlike") the evangelical churches founded new congregations in the same suburbs (36). Indeed, Diamond finds that of the 191 suburban congregations established around Indianapolis between 1941 and 1970, 58 percent were broadly evangelical (conservative Protestant, Pentecostal, or Holiness tradition) and only 29 percent had mainline affiliation (37).

50. Harvey S. Peters, "The Lutheran Church and Urban Ministry in North America: An Overview," in *The Experience of Hope: Mission and Ministry in Changing Urban Communities*, ed. Wayne Stumme (Minneapolis, MN: Augsburg Fortress, 1991), 28–29.

51. Ibid., 28.

52. Ibid.

53. "A Statement Regarding the Lutheran Church and Minority Groups—Adopted by the Southern Chicago District of the Augustana Lutheran Church on January 19, 1954," Church Federation of Greater Chicago Collection, Chicago History Museum.

54. Ibid.

55. Peters, "The Lutheran Church and Urban Ministry in North America," 29.

56. Ibid., 30.

57. Ibid., 31.

58. "Clergy Conference—Englewood, October 31, 1963," Church Federation of Greater Chicago Collection, Chicago History Museum.

CHAPTER 10   THE CONTRAST BETWEEN SISTER DENOMINATIONS

1. The Belgic Confession (1561), the Heidelberg Catechism (1563), and the Canons of Dort (1618–1619).

2. Robert P. Swierenga, "The Dutch Urban Experience," in *The Dutch in Urban America*, ed. Robert P. Swieringa, Donald Sinnema, and Hans Krabbendam (Holland, MI: Joint Archives of Holland, 2004), 6.

3. I.R.W., "Church in Transition: Brief Study of Emmanuel Reformed Church Program and Community," paper for a class at Trinity Evangelical Divinity School, 1987, 3, Joint Archives of Holland at Hope College and Western Seminary, Holland, MI (hereafter JAH).

4. Consistory Minutes, Emmanuel Reformed Church, February 5, 1963, JAH.

5. Consistory Minutes, Emmanuel Reformed Church, March 3, 1964.

6. Special Consistory Meeting Minutes, Emmanuel Reformed Church, July 29, 1963, 243.

7. Ibid.

8. Ibid.

9. Minutes of the Regular Consistory Meeting, Emmanuel Reformed Church, April 5, 1966.

10. Ibid.

11. Minutes of the Special Consistory Meeting, Emmanuel Reformed Church, May 16, 1966.

12. Minutes of Consistory Meeting, Emmanuel Reformed Church, November 1, 1966.

13. Minutes of Consistory Meeting, Emmanuel Reformed Church, October 6, 1970.

14. Correspondence dated June 2, 1967, located in the Minutes of Emmanuel Reformed Church.

15. Minutes of Regular Consistory Meeting, Emmanuel Reformed Church, September 3, 1968.

16. Agenda and Permanent Committee Reports, Classis of Chicago, Fall Session 1968, 14, JAH.

17. Minutes of Special Consistory Meeting, Emmanuel Reformed Church, September 10, 1968.

18. Agenda and Permanent Committee Reports, Classis of Chicago, Fall Session 1968, 16.

19. Agenda and Permanent Committee Reports, Classis of Chicago, Spring Session 1969, 28.

20. Ibid.

21. Agenda and Permanent Committee Reports, Classis of Chicago, Fall Session 1969, 10.

22. Minutes of the Particular Synod of Chicago, April 21 and 22, 1971, 33, JAH.

23. Ibid.

24. Minutes of the Particular Synod of Chicago, April 26 and 27, 1972, 28.

25. Announcement of Regular Fall Session of Classis Chicago, September 25, 1972.

26. Minutes of the Particular Synod of Chicago, April 26 and 26, 1973, 28–29.

27. Minutes of Regular Consistory Meeting, Emmanuel Reformed Church, December 1, 1970.

28. Minutes of Special Consistory Meeting, Emmanuel Reformed Church, August 28, 1977 and Minutes of Regular Consistory Meeting, Emmanuel Reformed Church, September 6, 1977.

29. Minutes of Regular Consistory Meeting, Emmanuel Reformed Church, February 7, 1978.

30. Ibid.

31. Minutes of Regular Consistory Meeting, Emmanuel Reformed Church, May 2, 1978.

32. Minutes of Regular Consistory Meeting, Emmanuel Reformed Church, March 6, 1979.

33. I.R.W., "Church in Transition," 6.

34. Ibid., 5, emphasis I.R.W.'s.

35. Ibid., 3.

36. Peter Y. DeJong, "Should the Church Follow Its Members?" *Torch and Trumpet* 10 (April 1961): 18–19.

37. Board of Domestic Mission Report, June 1952, 7, quoted by Noel Leo Erskine, *Black People and the Reformed Church in America* (New York: Reformed Church Press, 1978), 79.

38. *Acts and Proceedings of the General Synod of the Reformed Church in America* (Somerville, NJ: Somerset Press, 1959), 96.

39. Ibid.

40. Ibid., 102.

41. Ibid., 105.

42. *Acts and Proceedings*, 1957, 183–184.

43. Lynn Japinga, *Loyalty and Loss: The Reformed Church in America, 1945–1994* (Grand Rapids, MI: Eerdmans, 2013), 72.

44. *Acts and Proceedings*, 1959, 105–106.

45. Ibid., 108.

46. Ibid., 208.

47. *Acts and Proceedings*, 1960, 90.

48. Ibid., 179.

49. Ibid., 180.

50. *Acts and Proceedings*, 1962, 287–289 and 343–344.

51. *Acts and Proceedings*, 1969, 143.

52. Ibid., 102.

53. Ibid., 102–104.

54. Japinga, *Loyalty and Loss*, 149.

55. Edward Corwin, *A Digest of Constitutional and Synodical Legislation of the Reformed Church in America* (New York: Board of Publication of the RCA, 1906), 488.

56. Minutes of Classis Chicago South, May 19, 1971Articles 37 and 38, HHA.

57. Minutes of the Particular Synod of Chicago, April 23 and 24, 1969, 20–21.

58. *Acts and Proceedings*, 1968, 215–216.

59. Classical Home Missions Committee Report, Minutes of Classis Chicago South, May 21, 1968, Article 14 D, HHA; and Classical Home Missions Committee Report, September 17, 1969 Article 17 C.

60. Minutes of Classis Chicago South, September 15, 1971, Article 26.

61. Author's interview with Bob Jordan (alias), July 25, 2002, Chicago, IL.

62. Minutes of Classis Chicago South, January 19, 1972, Articles 42 and 45.

63. *Acts of Synod*, 1968, Overture 4, pp. 561–562.

64. Minutes of Classis Chicago South, May 21, 1968, Article 9 F.

65. Ibid.

66. Minutes of Classis Chicago South, January 15, 1968, Article 9 H.

67. Letter from Second CRC of Roseland dated December 18, 1968, Minutes of Classis Chicago South, January 15, 1969.

68. Minutes of Classis Chicago South, January 15, 1969, Article 10 C.

69. Minutes of Classis Chicago South, May 21, 1969, Article 13 D.

70. Letter from Second CRC of Roseland dated April 21, 1969, Minutes of Classis Chicago South, May 21, 1969.

71. Ibid., Article 18.

72. Letter from Synodical Delegate, Minutes of Classis Chicago South, September 17, 1969.

73. Report of Visiting Team I, Minutes of Classis Chicago South, May 19, 1971.

74. Minutes of the Particular Synod of Chicago, May 7 and 8, 1958, 13.

75. Minutes of the Particular Synod of Chicago, April 26 and 27, 1961, 10.

76. Agenda and Permanent Committee Reports, Classis of Chicago, Fall Session 1968, 13.

77. Agenda and Permanent Committee Reports, Classis of Chicago, Spring Session 1969, 28.

78. Ibid., 29.

79. Ibid.

80. Mission Committee Report in Agenda and Permanent Committee Reports Classis of Chicago, Fall Session 1969, 2.

81. Ibid.

82. Ibid., 4.

83. Ibid.

84. Ibid.

85. Ibid., 5.

86. Ibid., 6.

87. Ibid., 7.

88. *The Reformed Church in America, The Book of Church Order* (New York: Reformed Church Press, 1990), 13.

89. John Louis Schaver, *Christian Reformed Church Order: A Manual of the Church Order Adopted by the Synod of 1914* (Grand Rapids, MI: Zondervan, 1939), Article 32d.

90. Idzerd Van Dellen and Martin Monsma, *The Revised Church Order Commentary: An Explanation of the Church Order of the Christian Reformed Church* (Grand Rapids, MI: Zondervan, 1967), 140.

91. Ibid., 141.

92. Robert P. Swierenga, *Dutch Chicago: A History of Hollanders in the Windy City* (Grand Rapids, MI: Eerdmans, 2002), 242 and 311.

93. Nancy Tatom Ammerman, *Congregation and Community* (New Brunswick, NJ: Rutgers University Press, 1997); Omar McRoberts, *Streets of Glory: Church and Community in a Black Urban Neighborhood* (Chicago: University of Chicago Press, 2003); and Kevin D. Dougherty and Mark T. Mulder, "Congregational Responses to Growing Urban Diversity in a White Ethnic Denomination," *Social Problems* 56 (2009): 335–356.

94. For more on RCA congregations and niche switching, see Christopher P. Scheitle and Kevin D. Dougherty, "Density and Growth in a Congregational Population: Reformed Churches in New York, 1628–2000," *Review of Religious Research* 49 (March 2008): 233–250.

CHAPTER 11 CONCLUSION

1. Thomas Sugrue, *The Origins of the Urban Crisis: Race and Inequality in Postwar Detroit* (Princeton, NJ: Princeton University Press, 1996), 11.

2. James S. Bielo, "City of Man, City of God: The Re-urbanization of American Evangelicals," *City and Society* 23 (2011): 2–23.

3. "Segregation and Cities," *Society* 6 (September/October 1996): 2–3. This is an introductory article to an in-depth series on the topic.

4. John W. Frazier, Florence M. Margai, and Eugene Tettey-Fio, *Race and Place: Equity Issues in Urban America* (Boulder, CO: Westview, 2003).

5. Michael O. Emerson and Christian Smith, *Divided by Faith: Evangelical Religion and the Problem of Race in America* (New York: Oxford University Press, 2000). Emerson and Smith refer to the tendency of white evangelicals to hold the opinion that racism would dissolve if enough people would become Christians as the "miracle motif." See 117–118.

6. As mentioned in other instances, it might be plausible to assume that the differences among the RCA, CRC, PRC, and URC are also so relatively insignificant that an outsider would have great difficulty discerning which denomination was which.

7. "Learning from Timothy," *Banner* 148 (October 2013): 8.

8. Gerald Gamm, *Urban Exodus: Why the Jews Left Boston and the Catholics Stayed* (Cambridge, MA: Harvard University Press, 1999), 19.

9. Nancy Tatom Ammerman, *Congregation and Community* (New Brunswick, NJ: Rutgers University Press, 1997), 2, and Clifford Grammich, Kirk Hadaway, Richard Houseal, Dale E. Jones, Alexei Krindatch, Richie Stanley, and Richard H. Taylor, *2010 U.S. Religion Census: Religious Congregations and Membership Study* (Kansas City, MO: Nazarene Publishing House and Association of Statisticians of American Religious Bodies, 2012).

10. Stephen Warner, "The Place of the Congregation in Contemporary American Religious Configuration," in *American Congregations,* ed. James Wind and James Lewis (Chicago: University of Chicago Press, 1994), 54.

11. H. Richard Niebuhr, *The Social Sources of Denominationalism* (Cleveland, OH: Meridian, 1957).

BIBLIOGRAPHY

Acts and Proceedings of the General Synod of the RCA. New York: Board of Publication of the Reformed Church in America, 1957–1974.

Acts of Synod. Grand Rapids, MI: CRC Board of Publications, 1957–1974.

Ahlstrom, Sydney. *A Religious History of the American People.* New Haven, CT: Yale University Press, 1972.

Alba, Richard. *Ethnic Identity: The Transformation of White America.* New Haven, CT: Yale University Press, 1990.

Allen, Theodore W. *The Invention of the White Race, Vol. 1: Racial Oppression and Social Control,* 2nd ed. London: Verso, 2012.

Ammerman, Nancy Tatom. *Congregation and Community.* New Brunswick, NJ: Rutgers University Press, 1997.

——. *Fundamentalism in the Modern World.* New Brunswick, NJ: Rutgers University Press, 1987.

——. *Pillars of Faith: American Congregations and Their Partners.* Berkeley: University of California Press, 2005.

——. *Sacred Stories, Spiritual Tribes: Finding Religion in Everyday Life.* New York: Oxford University Press, 2014.

Avella, Steven. *This Confident Church: Catholic Leadership in the Life of Chicago.* South Bend, IN: University of Notre Dame Press, 1993.

Balmer, Randall. *Mine Eyes Have Seen the Glory: A Journey into the Evangelical Subculture in America.* New York: Oxford University Press, 1989.

Becker, Penny Edgell. "Making Inclusive Communities: Congregations and the 'Problem' of Race." *Social Problems* 45 (1998): 451–472.

Beets, Henry. *The Christian Reformed Church in North America: Sixty Years of Struggle and Blessing.* Grand Rapids, MI: Grand Rapids Printing Press, 1918.

Berger, Peter. *The Noise of Solemn Assemblies: Christian Commitment and the Religious Establishment in America.* Garden City, NY: Doubleday, 1961.

Bergsma, Derke. "A Tale of Two Churches: An Analysis and Critique of the Process of Decision Leading to Relocation from City to Suburb," Seminar paper, University of Chicago, 1968. Dutch Heritage Archives, Trinity Christian College, Palos Heights, IL.

Bielo, James S. "City of Man, City of God: The Re-urbanization of American Evangelicals." *City and Society* 23 (2011): 2–23.

Bishop, Bill. *The Big Sort: Why the Clustering of Like-Minded America Is Tearing Us Apart.* New York: Houghton Mifflin, 2008.

Blanchard, Troy C. "Conservative Protestant Congregations and Racial Residential Segregation: Evaluating the Closed Community Thesis in Metropolitan and Nonmetropolitan Counties." *American Sociological Review* 72 (2007): 416–433.

Bodnar, John. *The Transplanted: A History of Immigrants in Urban America.* Bloomington: Indiana University Press, 1985.

Bratt, James D. *Dutch Calvinism in Modern America: A History of a Conservative Subculture.* Grand Rapids, MI: Eerdmans, 1984.

Bratt, John H. "Dutch Calvinism in America." In *John Calvin: His Influence in the Western World,* ed. W. Stanford Reid, 289–306. Grand Rapids, MI: Zondervan, 1982.

Bray, Hiawatha. "Evangelical Racism?" *Christianity Today* 26 (1992): 42–44.

Brink, William P., and Richard R. De Ridder. *Manual of Christian Reformed Church Government*. Grand Rapids, MI: CRC Publications, 1987.

Buder, Stanley. *Pullman: An Experiment in Industrial Order and Community Planning 1880–1930*. New York: Oxford University Press, 1967.

Bureau of Research, Church Federation of Greater Chicago. *Englewood Study Area*. Chicago: Church Federation of Greater Chicago, 1963.

Cantrell, Randolph L., James F. Krile, and George A. Donohue, "Parish Autonomy: Measuring Denominational Differences." 22 (1983): 276–287.

Cashin, Sheryll. *The Failures of Integration: How Race and Class Are Undermining the American Dream*. New York: Public Affairs, 2004.

Chauncey, George. *Gay New York: Gender, Urban Culture, and the Making of the Gay Male Underworld, 1890–1940*. New York: Basic Books, 1994.

Chicago Local Community Fact Book. Chicago: Chicago Review Press, 1984, 1990.

Classis Holland: Minutes, 1848–1858. Translated by a Joint Committee of the CRC and RCA. Grand Rapids, MI: Grand Rapids Printing, 1943.

Clayton, Obie. "The Churches and Social Change: Accommodation, Moderation, or Protest." *Daedalus* 1 (1995): 101–119.

Cohen, Lizabeth. "From Town Center to Shopping Center: The Reconfiguration of Community Marketplaces in Postwar America." *American Historical Review* 23 (1996): 1050–1081.

Condit, Carl. *Chicago: 1930–1970*. Chicago: University of Chicago Press, 1974.

Conkin, Paul. *The Uneasy Center: Reformed Christianity in Antebellum America*. Chapel Hill: University of North Carolina Press, 1995.

Conn, Harvie M. *The American City and the Evangelical Church: A Historical Overview*. Grand Rapids, MI: Baker Books, 1994.

Connolly, Harold X. *A Ghetto Grows in Brooklyn*. New York: New York University Press, 1977.

Crawford, Margaret. *Building the Workingman's Paradise: The Design of American Company Towns*. London: Verso, 1995.

Dahm, Charles, and Robert Ghelardi. *Power and Authority in the Catholic Church: Cardinal Cody in Chicago*. South Bend, IN: University of Notre Dame Press, 1982.

Day, Katie. *Faith on the Avenue: Religion on a City Street*. New York: Oxford University Press, 2014.

Degler, Carl N. "Remaking American History." *Journal of American History* 67 (1980): 7–25.

De Jong, Gerald F. *The Dutch in America: 1609–1974*. Boston: Twayne, 1975.

Dekker, Gerard. "A Changing World Asks for Changing Congregations." Paper presented at the Fourth Triennial Conference of the International Society for the Study of Reformed Communities, Edinburgh, Scotland, June 28–July 2, 2003.

Diamond, Etan. *And I Will Dwell in Their Midst: Orthodox Jews in Suburbia*. Chapel Hill: University of North Carolina Press, 2000.

———. *Souls of the City: Religion and the Search for Community in Postwar America*. Bloomington: Indiana University Press, 2003.

Dochuk, Darren. "'Praying for a Wicked City': Congregation, Community, and the Suburbanization of Fundamentalism." *Religion and Culture: An Interpretative Journal* 13 (2003): 167–203.

Dougherty, Kevin D., and Mark T. Mulder. "Congregational Responses to Growing Urban Diversity in a White Ethnic Denomination." *Social Problems* 56 (2009): 335–356.

Drake, St. Clair and Horace R. Cayton. *Black Metropolis: A Study of Negro Life in a Northern City*. New York: Harcourt, Brace, and Company, 1945.

Dudley, Carl S. *Where Have All Our People Gone?* New York: Pilgrim Press, 1979.

Dudley, Carl S., Jackson W. Carroll, and James P. Wind, eds. 1991. *Carriers of Faith: Lessons from Congregational Studies.* Louisville, KY: Westminster/John Knox.

Ebaugh, Helen Rose, and Janet Saltzman Chafetz. "Structural Adaptations in Immigrant Congregations." *Sociology of Religion* 61 (2000): 135–153.

Ecumenical Creeds and Reformed Confessions. Grand Rapids, MI: CRC Publications, 1988.

Ehrenhalt, Alan. *The Great Inversion and the Future of the American City.* New York: Alfred A. Knopf, 2012.

Eisland, Nancy L. *A Particular Place: Urban Restructuring and Religious Ecology in a Southern Exurb.* New Brunswick, NJ: Rutgers University Press, 2000.

Elisha, Omri. *Moral Ambition: Mobilization and Socialization in Evangelical Megachurches.* Berkeley: University of California Press, 2011.

Emerson, Michael O. *People of the Dream: Multiracial Congregations in the United States.* Princeton, NJ: Princeton University Press, 2006.

Emerson, Michael O., and Christian Smith. *Divided by Faith: Evangelical Religion and the Problem of Race in America.* New York: Oxford University Press, 2000.

Engelhard, David H., and Leonard J. Hofman, eds. *Manual of Christian Reformed Church Government.* Grand Rapids, MI: CRC Publications, 2001.

Finke, Roger, and Rodney Stark. *The Churching of America, 1776–1990: Winners and Losers in Our Religious Economy.* New Brunswick, NJ: Rutgers University Press, 1992.

Fish, John, Gordon Nelson, Walter Stuhr, and Lawrence Witmer. *The Edge of the Ghetto: A Study of Church Involvement in Community Organization.* New York: Seabury, 1968.

Frazier, John W., Florence M. Margai, and Eugene Tettey-Fio. *Race and Place: Equity Issues in Urban America.* Boulder, CO: Westview, 2003.

Gamm, Gerald. *Urban Exodus: Why the Jews Left Boston and the Catholics Stayed.* Cambridge, MA: Harvard University Press, 1999.

Gaustad, Edwin Scott. *A Religious History of America.* 3rd ed. San Francisco: Harper & Row, 1990.

Gibson, Winter. *The Suburban Captivity of the Church: An Analysis of Protestant Responsibility in the Expanding Metropolis.* New York: Macmillan, 1962.

Gotham, Kevin Fox. *Race, Real Estate, and Uneven Development: The Kansas City Experiment, 1900–2000.* Albany: State University of New York Press, 2002.

Greeley, Andrew. *The Denominational Society: A Sociological Approach to Religion in America.* Glenview, IL: Scott, Foresman, 1972.

Green, Constance. *The Secret City: A History of Race Relations in the Nation's Capital.* Princeton, NJ: Princeton University Press, 1967.

Grossman, James R. *Land of Hope: Chicago, Black Southerners, and the Great Migration.* Chicago: University of Chicago Press, 1989.

Hadden, Jeffery K. *The Gathering Storm in the Churches.* Garden City, NY: Doubleday, 1969.

Handlin, Oscar. *The Uprooted.* Boston: Little, Brown, 1951.

Hart, Darryl G. *That Old-Time Religion in Modern America: Evangelical Protestantism in the Twentieth Century.* Chicago: Ivan R. Dee, 2002.

———. *The Lost Soul of American Protestantism.* New York: Rowman and Littlefield, 2002.

Hartley, Loyde. *Cities and Churches: An International Bibliography, 1800–1991,* vols. 1–3. Metuchen, NJ: American Theological Library Association and Scarecrow Press, 1992.

Hatch, Nathan O. *The Democratization of American Christianity.* New Haven, CT: Yale University Press, 1989.

Helper, Rose. *Racial Policies and Practices of Real Estate Brokers.* Minneapolis: University of Minnesota Press, 1969.

Herberg, Will. *Protestant, Catholic, Jew: An Essay in American Religious Sociology.* Garden City, NY: Doubleday, 1955.

Hirsch, Arnold. *The Making of the Second Ghetto: Race and Housing in Chicago, 1940–1960.* New York: Cambridge University Press, 1983.

Hoeksema, Herman. *The Protestant Reformed Churches in America: Their Origin, Early History, and Doctrine.* Grand Rapids, MI: First Protestant Reformed Church, 1947.

Hoezee, Scott, and Christopher H. Meehan. *Flourishing in the Land: A Hundred-Year History of Christian Reformed Missions in North America.* Grand Rapids, MI: Eerdmans, 1996.

Holifield, E. Brooks. "Toward a History of American Congregations." In *American Congregations*, vol. 2, *New Perspectives in the Study of Congregations*, ed. James P. Wind and James W. Lewis, 25–53. Chicago: University of Chicago Press, 1994.

Hopewell, James. *Congregation: Stories and Structures.* Philadelphia: Fortress, 1987.

Iannaccone, Laurence R. "Why Strict Churches Are Strong." *American Journal of Sociology* 99 (1994): 1180–1211.

Ignatiev, Noel. *How the Irish Became White.* New York: Routledge, 1995.

Jackson, Carroll, and David R. Roozen. "Congregational Identities in the Presbyterian Church." *Review of Religious Research* 31 (1990): 351–369.

Jackson, Kenneth T. *Crabgrass Frontier: The Suburbanization of the United States.* New York: Oxford University Press, 1985.

Jacobson, Matthew. *Whiteness of a Different Color: European Immigrants and the Alchemy of Race.* Cambridge, MA: Harvard University Press, 1999.

Japinga, Lynn. *Loyalty and Loss: The Reformed Church in America, 1945–1994.* Grand Rapids, MI: Eerdmans, 2013.

Johnson, Douglas W., and George W. Cornell. *Puncture Preconceptions: What North American Christians Think about the Church.* New York: Friendship Press, 1972.

Katz, Michael. *The Undeserving Poor: From the War on Poverty to the War on Welfare.* New York: Pantheon, 1989.

Kloetzli, Walter. *The City Church—Death or Renewal: A Study of Eight Urban Lutheran Churches.* Philadelphia: Muhlenberg, 1961.

Kromminga, D. H. *The Christian Reformed Tradition: From the Reformation to the Present.* Grand Rapids, MI: Eerdmans, 1943.

Kromminga, John. *The Christian Reformed Church: A Study in Orthodoxy.* Grand Rapids, MI: Baker Book House, 1949.

Kruse, Kevin. *White Flight: Atlanta and the Making of Modern Conservatism.* Princeton, NJ: Princeton University Press, 2005.

Krysan, Maria. "Whites Who Say They'd Flee: Who Are They, and Why Would They Leave?" *Demography* 39 (2002): 675–696.

Lecky, Robert S., and H. Elliot Wright, eds. *Black Manifesto: Religion, Racism, and Reparations.* New York: Sheed and Ward, 1969.

Lee, Robert. *The Church and the Exploding Metropolis.* Richmond, VA: John Knox, 1965.

———, ed. *Cities and Churches: Readings on the Urban Church.* Philadelphia: Westminster, 1962.

Lehman, Nicholas. *The Promised Land: The Great Black Migration and How It Changed America.* New York: Alfred A. Knopf, 1991.

Lewis, James W. *The Protestant Experience in Gary, Indiana, 1905–1975: At Home in the City.* Knoxville: University of Tennessee Press, 1992.

Lincoln, C. Eric. *Race, Religion, and the Continuing American Dilemma.* New York: Hill and Wang, 1984.

Little, James T., Hugh O. Nourse, R. B. Read, and Charles L. Leven. *The Contemporary Neighborhood Succession Process: Lessons in the Dynamic of Decay from the St. Louis Experience.* St. Louis: Institute for Urban and Regional Studies, 1975.

Loescher, Frank. *The Protestant Church and the Negro: A Pattern of Segregation.* Westport, CT: Negro Universities Press, 1948.

Lucas, Henry. *Dutch Immigrant Memoirs and Related Writings.* Grand Rapids, MI: Eerdmans, 1997.

———. *Netherlanders in America: Dutch Immigration to the United States, 1879–1850.* Ann Arbor: University of Michigan Press, 1955.

Manning, Thomas, and Marsha Rizdorf, eds. *Urban Planning and the African American Community: In the Shadows.* Thousand Oaks, CA: Sage Publications, 1997.

Marks, Carole. *Farewell—We're Good and Gone: The Great Black Migration.* Bloomington: Indiana University Press, 1989.

Marsden, George M. *Understanding Fundamentalism and Evangelicalism.* Grand Rapids, MI: Eerdmans, 1991.

Marty, Martin E. "Ethnicity: The Skeleton of Religion in America." *Church History* 41 (1972): 5–21.

———. *Pilgrims in Their Own Land: 500 Years of Religion in America.* Boston: Little, Brown, 1984.

———. *Religion and Republic: The American Circumstance.* Boston: Beacon, 1987.

———. *Righteous Empire: The Protestant Experience in America.* New York: Dial, 1970.

Massey, Douglas S., and Nancy A. Denton. *American Apartheid: Segregation and the Making of the Underclass.* Cambridge, MA: Harvard University Press, 1993.

May, Henry F. *Protestant Churches and Industrial America.* New York: Harper & Row, 1949.

McDaniel, Antonio. "The Dynamic Racial Composition of the United States." In *An American Dilemma Revisited: Race Relations in a Changing World,* ed. Obie Clayton Jr., 269–287. New York: Russell Sage, 1996.

McGreevy, John. *Parish Boundaries: The Catholic Encounter with Race in the Twentieth Century Urban North.* Chicago: University of Chicago Press, 1996.

McKee, James B. *Sociology and the Race Problem: The Failure of a Perspective.* Urbana: University of Illinois Press, 1993.

McKinney, William, and Dean R. Hodge. "Community and Congregational Factors in the Growth and Decline of Protestant Churches." *Journal for the Scientific Study of Religion* 22 (1983): 51–66.

McMahon, Eileen M. *What Parish Are You From? A Chicago Irish Community and Race Relations.* Lexington: University of Kentucky Press, 1995.

McMullen, Mike. "Religious Polities as Institutions." *Social Forces* 73 (1994): 709–728.

McRoberts, Omar. *Streets of Glory: Church and Community in a Black Urban Neighborhood.* Chicago: University of Chicago Press, 2003.

Meagher, Timothy J., ed. *Urban American Catholicism: The Culture and Identity of the American Catholic People.* New York: Garland, 1988.

Meehan, Chris. "Learning from Timothy." *Banner* 148 (2013): 50–53.

Meyer, Stephen Grant. *As Long as They Don't Move Next Door: Segregation and Racial Conflict in American Neighborhoods.* Lanham, MD: Rowman & Littlefield, 2000.

Mohl, Raymond A. "Making the Second Ghetto in Metropolitan Miami, 1940–1960." *Journal of Urban History* 21 (1995): 395–427.

Mouw, Richard. *He Shines in All That's Fair: Culture and Common Grace.* Grand Rapids, MI: Eerdmans, 2001.

Mulder, Arnold. *Americans from Holland.* Philadelphia: J. B. Lippincott, 1947.

Mulder, Mark T. "Evangelical Church Polity and the Nuances of White Flight: A Case Study from the Roseland and Englewood Neighborhoods in Chicago." *Journal of Urban History* 38 (2012): 16–38.

———. "Mobility and the (In)Significance of Place: A Case Study from the South Side of Chicago." *Geographies of Religion and Belief Systems* 3 (2009): 1643.

Niebuhr, H. Richard. *The Kingdom of God in America*. Middletown, CT: Wesleyan University Press, 1937.

———. *The Social Sources of Denominationalism*. Cleveland, OH: Meridian, 1929.

Noll, Mark A. *American Evangelical Christianity: An Introduction*. Malden, MA: Blackwell, 2001.

Orser, Edward. *Blockbusting in Baltimore: The Edmondson Village Story*. Lexington: University of Kentucky Press, 1994.

Osborne, William A. *The Segregated Covenant: Race Relations and American Catholics*. New York: Herder and Herder, 1967.

Patillo, Mary. *Black on the Block: The Politics of Race and Class in the City*. Chicago: University of Chicago Press, 2007.

Patillo-McCoy, Mary. *Black Picket Fences: Privilege and Peril among the Black Middle Class*. Chicago: University of Chicago Press, 1999.

Portes, Alejandro. "Social Capital: Its Origins and Applications in Modern Sociology." *Annual Review of Sociology* 24 (1998): 1–24.

Pritchett, Wendell. *Brownsville, Brooklyn: Blacks Jews, and the Changing Face of the Ghetto*. Chicago: University of Chicago Press, 2002.

Putnam, Robert D., and David E. Campbell. *American Grace: How Religion Divides and Unites Us*. New York: Simon and Schuster, 2010.

Quillian, Lincoln. "Migration Patterns and the Growth of High Poverty Neighborhoods, 1970–1990." *American Journal of Sociology* 105 (1999): 1–37.

Rapkin, Chester, and William G. Grigsby. *The Demand for Housing in Racially Mixed Areas: A Study of the Nature of Neighborhood Change*. Berkeley: University of California Press, 1960.

Roedigger, David R. *The Wages of Whiteness: Race and the Making of the American Working Class*, 2nd ed. New York: Verso, 1999.

Roozen, David A., William McKinnney, and Jackson W. Carroll. *Varieties of Religious Presence: Mission in Public Life*. New York: Pilgrim Press, 1988.

Rowlands, Marie K. "Down an Indian Trail: The Story of Roseland." *Calumet Index* (June). Reprinted for the Dutch Heritage Center, Palos Heights, IL, 1949.

Sack, Robert David. *Homo Geographicus: A Framework for Action, Awareness, and Moral Concern*. Baltimore: Johns Hopkins University Press, 1997.

Sampson, Robert J. *Great American City: Chicago and the Enduring Neighborhood Effect*. Chicago: University of Chicago Press, 2012.

Schaver, J. L. *The Polity of Churches*. Chicago: Chicago Polity Press, 1947.

Scheitle, Christopher P., and Kevin D. Dougherty. "Density and Growth in Congregational Population: Reformed Churches in New York, 1628–2000." *Review of Religious Research* 49 (2008): 233–250.

Seligman, Amanda I. *Block by Block: Neighborhoods, Public Policy, and "White Flight" in Richard J. Daley's Chicago*. Chicago: University of Chicago Press, 2005.

Sharkey, Patrick. *Stuck in Place: Urban Neighborhoods and the End of Progress toward Equality*. Chicago: University of Chicago Press, 2013.

Shelton, Jason E., and Michael O. Emerson. *Blacks and Whites in Christian America: How Racial Discrimination Shapes Religious Convictions*. New York: New York University Press, 2012.

Smidt, Corwin, Don Luidens, James Penning, and Roger Nemeth. *Divided by a Common Heritage: The Christian Reformed Church and the Reformed Church in America at the Beginning of the New Millennium*. Grand Rapids, MI: Eerdmans, 2006.

South, Scott J., and Kyle D. Crowder. "Escaping Distressed Neighborhoods: Individual, Community, and Metropolitan Influences." *American Journal of Sociology* 102 (1997): 1040–1084.

Squires, Gregory D., Larry Bennet, Kathleen McCourt, and Philip Nyden. *Chicago: Race, Class, and the Response to Urban Decline*. Philadelphia: Temple University Press, 1987.

Stanger-Ross, Jordan. "Neither Fight nor Flight: Urban Synagogues in Postwar Philadelphia." *Journal of Urban History* 32 (2006): 791–812.

Steinberg, Stephen. *The Ethnic Myth: Race, Ethnicity, and Class in America*. Boston: Beacon, 1981.

———. *Turning Back: The Retreat from Racial Justice in American Thought*. Boston: Beacon, 1995.

Stumme, Wayne, ed. *The Experience of Hope: Mission and Ministry in Changing Urban Communities*. Minneapolis, MN: Augsburg Fortress, 1991.

Sugrue, Thomas. *The Origins of the Urban Crisis: Race and Inequality in Postwar Detroit*. Princeton, NJ: Princeton University Press, 1996.

Swierenga, Robert P. *Dutch Chicago: A History of the Hollanders in the Windy City*. Grand Rapids, MI: Eerdmans, 2002.

———. "The Dutch Urban Experience." In *The Dutch in Urban America*, ed. Robert P. Swierenga, Donald Sinnema, and Hans Krabbendam, 1–12. Holland, MI: JAH, 2004.

———. *Faith and Family: Dutch Immigration and Settlement in the United States, 1820–1920*. New York: Holmes and Meier, 2000.

———. "A Tale of Two Cities: Acculturation and Its Long-Term Impact on Chicago's West Side Reformed Churches." *Origins* 23 (2005): 12–21.

———. "Walls or Bridges? Acculturation Processes in the Reformed and Christian Reformed Churches in North America." In *Morsels in Melting Pot: The Persistence of Dutch Immigrant Communities in North America*, ed. George Harinck and Hans Krabbendam, 33–54. Amsterdam: VU University Press, 2006.

Swierenga, Robert P., ed. *The Dutch in America: Immigration, Settlement, and Cultural Change*. New Brunswick, NJ: Rutgers University Press, 1985.

Thompson, Heather Ann. "Rethinking the Politics of White Flight in the Postwar City: Detroit, 1945–1980." *Journal of Urban History* 25 (1999): 163–199.

Tiemersma, Richard R. "Growing Up in Roseland in the Twenties and Thirties." *Origins* 5 (1987): 2–19.

Tobin, Gary, ed. *Divided Neighborhoods: Changing Patterns of Racial Segregation*. Newbury Park, CA: Sage, 1987.

Tuan, Yi-Fu. *Topophilia: A Study of Environmental Perception, Attitudes, and Values*. Englewood Cliffs, NJ: Prentice-Hall, 1974.

Van Dellen, Idzerd, and Martin Monsma. *The Church Order Commentary*. Grand Rapids, MI: Zondervan, 1941.

———. *The Revised Church Order Commentary: An Explanation of the Church Order of the Christian Reformed Church*. Grand Rapids, MI: Zondervan, 1967.

Vanden Bosch, Amry. *Dutch Communities of Chicago*. Chicago: Knickerbocker Society of Chicago, 1927.

Van Hinte, Jacob. *Netherlanders in America: A Study of Emigration and Settlement in the 19th and 20th Centuries in the United States of America*. Grand Rapids, MI: Baker Book House, 1985.

Venkatesh, Sudhir Alladi. *American Project: The Rise and Fall of a Modern Ghetto*. Cambridge, MA: Harvard University Press, 2000.

Warner, R. Stephen. *A Church of Our Own: Disestablishment and Diversity in American Religion*. New Brunswick, NJ: Rutgers University Press, 2005.

———. *New Wine in Old Wineskins: Evangelicals and Liberals in a Small-Town Church.* Berkeley: University of California Press, 1988.

———. "The Place of the Congregation in the Contemporary American Religious Configuration." In *American Congregations*, vol. 2: *New Perspectives in the Study of Congregations*, ed. J. P. Wind and J. W. Lewis, 54–99. Chicago: University of Chicago Press, 1994.

———. "A Work in Progress toward a New Paradigm for the Sociological Study of Religion in the United States." *American Journal of Sociology* 98 (1993): 1044–1093.

Wedam, Elfriede. "'If We Let the Market Prevail, We Won't Have a Neighborhood Left': Religious Agency and Urban Restructuring on Chicago's Southwest Side." *City and Society* 17 (2005): 211–233.

Wellman, James K. Jr. *The Gold Coast Church and the Ghetto: Christ and Culture in Mainline Protestantism.* Chicago: University of Illinois Press, 1999.

Wells, David F. *Reformed Theology in America: A History of Its Modern Development.* Grand Rapids, MI: Baker Book House, 1997.

Wheeler, Barbara. "Uncharted Territory: Congregational Identity and Mainline Protestantism." In *The Presbyterian Predicament: Six Perspectives*, ed. Milton J. Coalter, John M. Mulder, and Louis B. Weeks, 67–89. Louisville, KY: Westminster/John Knox, 1990.

Wilford, Justin G. *Sacred Subdivisions: The Postsuburban Transformation of American Evangelicalism.* New York: New York University Press, 2012.

Wilson, William Julius. *The Declining Significance of Race: Blacks and Changing American Institutions.* Chicago: University of Chicago Press, 1978.

———. *When Work Disappears: The World of the New Urban Poor.* New York: Vintage, 1996.

Wilson, William Julius, and Richard Taub. *There Goes the Neighborhood: Racial, Ethnic, and Class Tensions in Four Chicago Neighborhoods and Their Meaning for America.* New York: Alfred A. Knopf, 2006.

Winant, Howard. *Racial Conditions: Politics, Theory, Comparisons.* Minneapolis: University of Minnesota Press, 1994.

Wind, James P. and James W. Lewis. *American Congregations*, vol. 1, *Portraits of Twelve Religious Communities* and vol. 2, *New Perspectives in the Study of Congregations.* Chicago: University of Chicago Press, 1994.

Winston, Diane. "Babylon by the Hudson; Jerusalem on the Charles: Religion and the American City." *Journal of Urban History* 25 (1998): 122–129.

Woldoff, Rachael. *White Flight/Black Flight: The Dynamics of Racial Change in an American Neighborhood.* Ithaca, NY: Cornell University Press, 2011.

Wood, Forrest. *Arrogance of Faith.* New York: Alfred A. Knopf, 1991.

Wood, James R., and Mayer N. Zald. "Aspects of Racial Integration in the Methodist Church: Sources of Resistance to Organizational Policy." *Social Forces* 45 (1966): 255–264.

Wuthnow, Robert. *Producing the Sacred: An Essay on Public Religion.* Chicago: University of Illinois Press, 1994.

———. *The Restructuring of American Religion: Society and Faith since World War II.* Princeton, NJ: Princeton University Press, 1988.

INDEX

ABOUT THE AUTHOR

MARK MULDER is an associate professor of sociology at Calvin College in Grand Rapids, Michigan. He is the author of numerous articles that examine urban congregations, race, and place. At Calvin, he teaches classes ranging from urban sociology to diversity and inequality to church and society. Dr. Mulder is also co-director of the Latino Protestants Congregation Project, a national-scope ethnographic study exploring this growing wing of Protestantism in the United States.

CPSIA information can be obtained
at www.ICGtesting.com
Printed in the USA
LVHW030903010921
696600LV00013B/829